T0336481

Japanese Companies

JAPANESE SOCIETY SERIES

General Editor: Yoshio Sugimoto

Lives of Young Koreans in Japan
Yasunori Fukuoka

Globalization and Social Change in Contemporary Japan
J.S. Eades Tom Gill Harumi Befu

Coming Out in Japan: The Story of Satoru and Ryuta
Satoru Ito and Ryuta Yanase

Japan and Its Others:
Globalization, Difference and the Critique of Modernity
John Clammer

Hegemony of Homogeneity:
An Anthropological Analysis of *Nihonjinron*
Harumi Befu

Foreign Migrants in Contemporary Japan
Hiroshi Komai

A Social History of Science and Technology in
Contempory Japan, Volume 1
Shigeru Nakayama

Farewell to Nippon: Japanese Lifestyle Migrants in Australia
Machiko Sato

The Peripheral Centre:
Essays on Japanese History and Civilization
Johann P. Arnason

A Genealogy of 'Japanese' Self-images
Eiji Oguma

Class Structure in Contemporary Japan
Kenji Hashimoto

An Ecological View of History
Tadao Umesao

Nationalism and Gender
Chizuko Ueno

Native Anthropology: The Japanese Challenge
to Western Academic Hegemony
Takami Kuwayama

Youth Deviance in Japan: Class Reproduction of Non-Conformity
Robert Stuart Yoder

Japanese Companies: Theories and Realities
Masami Nomura and Yoshihiko Kamii

Japanese Companies

Theories and Realities

Edited by

Masami Nomura

and

Yoshihiko Kamii

Translated by

Brad Williams

Trans Pacific Press

Melbourne

This English edition first published in 2004 by
Trans Pacific Press, PO Box 120, Rosanna, Melbourne, Victoria 3084, Australia
Telephone: +61 3 9459 3021 Fax: +61 3 9457 5923
Email: info@transpacificpress.com
Web: http://www.transpacificpress.com

Designed and set by digital environs Melbourne.
enquiries@digitalenvirons.com

Printed by BPA Digital, Burwood, Victoria, Australia

Distributors

Australia
Bushbooks
PO Box 1958, Gosford, NSW 2250
Telephone: (02) 4323-3274
Fax: (02) 4323-3223
Email: bushbook@ozemail.com.au

USA and Canada
International Specialized Book
Services (ISBS)
920 NE 58th Avenue, Suite 300
Portland, Oregon 97213-3786
USA
Telephone: (800) 944-6190
Fax: (503) 280-8832
Email: orders@isbs.com
Web: http://www.isbs.com

Japan
Kyoto University Press
Kyodai Kaikan
15-9 Yoshida Kawara-cho
Sakyo-ku, Kyoto 606-8305
Telephone: (075) 761-6182
Fax: (075) 761-6190
Email: sales@kyoto-up.gr.jp
Web: http://www.kyoto-up.gr.jp

UK and Europe
Asian Studies Book Services
Franseweg 55B, 3921 DE Elst,
Utrecht, The Netherlands
Telephone: +31 318 470 030
Fax: +31 318 470 073
Email: info@asianstudiesbooks.com
Web: http://www.asianstudiesbooks.com

ISBN 1-8768-4355-1 (Hardback)
ISBN 1-8768-4361-6 (Paperback)

National Library of Australia Cataloging in Publication Data

Japanese companies: theories and realities.
Bibliography.
Includes index.
ISBN 1 876843 55 1.
ISBN 1 876843 61 6 (pbk.).

1. Corporations – Japan. I. Nomura, Masami, 1948–. II.
Kamii, Yoshihiko, 1947–. (Series: Japanese society
series).
338.740952

Contents

Tables   vi
Figures   vi
Contributors   vii
Translators   vii
A note on Japanese names   vii
Preface
Masami Nomura and Yoshihiko Kamii   ix

1   Are Personnel Assessments Fair?
    Kōshi Endō   1
2   Is Workshop Information Shared?
    Uichi Asao   20
3   People in Irregular Modes of Employment: Are They
    Really Not Subject to Discrimination?
    Mari Ōsawa   39
4   Is Subcontracting Risk Sharing?
    Hirofumi Ueda   64
5   Do Japanese Labour Unions Bargain?
    Yoshihiko Kamii   82
6   A Critical Analysis of Koike Kazuo's Skill Theory
    Masami Nomura   102
7   Aoki's Theory and the Reality of Japanese Companies
    Masaru Kaneko   121
8   The Failure of J-Firm Theory
    Shigeo Takeda   142

Notes   172
References   175
Index   185

Tables

Table 2-1 Comparison of annual working hours between
major Japanese and European automobile
manufacturers (production workers, 1990)   35

Table 3-1 Proportion of workplaces applying various
kinds of treatment to 'part-time workers:
2001, 1995 and 1990 (where available)   45

Table 3-2 Scheduled wage per hour for part-timers as a
percentage of full-time pay, 1990–2000 (at
June in each year, for all industries, company-
sizes and job descriptions)   46

Table 3-3 Reasons given by 'part-timers for present
mode of employment   47

Table 6-1 Job Matrix   118

Figures

Figure 4-1 Designs approved/Designs supplied system   72
Figure 4-2 Overseas production   77

Contributors

Asao, Uichi, Professor, Faculty of Business Administration, Toho Gakuen University

Endō, Kōshi, Professor, School of Business Administration, Meiji University

Kamii, Yoshihiko, Professor, Faculty of Economics, Saitama University

Kaneko, Masaru, Professor, Faculty of Economics, Keio University

Nomura, Masami, Professor, Graduate School of Economics and Management, Tohoku University

Ōsawa, Mari, Professor, Institute of Social Science, The University of Tokyo

Takeda, Shigeo, Professor, Faculty of Economics, Hosei University

Ueda, Hirofumi, Associate Professor, Graduate School for Creative Cities, Osaka City University

Translators

The book was translated by Dr Brad Williams from Monash University, except chapter 8 which was translated by Associate Professor David Askew from Monash University and Ritsumeikan Asia Pacific University.

A note on Japanese names

Japanese words have been transcribed in the conventional Hepburn system. Generally, Japanese names have been given in the usual Japanese order, with family names first. The main exception is that of Japanese names on the cover and in the title page, the table of contents and chapter headings, where the western order has been retained to avoid confusion in citations.

Preface

'Why are Japanese companies the best in the world? What is the driving force behind their strength?' These were the catchwords of a bestseller published by Nihon Keizai Shimbunsha entitled *Seminar: A Guide to Modern Companies*. These watchwords summed up fully in a few short words the perception of Japanese companies during the bubble period in the late 1980s. However, such a perception of Japanese companies did not exist that long ago. It was a new perspective that was propagated during the 1980s.

The perception of Japanese corporations during the period of high growth

From 1955, the Japanese economy achieved high growth for nearly two decades. During this period, large Japanese companies recovered from the chaos of the early post-war years and grew rapidly. In industries such as steel, shipping and electronics Japanese companies became world leaders. Despite such rapid growth, the general view, not only among critical researchers but also among governments, was that Japan's economy and companies, indeed Japanese society as a whole, was 'dated' and required 'modernisation.' There are several reasons for this.

Immediately after the war, Japan was a developing country in a sense, with half of the total workforce employed in agriculture and the forestry industry. While Japanese companies certainly grew rapidly during the period of high growth, problems of over-employment and potential unemployment in agriculture and small urban businesses remained. As a result, a dual structure comprising large modern corporations on the one hand, and small business and the self-employed on the other, existed. The exploitation of subcontractors in this dual structure is seen as having made the development of large companies possible. It is clear that high growth also brought about social distortions. Large cities became overpopulated, while rural villages suffered from depopulation.

The large number of low-income earners from rural Japan travelling to other towns and cities in order to work was also considered a serious problem. Japan's economic revitalisation was beset by severe air and water pollution caused by companies and economic activities.

At the end of the high growth period in the early 1970s, criticism of the Japanese economy and companies reached a peak. In 1970, the *Asahi Shimbun*, then the biggest newspaper in Japan, featured a series of articles that were critical of high growth. The articles were entitled 'go to hell GNP' (*kutabare* GNP), which became a popular catchphrase. In fact, beginning with Tokyo, reformist governors supported by the Japan Socialist Party and Japan Communist Party were victorious in several important local government elections, which resulted in an era of progressive local government. Reformist local governments were critical of high growth and forced companies to adhere to strict environmental standards.

The first oil shock as a turning point

However, these criticisms were swept away by the first oil shock in 1973. Japanese society, which had become accustomed to double-digit growth, recorded negative growth in 1974 – the first since the end of the war – and people were subsequently panic-stricken. If we look calmly, the Japanese economy recorded negative growth for only one year. But the awareness that the period of high growth was over changed the atmospherics of Japanese society considerably. Criticisms of economic growth quickly subsided. Public opinion calling for 'lifestyle rather than production' and 'welfare rather than growth' was replaced by calls for 'perseverance' and criticism of 'reckless welfare' (*baramaki fukushi*). Reformist local governments that prioritised welfare disappeared one after the other.

The negative growth caused by the oil shock lasted only one year. Casting a contemptuous glance at Europe and America, which had fallen into severe economic stagnation as a result of the oil shock, the Japanese economy, on the back of a concentrated export drive, was headed for recovery, boasting the highest growth rate among the industrialised countries. The more severe the economic stagnation in the advanced industrialised countries, the more Japan became conspicuous in its growth. This led many

Japanese citizens to feel confident and proud of Japan's economy and companies. From the late 1970s to the early 1980s, criticisms of Japan's economy and companies were overshadowed by an atmosphere in which their strength and wonderful features were emphasised.

The dominant tone of the 1980s

Against the backdrop of an improving Japanese economy, the 1980s was a period in which theories of Japanese companies became extremely popular. Novel concepts such as 'peoplistic firm' and 'humanware' were proposed one after the other. These theories were developed from the perspective of explaining why Japanese companies were so competitive, and how they were able to achieve such high efficiency, ignoring many problems that would appear soon after the burst of the bubble in the early 1990s. The watchword quoted at the beginning of this preface: 'Why are Japanese companies the best in the world?' was an obvious manifestation of the prevailing mood in Japan.

Two particular aspects of companies became the focus of the various theories espoused. One concerned labour relations and the other inter-company relations, especially subcontracting within the *keiretsu* system. Both had a long tradition of research, but in the 1980s a new interpretation was presented and widely accepted.

From the perspective of relations between management and labour unions, Japanese enterprise unions were not strong enough to regulate labour practices in the workplace. The fact that enterprise unions' workplace regulations were weak meant that corporate management could achieve what it wished. Unlike in America and Europe, labour-management relations were interpreted as contributing to high corporate efficiency in Japan. While labour-management relations were certainly an important part of labour relations, it remained of limited significance when explaining corporate efficiency.

A new theory in the 1980s refuted such explanations and emphasised that Japanese companies were strong because they possessed crucial resources that contributed to their com-petitiveness, namely the skills of Japanese workers. Japanese companies had a tradition of long-term employment, and production workers accumulated skills specific to a particular company that could not be used in other workplaces. It was claimed that these high skills contributed significantly to the competitiveness of the Japanese manufacturing industry.

Until the 1970s, subcontracting in the *keiretsu* system was seen as the exploitation of small and medium-sized firms by big business, which was premised on a dual structure. However, in the 1980s, the notion of exploitation was refuted. Instead, it was argued that subcontracting in the *keiretsu* system was a relationship of coexistence and co-prosperity in which the parent company and the subsidiary shared the risks. It was emphasised that a long-term risk-sharing business relationship contributed to the international competitiveness of Japanese companies.

Market fundamentalism in the 1990s

Concomitant with the collapse of the bubble economy in the early 1990s, the assessment of Japanese companies again changed. Harsh criticism of the Japanese economic system and Japanese-style management assumed greater prominence in place of the earlier arguments extolling their virtues. Those condemning the Japanese economic system and Japanese-style management were market fundamentalists who worshipped the American model, arguing that the Japanese economic system and Japanese-style management are good for the period of high economic growth. In an era of a stagnating economy and/or global capitalism, however, the Japanese economic system and Japanese-style management are no longer economically rational. Life-time employment and a seniority-oriented wage system can no longer be maintained under severe economic conditions in the post-bubble recession. Employment will and should become fluid. The closed nature of subcontracting in the *keiretsu* system will probably be replaced by global procurement. Moreover, the development of information technology will probably accelerate internet procurement. In a word, the Japanese economic system and Japanese-style management have reached an end, replaced by a universal economic and management system that exists in the U.S.

In this manner, market fundamentalism was critical of the Japanese economic system and Japanese-style management. However, it should be noted that market fundamentalism did not criticise the theories of the 1980s as being empirically incorrect, nor as being one-sided assertions. Rather, the Japanese economic system and Japanese-style management were criticised as being outdated in an era of global capitalism; the conditions sustaining them no longer exist; they are based on undesirable values of collectivism, impeding individual responsibility and autonomy.

For instance, the theory of the 1980s attributed Japan's strong competitiveness to highly firm-specific skills. Market fundamentalists, while acknowledging this, claimed that companies could not bear training costs for such skills in a stagnating economy. They also argued that the number of workplaces requiring high skills had been reduced and that the flexible labour market had expanded. They did not discuss whether Japanese workers really possessed highly firm-specific skills. Market fundamentalists, in a word, accepted the theory of the 1980s but insisted that the conditions had changed in an era of global capitalism. In this sense, the widely-shared theory of the 1980s has not been challenged seriously by market fundamentalists until now.

Aoki Masahiko, Koike Kazuo and Asanuma Banri

It was Aoki Masahiko, Koike Kazuo and Asanuma Banri who formulated the widely-accepted theory in the 1980s. The three collaborated based on a division of labour. Koike examined labour relations, while Asanuma explored relations within the *keiretsu* system. Relying completely on Koike and Asanuma's research, Aoki established a theory of Japanese companies, using 'organisational economics,' which was based on game theory.

That Koike and Asanuma were seen to be conducting detailed empirical research, which was also outstanding in terms of substantiation, is a reason for the influence of Aoki, Koike and Asanuma's argument. Another significant reason is that Aoki, cleverly employing game theory, combined Koike and Asanuma's arguments and clearly outlined the features of Japanese companies compared with American firms. However, these are not the only reasons for their influence. The main reason their work was widely accepted was because their argument was based on an extremely popular image spreading throughout Japanese society.

Koike named his theory the 'theory of intellectual skill' (*chiteki jukurenron*). By using the name of 'intellectual skill,' Koike conferred an academic meaning to the old image of Japanese workers who worked diligently and were able to respond skilfully in adapting to new technology. Asanuma defined the core concept of 'relational skill' (*kankeiteki ginō*) as 'the ability to be able to respond efficiently to a specific customer's needs and demands and to supply them.' This is commonsense theorising. It is a matter of course that, where a company has a long-term business relationship with suppliers, suppliers are able to efficiently respond because they know what requests the company is going to make. Aoki's theory, which drew from Koike and Asanuma's research, was also based on a popular image. It is because they adroitly theorised about a popular image that Aoki, Koike and Asanuma's argument was widely accepted.

The Aim and Structure of the Book

We believe that Aoki, Koike and Asanuma's argument is empirically incorrect in some parts, one-sided in other parts, and also theoretically erroneous. In order to elucidate this point, this book critiques the arguments of Aoki, Koike and Asanuma empirically as well as theoretically.

The first section explores the realities of Japanese companies. Chapter one (Endō Kōshi) notes that employees do not have the right to know the results of their assessment and highlights how this is a decidedly unfair feature of assessments in Japanese companies. He is critical of the ignorance and lack of interest shown by Koike and Aoki regarding this point. Chapter two (Asao Uichi) examines whether workers, as a whole, share workplace information (knowledge) and whether data processing is decentralised in Japanese factories. Asao argues that information is shared only among a limited number of workers and that Koike and Aoki ignore the centralised aspect of data processing. Chapter three (Ōsawa Mari) focuses mainly on female part-time workers and expresses fundamental doubts regarding the popular notion that differences in the treatment of non-regular and regular employees is neither discriminatory nor legally unjustifiable. Chapter four (Ueda Hirofumi) argues that Asanuma's claim that *keiretsu* subcontracting is a relationship of risk-sharing is one-sided. Ueda also argues that this derives from a methodological error in which Asanuma classifies suppliers into two categories: suppliers with supplied drawings (*taiyozu*) and suppliers with approved drawings (*shōninzu*). Chapter five (Kamii Yoshihiko) examines the validity of the common assumption that Japanese enterprise unions engage in broad negotiations with companies. Kamii argues that such a view is empirically incorrect.

The second section focuses on theory. Chapter six (Nomura Masami) examines broadly the problems associated with Koike Kazuo's 'theory of intellectual skill.' Nomura notes that the popularity of the 'theory of intellectual skill' derives from its conceptual ambiguity. Chapter seven (Kaneko Masaru) argues that the J-firm theory of Aoki Masahiko is methodologically wrong and empirically incorrect. Chapter eight (Takeda Shigeo) explains from a theoretical perspective that the game theory employed by Aoki is fundamentally deficient in terms of systems analysis.

The research project from which this book was edited was supported by a 1997–1999 Grant-in-Aid from the Japan Society for the Promotion of Science/Basic Research (B-1). The publication of this book was also supported by a 2003–2004 Grant-in-Aid for Publication of Scientific Research Results from the Japan Society for the Promotion of Science.

In this book we have attempted to critique comprehensively the widely-shared theories concerning Japanese companies. While the book reconstructs theories of Japanese companies and the Japanese economy, it is merely a first – albeit necessary – step. We go beyond critiquing these theories by offering an alternative view of the Japanese economy and Japanese-style management. We will further pursue research on political, social and economic changes in the 1990s and will, hopefully in the near future, present comprehensive views on Japan's economy.

Masami Nomura and Yoshihiko Kamii
20 February 2004

1 Are Personnel Assessments Fair?

Kōshi Endō

Presenting the problem

Personnel assessments – the Japanese equivalent of performance appraisals – are conducted fairly in Japanese companies. The number of economists and business administration scholars who shared this view increased from the mid-1980s to the mid-1990s. This was a significant shift considering that before this, a majority were sceptical of the fairness of personnel assessments.

The claim that personnel assessments are conducted fairly in Japanese companies was not substantiated by proper empirical research into the features of these assessments. Instead, it was an assumption based on the strong international competitiveness of Japanese companies in the 1980s. First, a theory was constructed to explain the above fact. Then, a natural 'corollary' of the above theory resulted in the assumption that personnel assessments in Japanese companies had to be fair.

The reasoning behind 'fair assessments'

According to one of the most influential theories that sought to explain the competitiveness of Japanese companies, the high-level of work skills possessed by employees are an important managerial resource, which contribute decisively to the strong international competitiveness of Japanese companies. That is, working for long periods in the same company, employees are able to experience various types of work due to frequent job reassignment and rotation in Japanese companies. As a result of this on-the-job training (OJT), employees, in addition to being able to perform a wide range of tasks, acquire the ability to be able to adapt to work-related changes and abnormal situations. It was Koike Kazuo who noted a high-level work capacity of adapting to work-related changes and abnormal situations acquired by employees. He conceptualised it as 'intellectual skill' and contributed most to the theory explaining the strong competitiveness of Japanese companies.

Having theorised the issue in the manner described above, the fairness of personnel assessments must be subsequently demonstrated. The personnel assessment ought to be a system of evaluating the work capacity of employees. Therefore, failure to evaluate work capacity fairly not only reflects unfair treatment of employees but more importantly, makes it difficult for companies to push their employees to acquire a high-level work capacity. The reason is that if it is not evaluated fairly, employees will be lax in their efforts to acquire a high-level work capacity. Incidentally, because Japanese companies maintained strong international competitiveness throughout the 1980s, their employees should have acquired high-level work capacity. Accepting this argument, the evaluation of work capacity, that is, personnel assessments must be conducted fairly.

Are such assumptions correct? Similarly, has the system of personnel assessments in Japanese companies been designed fairly? Moreover, are they managed fairly? This chapter addresses these questions. This chapter draws mainly from my research that claims to clarify most accurately the characteristics of personnel assessments in Japanese companies (Endō 1999).

In examining the fairness of personnel assessments, it is necessary to consider what 'intellectual skill' or high-level work capacity of adapting to work-related changes and abnormal situations – the objects of assessment – actually imply. Moreover, it is necessary to critically examine the narrow view that focuses only on employees' 'intellectual skill' as the source of international competitiveness. This is because there are many factors beyond 'intellectual skill' that influence international competitiveness. However, due to space limitations, this chapter will not consider these. For a discussion of the former, please refer to chapter six and Endō's research (2001). For a discussion of the latter, please consult the rest of this book.

The reasons for 'fairness'

I stated that the theory of 'fair assessments' was simply based on certain assumptions. However, this does not mean that the argument for 'fairness' has no basis. Many reasons have been cited. They all claimed that the personnel assessments of Japanese companies are fairer than performance appraisals of foreign companies. However, the reasons cited were not based on solid empirical research.

I will divide the reasons behind the assertion of 'fairness' into two groups, and critically examine both. Dividing these into two groups is done for the sake of convenience, as both share common features in kind. The first group consists of two unique and sophisticated reasons, which Koike was the first person to highlight. I point out beforehand that the 'job-matrix chart' (*shigotohyō*), which Koike regards as important material evidence for one of the reasons, does not in fact exist; Koike 'made it up.' The second group consists of various reasons listed by various researchers without rhyme or reason, which are clearly more unsophisticated than Koike's. I use the words 'various reasons listed without rhyme or reason,' because their thinking is shallow and therefore easily criticised. They also borrow from Koike's reasons frequently without care. Nevertheless, there are eminent researchers among them, who repeat the various reasons of 'fair assessments' in their widely-read works. They became influential and could not be ignored.

Critiques of Koike Kazuo's theory of 'fair assessments'

Assessment by multiple bosses over a long period of time

One of the two reasons Koike cites for the 'fairness' of assessments was put forward as a hypothesis in 1981 (Koike1981: 27–45). According to this hypothesis, Japanese assessments are conducted over a long period of time. Because there are changes in company bosses and their subordinates due to personnel reshuffling during this period, assessments are conducted by 'multiple assessors.' As a result, 'it is easy to create a 'market' (*sōba*) for assessment standards, which diminishes arbitrariness based on subjectivity.' That is, it increases the 'fairness' of assessments. According to Koike's hypothesis, however, this is not the case with European and American companies where appraisals are conducted by bosses who have considerable discretionary and arbitrary powers. The hypothesis displayed a level of certain sophistication as it combined several features of employment practices in Japanese companies: long service, frequent personnel reshuffling (transfers, reassignments and rotations) and employees' acquiring a work capacity due to OJT.

This is undoubtedly a hypothesis that is not based on empirical research. Koike himself emphasised that it was 'dogmatic and biased' and 'complete speculation' (Koike 1981: 29, 31). Even after that, Koike never conducted empirical, comparative research into foreign companies. In fact, Koike's understanding of European and American companies was nothing more than a subjective impression. For instance, in America performance appraisals are heavily regulated by laws prohibiting employment discrimination. This has led to the elimination of arbitrary appraisals (Endō 1999: 107–110; Nagayoshi 2000–01). In Germany performance appraisals are heavily regulated by labour unions based on labour-management agreements and discretionary appraisals have been eliminated (Asao 1993; Tōnai 1995). It is the various provisions of the Works Constitution Act (*Betriebsverfassungsgesetz*) that provide security against this (Ogata 1999).

However, as this sophisticated hypothesis was congruent with trends in the 1980s, it can be said that it was only the notion that 'personnel assessments of Japanese companies are fairer than performance appraisals of foreign companies' that became popular among researchers. Moreover, from around 1986, Koike himself began speaking to Aoki as if it was a verified hypothesis, or an established theory (Koike 1986; Aoki, Koike and Nakatani 1986). The spread of this hypothesis was the beginning of all theories concerning 'fair assessments.'

Criticism

Are the reasons Koike cites correct? Based on Koike's reasoning, it is necessary to fulfil the following conditions in order to increase the assessment's degree of fairness. First, multiple assessors should conduct each assessment independently without referring to or being influenced by other assessors' results. Second, the mean value of the assessment results should be used. If this is done, it is believed it will offset errors in the individual assessment results and also increase their accuracy. On the other hand, if the assessments are conducted while referring to other assessors' results, it is feared they will be influenced by these. Although this will improve the consistency of the assessment results among the assessors, there is a fear it may also lead to consistently erroneous results.

How then are personnel assessments actually conducted? The assessors' manual frequently instructs them to 'refer to your predecessor's assessment results.' Previous assessment results are sometimes written down in the assessment form in advance for the sake of the present assessor's convenience. For instance, a certain company's assessment form that was made public in 1996 contained three years worth of assessment results. The reason given for this was 'listing three years worth of assessment results will reduce the impact of changes in one's superiors, duties and place of work' (Nikkeiren-Kōhōbu ed. 1996: 256). That is, it recommends that assessors refer to other assessors' results. In other words, it is believed individual assessors should not conduct assessments independently.

Although this system leads to more consistent assessment results among assessors, it can also result in an increase in erroneous results. Moreover, a system has not been established that will prevent this. A 'market' for erroneous results is not only a theoretical possibility, it actually occurs. To cite an obvious example, the personnel assessments of female employees who provide long service to large companies are frequently viewed negatively when determining promotions and wage increases. This has led to appeals from female employees to rectify their assessments. A part of this phenomenon can be explained by prejudice against long serving female employees and the absence of a mechanism to protect against the establishment of a 'market' for consistently biased assessment results.

In fact, the assessors themselves believe the results vary according to the individual assessors. According to a recent survey of section chiefs (1604 in total) from 24 companies, which asked the greatest number of levels by which the results of a five-level survey changed following a change in assessors, 58.6% replied one level; 32.8% – two levels; 3.7% – greater than three levels; and 4.2% – no change (Nihon Rōdō Kenkyū Kikō 1998: 113). It may be 'common sense' among assessors that assessment results vary according to individual assessors. Yet, I would like to pay attention to the fact that it is precisely because the respondents know their predecessors' assessment results that these responses were obtained.

I can surmise that the reason the assessment results vary is that there are many evaluation items such as 'passion/will' and 'ability' used in the personnel assessments of Japanese companies, which require subjective judgment. Because judgment is subjective, there is considerable variation. Japanese companies leave the excessive subjectivity inherent in personnel assessments intact, but pursue consistency of assessment results and require assessors to refer to other assessors' results. However, this can also lead to an increase in erroneous assessment results. This is the 'market' for assessments that Koike gave as a reason for the fairness of Japanese assessments – it does not necessarily imply a 'fair assessment,' but can imply an unfair one.

The 'job-matrix chart'

The second reason Koike cites for the 'fairness' of assessments is a practice he refers to as the 'job-matrix chart' for production workers (Koike 1989: 319–338, Koike 1994: 261–274). According to Koike, there are two types of 'job-matrix charts.' One is a form that displays production workers' 'breadth of experience,' and the other shows 'depth of experience.' In addition, a factory manager evaluates production workers' 'breadth of experience' and 'depth of experience' 'every three months' and 'sometimes displays these on the factory wall.' Koike points out that this practice reduces the arbitrariness of assessments. It was Koike who pointed out for the first time that the chart, which is understood as a practice that promotes skill training, increases the assessments' degree of fairness. The paper of Koike's in which this was noted was included in a volume of articles entitled *Japanese Companies* (Japanese version) or *Business Enterprise in Japan* (English version) that resulted from a conference attended by eminent economists and business administration scholars (Imai and Komiya 1989, 1994). *Japanese Companies* went through many reprints in Japan, which is probably why the second reason Koike cites for the 'fairness' of assessments became so popular.

Other criticisms

How important are the reasons Koike cites for the 'fairness' of assessments? I do not believe they are so important. This is because the skill evaluation criteria, which are only dealt with by the 'job-matrix chart,' are limited to part of these criteria. As is well known, there are many evaluation criteria in Japanese personnel assessments, which are classified into three broad categories: 'results,' 'passion/will' and 'ability.' Skill evaluations are limited to part of these criteria. Therefore, assessment results are not determined by merely evaluating skill. They are strongly influenced by the criteria in the 'passion/will' category. The claim that 'simply being skilled will not improve assessments' can often be heard when conducting survey interviews at factories. Indeed, not determining results merely based on skill evaluation is a feature of personnel assessments in Japanese companies. One cannot attach too much importance to the practice of 'job-matrix charts' as a reason for 'fairness.'

Incidentally, in what is truly surprising, of the two types of 'job-matrix charts' that Koike highlights as documented evidence, 'the job-matrix chart for depth of experience,' does not actually exist. It is now clear that Koike 'made up' this evidence. It was Endō who first raised suspicions regarding this (Endō 1999: 23–26). Nomura Masami made it clear from what information Koike 'made up' the evidence (Nomura 2001). 'The job-matrix chart for depth of experience' was an essential piece of documented evidence that substantiated the theory of 'intellectual skill.' However, the act of 'making up' evidence to substantiate one's own argument can only be called a rare scandal. At a time now when it has been revealed that all of Koike's arguments, namely, the theories of 'intellectual skill' and 'fair assessments,' would not stand up without 'making up' this evidence, it is only natural to scrutinise closely the essence of Koike's arguments and why they had formerly gained considerable influence in academia.

Criticism of the various reasons for 'fair assessments'

Aoki Masahiko's reasons for 'fairness'

The first person who listed the reasons for 'fairness' without rhyme or reason was Aoki Masahiko – a researcher who had gained international acclaim. Aoki cited four reasons for the 'fairness' of assessments in Japanese companies after making a comparison with appraisals in American companies (Aoki 1988: 56). According to Aoki, although one 'cannot deny the partiality' associated with assessments in Japanese companies, there are four reasons why this 'can be deterred to a certain extent.' First, assessors cannot make arbitrary decisions because assessment procedures are regularised and standardised by the personnel division. Second, multiple assessors evaluate employees over a long period of time. Third, dissatisfied employees can appeal to the personnel division to be relocated. Fourth, the informal reputation of bosses among their subordinates influences their career prospects.

Criticism

Are the reasons Aoki cited correct? Because the first and fourth reasons also apply to appraisals in other advanced industrialised countries such as America, they do not explain why assessments in Japan are fairer than appraisals conducted overseas. On the contrary, as will be discussed later, these reasons are linked to those features that reveal distinct unfairness associated with assessments in Japan. Therefore, if Aoki was to point out the first and fourth reasons, he would be asked for his opinion of this fundamental problem. However, Aoki makes no mention of this at all.

The second reason is a rehash of one Koike cites for 'fairness.' However, Aoki did not write down that this reason was Koike's idea. Why did Aoki not make this clear? Is it because he directly heard Koike speak as if it was an established theory (Aoki, Koike, and Nakatani 1986)? Did Aoki judge that it was not necessary to point this out because it was an established theory? If this is the case, Aoki's judgement was thoughtless for a researcher. This reason has already been criticised because of the problems associated with it.

The third reason is incorrect. It is understood that Japanese companies are clearly authorised to order employees to relocate without promoting them. The basis for this does not lie in seeking employees for particular types of work, but in an employment practice whereby companies take on employees without specifying the nature of the job. It is precisely because of this that companies are authorised to relocate employees. This practice has the support of the courts. It is rare for the personnel division in Japanese companies to fulfil employees' wishes regarding job relocation. In addition, dissatisfied employees in Japanese companies are deterred from seeking to resolve their problems through job changes because the seniority-based wage system makes this disadvantageous. Incidentally, because American companies seek employees to fill specific jobs, it is unusual for them to order employees to relocate without promoting them. Unlike Japanese companies, American companies arrange a 'job-posting program' to give incumbent employees opportunity to fulfil their wishes to be relocated. Moreover, it is possible for dissatisfied employees in American companies to resolve their problems through job changes, because there is no seniority-based wage system. If the 'job-posting program' is common practice in American companies, the third reason accords fully with American companies, but not their

Japanese counterparts. Aoki does not understand the differences in employment practices between Japanese and American companies.

Looking back from the present, it is even surprising that Aoki was satisfied with this set of reasons. According to my understanding, it is because these reasons are either simply casual ideas or are a rehash of Koike's work. Aoki may not have been satisfied completely, because he originally used the words 'can deter to a certain extent.' However, he did not properly examine the 'fear of partiality.' Ultimately, the reason for this is that he initially assumed that personnel assessments in Japanese companies are undoubtedly fair based on the fact that Japanese companies are extremely competitive in international markets. The Four reasons Aoki cites were certainly a product of the times.

Koike Kazuo and Aoki Masahiko, both eminent scholars, developed the theory of 'fair assessments.' Moreover, Koike spoke as if it was an established theory, and Aoki borrowed from what he thought was an established theory. If this is the case, it is not surprising that other economists and business management scholars believed the notion that personnel assessments in Japanese companies are conducted fairly to be already an established theory that did not require substantiation.

Fujimura Hiroyuki's article

The first 'academic thesis' to openly display such bias was Fujimura Hiroyuki's 'An International Comparison of Performance Appraisals' (Fujimura 1989). Fujimura put forward the proposition that 'in order to secure the fairness of personnel assessments in Japanese companies, three systems: the self-reporting system, the interview system and assessor training, have been established.' In order to advocate this, Fujimura's research should have featured a comparison with overseas cases to demonstrate that either these systems have not been introduced in other advanced industrialised countries, or even if they have, their content and level are lower than in Japan. However, Fujimura not only came to this conclusion without comparing these three systems overseas, but also without making any mention of them at all. Therefore, despite giving it the title 'international comparison,' the article was a curious 'academic thesis' that displayed little concern for overseas systems. Because the 'fair assessments' assertion had already become an established theory, did Fujimura think that it probably required neither substantiation nor mention?

The 'self-reporting system' is the modification of the Management by Objectives (MBO) system, which was developed and is widely used at present in America. This is not particularly specialised knowledge. Fujimura does not understand it. The 'self-reporting system' also exists overseas, as does 'assessor training.' Fujimura did not conduct research into the content and level of both systems overseas, so we must wait for future investigation. It is certain, however, that these systems do not only exist in Japan. Moreover, the 'interview system' that Fujimura made note of 'backfired.' As will be discussed later, this is because this system is linked to the significant unfairness of assessments in Japan.

Itami Hiroyuki and Kagono Tadao's textbook

Even textbooks treated the theory of 'fair assessments' as an established theory. In one of the most widely read business management textbooks today, Itami Hiroyuki and Kagono Tadao, after making a comparison with American companies, gave three reasons for the fairness of assessments in Japanese companies (Itami and Kagono 1989: 508–509; 1993: 542–43). First, multiple bosses conduct assessments over a long period of time. Second, because Japanese companies concentrate personnel management into their personnel division of head office, the personnel division can re-evaluate bosses' assessments. Third, a market for assessments develops because many of them are collected in the personnel division.

Are these reasons correct? The first is a rehash of Koike's reason. While this may also apply to the second and third reasons, Itami and Kagono did adopt a novel approach by focusing on an organisational feature of Japanese companies, that is, the centralisation of personnel management into the personnel division of head office. In addition, based on this, they pointed out a third reason: a 'market' for assessments develops in the personnel division. However, the problems associated with Koike's reasons have already been critiqued and are still valid even if a 'market' for assessments develops in the personnel division.

The second reason is that the personnel division 'monitors' bosses. If Itami and Kagono point out this 'monitoring,' which takes place during the assessment process, why do they not refer to the importance of 'monitoring' of final assessment results that have been determined by the personnel division? It is precisely the 'monitoring' of final assessment results, to be discussed later, that is related to the significant unfairness of assessments in Japan.

The second and third reasons concern the distinctive practice of 'adjustment' in Japanese companies. Here, assessments conducted by employees' direct bosses are not final; the personnel division 'adjusts' these and turns them into final results. 'Adjustment' often involves changing first-stage assessments, which are conducted as absolute evaluations (there is an evaluation standard outside the group being evaluated), into relative evaluations (there is an evaluation standard within the group being evaluated). Therefore, under the practice of 'adjustment,' the assessment results of the first-stage assessors, who are employees' direct bosses, may not become the final results. Because of this possibility, the practice of 'adjustment' is also related to the definite unfairness of assessments in Japan, which is discussed later.

Aoki Masahiko and Okuno Masahiro's textbook

An advanced textbook in comparative institutional economic analysis is similar in this regard. After considering appraisals in American companies, Aoki Masahiko and Okuno Masahiro stated that with assessments in Japanese companies, 'efforts are made to establish objective and fair assessment standards under the supervision of the personnel division.' As an example, they provide a detailed introduction of two types of 'job-matrix charts' (Aoki and Okuno 1996: 133–134). 'Fair assessment standards' is the first reason Aoki cites for 'fairness' and the 'job-matrix chart' is a rehash of Koike's reason. The problems associated with these reasons have already been criticised.

What deserves special mention is that this textbook illustrates how dangerous 'borrowing' is for researchers. Although one type of 'job-matrix chart' was 'made up' by Koike, because they accepted and borrowed from this 'job-matrix chart,' Aoki and Okuno should have been aware that every time readers scanned the text's narrative, they would probably smile wryly or derisively.

Influencing court decisions?

At the end of the 1990s, the theory of 'fair assessments' may have begun to influence court decisions. In recent court cases involving wage discrimination in which the judges ruled against employees, the judges cited 'fair assessments' as an important reason for their decision. That is, the judges stated that 'detailed systemic preparation has been undertaken with regards to the evaluation methodology, procedures, and subjects etc. of the assessments,' enumerating various particulars of these systems without rhyme or reason. They also ruled that the assessments of the cases involved were fair (National Life Finance Corporation Case Tokyo District Court Decision – presiding judge Takase Saburō – 2 February 2000). This ruling is the theory of 'fair assessments' itself. This may be a new sign of the situation ahead because it was uncommon for courts to rule on the theory of 'fair assessments' until this time. I believe this to be a serious matter.

An insufficient right to know assessment results

When making claims about the fairness of personnel assessments in Japanese companies, there is an assessment mechanism that Koike, Aoki, other researchers and judge Takase did not make any mention of. This mechanism is also seen as an integral component in attaining fairness of performance appraisals in advanced industrialised countries such as America. This mechanism is employees' right to know their appraisal results. Moreover, it involves the preparation of a series of procedures premised upon this right.

The right to know in America

Because scholars advocating a theory of 'fair assessments' normally do so after making comparisons with appraisals in American companies, I will explain employees' right to know their appraisal results, highlighting examples of the situation in America (Endō 1999: 97–101).

'The employees' signature column'

There is an 'employees' signature column' in perhaps all appraisal forms in American companies. After companies show employees the forms in which the appraisal results are recorded, they request a signature from the employees signifying that they have reviewed it. Because of the development of laws prohibiting employment discrimination, in the event that employees do not review the appraisal results, a precedent is set whereby the court rules the appraisal to be discriminatory. This is the reason why employees' signature columns have become an established practice in America. When this precedent is established, American companies have to obtain employee's signatures, which are to be submitted as explicit documentary evidence to the court demonstrating that employees have reviewed the appraisal results. It is essential for American companies to do so in order for appraisals not to be judged discriminatory in court in the event an employee files a suit claiming these are unfair. In other words, the burden of proof that employees have reviewed the appraisal results lies with the companies. What the 'employees' signature column' shows is that employees have the legal right to know their appraisal results. This right is not only valid in terms of legal precedent, but also statute. In more than ten states, beginning with Massachusetts, the right of employees to examine company personnel records is recognised by state laws.

If companies lose a case without being able to prove that they informed employees of their appraisal result, they not only have to pay compensation to the employees (who are the plaintiffs) for damages, but in some cases, must also pay punitive damages that can amount to several times the cost of the damage incurred. Ordering punitive damages is a legal measure designed to force companies not to undertake discriminatory employment practices. This ensures companies will make efforts to show employees appraisal results.

'Notice about allowing for disapproval'

Creating a precedent whereby companies lose a case if employees do not review their appraisal results, and ensuring the burden of proof that employees have reviewed these rests with the companies led to the establishment of a new practice. It is a 'notice about allowing for disapproval' appended to the 'employees' signature column.' The note, for example, states 'Your signature does not necessarily mean that you agree with the appraisal result. What it simply means is that the appraisal result was reviewed by you.' On reviewing their appraisal results, there may be employees who are dissatisfied or disagree with them and refuse to sign in the fear that doing so will be interpreted as their agreeing with it. If those employees should not sign and later file a suit in the court claiming discriminatory assessments, the companies would certainly lose the case because of the absence of evidence that the companies informed them of their appraisal results. Therefore, companies must make considerable effort to get employees not to refuse to sign their appraisal forms, that is, to obtain evidence in order not to lose cases fought in court over the fairness of appraisals. The existence of a 'notice about allowing for disapproval' symbolises the significance of the burden of proof that rests with companies.

Presently in court cases in America where the fairness of appraisals is in dispute, it could even be the case that informing employees of their appraisal results is the very precondition for companies to decide to fight. Because it can be reasonably predicted that the decision will go against companies if they do not show employees their appraisal results, fighting the matter out in court may be futile for companies. It is fair to say that while a case is fought after fulfilling this precondition, there are several precedents that have been established concerning other mechanisms linked to the fairness of appraisals. For instance, when appraisals are not conducted based on job analysis, companies will lose the case (Endō 1999: 107–110).

The absence of a right to know in Japan

In Japan employees do not have the right to know their assessment results. As the various surveys reveal, Japanese companies that inform employees of their assessment results are a minority. Because those companies surveyed frequently include so-called foreign-affiliated firms, when one excludes these and picks out companies that only go as far as to inform employees of their assessment results, the number is really extremely small. At the highest estimate, this equated to only about one percent of Japanese companies in the 1980's. However, it should be noted that this figure has risen somewhat since the late 1990s. This situation reflects the fact that the right for employees to know their assessment results does not even exist legally as an intra-company right. Even though there are many court cases in Japan fought over fair assessments, and also employees (who are the plaintiffs) who demand that companies present the assessment results as evidence to the court, there are virtually no companies that comply with these requests.

The advocates of the theory of 'fair assessments' ignore employees' right to know their assessment results. They are also ignorant of the fact that employees' right to know their appraisal results in advanced industrial countries such as America is seen as pivotal in achieving fair performance appraisals. When one takes this right into consideration, the reasons frequently cited for 'fairness' are exposed as hollow.

Without the right to know: The hollow reasons cited for 'fairness'

As discussed previously, among the four reasons Aoki cites for 'fairness,' the first and the fourth are applicable to appraisals in America and other advanced industrial countries. However, in Japanese companies the first of these: 'the regularisation and standardisation of assessment procedures,' does not include making it obligatory for them to notify employees of their assessment results. Aoki is ignorant of this. Therefore, Aoki should have stated why the assessments in Japanese companies (which lack processes by which employees are notified of assessment results) 'can deter partiality' more than the appraisals in American companies (which do have these processes, and where the employees' right to access information is guaranteed). Moreover, when Aoki pointed out the fourth reason: 'the informal reputation among subordinates,' he should have stated why this feature of Japanese companies (where employees are not notified of assessment results) 'can deter partiality' more successfully than the same feature developed in American companies (where the employees' right to access their appraisal results is guaranteed).

When Fujimura pointed out 'the interview system,' he was ignorant of the fact that it is common for Japanese companies not to notify employees of their assessment results during 'interviews.' Therefore, his understanding is that personnel assessments in Japanese companies (where 'interviews' are conducted but employees are not notified of their assessment results) are fairer than performance appraisals in American companies (where 'interviews' are conducted and employees have the right to be notified of their appraisal results).

If Itami and Kagono were to point out the effects of 'monitoring' by the personnel division on bosses' assessments in the process, they should have also referred to the effects of 'monitoring' by the assessed employees on the final assessment results that had been determined by the personnel division. In addition, in order for employees to be able to 'monitor,' of course, it is necessary for them to be notified of their assessment results.

Moreover, when Itami and Kagono point out the practice of 'adjustment,' they do not consider that a failure to notify employees of their assessment results is not unrelated to the practice of 'adjustment.' This relationship means that the practice of 'adjustment' makes it difficult to notify employees of their final assessment results. That is, when the final result is more poorly 'adjusted' than the first stage result, and when the first stage assessors notify employees of their final results, it is difficult for the first stage assessors to convince employees of the reasons for the poor, final results because they do not know the reasons. When an absolute evaluation is changed into a relative evaluation during the 'adjustment' process, the difficulties may further increase. Do Japanese companies fail to notify employees of their assessment results because many of them prioritise the practice of 'adjustment,' which makes notification difficult? Itami and Kagono should have examined such an issue.

Assessment discrimination against long-serving employees

Thus far, I have examined and critiqued the various reasons highlighted in the theory of 'fair assessments.' However, there is a simpler and easier method of pointing out the errors of this theory. This is by noting the significant possibility that personnel assessments in Japanese companies are used as a tool for employment discrimination and, as a result, there are not a few instances in which employees claim assessment discrimination and file a suit in court. This completely contradicts the theory of 'fair assessments.'

Employees filing a suit in court

Among employees working in Japanese companies for a long period of time, there is a certain group who are treated in such a way that their promotions take longer and salary increases are smaller than most other employees. While the influence on the treatment of assessment results is minor in a year, it becomes significant after a decade. After a decade or more, there are occasions when this group of employees feels they can no longer endure the consistently poor treatment. They then claim employment discrimination and take companies to court seeking a resolution to this problem. Such court cases increased from the mid-1960s. Initially, there were many cases in which employees claimed they had been discriminated against because of their beliefs and ideologies – although the companies did not acknowledge this as a cause of discrimination. However, from the mid-1980s, just when the theory of 'fair assessments' was being propagated, cases emerged in which women claimed they faced discrimination because of their gender.

When these cases were taken to court, the companies often claimed the reason for the poor treatment was that these employees' past assessment results were consistently poor. Moreover, the companies of course claimed that the assessments were conducted fairly. Although the companies made such assertions, there are virtually no instances in which they presented employees past assessment results as evidence to the court – even when the employees (who were the plaintiffs) demanded that the companies present their assessment results as evidence to the court. Instead, the companies highlighted employees' minor errors and failures and claimed they had a low work capacity. There are not a few instances in which the evidence to support these claims rested with the testimony of their boss.

The manner in which judges preside over the proceedings

Judges rarely order companies to present assessment results as evidence to substantiate their claims. They usually permit companies to arrange the testimony of many bosses, and employees to make a counterargument. Therefore, each party concerned needs considerable time. This is typical of the way in which judges preside over the proceedings in Japan. It is not uncommon for these cases to take more than 10 years to resolve. Moreover, the costs of going to trial are exorbitant. In my opinion, this procedure in Japan is difficult to understand. While companies emphasise employees' mistakes and failures, they do not demonstrate how these are reflected in actual assessment results or influence employee treatment. Therefore, I think the alleged employees' mistakes and failures cannot substantiate actual assessment results, whether they are right or wrong. This is the case particularly when a relative evaluation is used. Judges' 'beliefs,' or judges making an inference about actual assessment results from mistakes and failures alleged by companies, I think, runs counter to the principle of 'trial by evidence' and is something judges fundamentally 'should not do.' In any case, such an approach greatly influences court cases concerning assessment discrimination in Japan.

If it was an American judge...

Based on an established legal precedent in America today, what ruling would an American judge hand down in a case concerning assessment discrimination in Japan? One can easily imagine the ruling. It would almost certainly be a victory for the employees (the plaintiffs). The reason is simple: employees were not informed of their assessment results. Indeed, the ruling may be that 'the courts themselves are not set up' to handle these cases. It is because the courts in Japan do not recognise employees' right to know their assessment results – a right that is seen as critical for the fairness of performance appraisals in America. In other words, it is because American judges cannot understand that without demanding that companies present the assessment results to the court as material evidence, Japanese judges give the parties concerned considerable time to fight each other over the fairness of assessments on the other 'evidence.' Significant differences exist between Japan and America with regards to court cases fought over assessment discrimination. If we compare the fairness of assessments in Japan and America, we must take into consideration this difference in legal rights.[1]

Employees' determination to present a case to the court claiming assessment discrimination in Japan means they realise they have to bear a heavy burden. It is more burdensome than in America. This is because it costs employees (who are plaintiffs) considerable time and money. In addition, the psychological burden is not insignificant. Moreover, employees' chances of winning are lower than in America. This is because the manner in which judges preside over proceedings in court in Japan is disadvantageous for employees. As a result, there are relatively fewer cases in Japan fought over assessment discrimination than in America. This is not because discrimination does not exist, but because the court system preventing discrimination is weak in Japan. Therefore, in Japan employees only take their claims to court in 'extreme cases.'

Scholars such as Koike Kazuo and Aoki Masahiko who claimed that personnel assessments in Japan were fair should not ignore the fact that personnel assessments may have been used as a tool for employment discrimination, and also that employees' right to know their assessment results does not exist. Moreover, if they refer to performance appraisals in America, they should not overlook the development of laws prohibiting employment discrimination, which strongly suppresses the arbitrariness of performance appraisals, and the establishment of employees' right to know their appraisal results.

Koike and Aoki based their analyses on the premise that Japanese companies were highly competitive internationally in the 1980s. They were convinced that 'personnel assessments in Japanese companies must be fair.' Meanwhile, they did not conduct any research on the various features of personnel assessments adequately. However, these ideas should be quickly dispelled today. Not only is the prejudicial theory of 'fair assessments' incorrect, but it also impedes the realisation of social justice in the sense of making personnel assessments as fair as possible.

2 Is Workshop Information Shared?

Uichi Asao

'Theory of horizontal information structure'

The strength of Japanese companies, particularly the export manufacturing industry, is that in addition to operating workers sharing information (knowledge), they raise product quality and productivity as a result of personally resolving and coping with the various problems that occur in each workshop. This theory of Japanese companies was widely disseminated from the 1980s to the early 1990s. Aoki Masahiko's 'theory of horizontal information structure' was an exemplar of this.

According to Aoki, the information structure (the way in which work is coordinated) in Japanese companies in characterised by decentralised and horizontal coordination based on knowledge sharing. The information structure in American companies is characterised by centralised and vertical coordination based on specialisation (Aoki 1988: mostly from chapter two). The notable differences in the ways in which work is coordinated in Japanese and American companies are highlighted by the following 'stylised facts' (p. 10) based on a comparison of large Japanese and American companies with labour unions in the manufacturing industry (automobiles and steel) until the mid-1970s.

The following three points are characteristic of the way in which work is coordinated in American companies. First, because of the importance attached to specialisation and job classification in American companies, coping with emergencies (workshop coordination) such as worker absenteeism, malfunctioning machines and the production of defective products is left to specialists (eg. reliefmen, repairmen and inspectors) under the instruction of the on-the-job superintendent. Operating workers are not responsible for coping with such emergencies (according to the principle of specialisation, knowledge is not shared between specialists and operating workers). For instance, operating workers cannot stop the production line based on their own judgement, even when the section for which they are responsible produces defective products. In other words, the everyday tasks performed by operating workers (executive function) and the job of coping with emergencies (coordinated function) are separated (separated system).

Second, this principle of specialisation is also dominant in the area of intershop coordination. Exchanging necessary information for the purpose of coordinating each workshop's production in coping with market fluctuations and emergencies in the manufacturing process becomes a specialised function of management, which is structured as a ranking hierarchy (eg. a central planning division and delivery division for the manufacturing sector). Each workshop is not directly involved (in other words, information is not shared between each workshop). Therefore, intermediate stock such as materials, parts and in-process products functions as a buffer for coordinating production.

To sum up, in American companies coordinating work within and between workshops becomes a specialised task for super-intendents and managers. As a result, professional and hierarchical control is more complex. This method of work coordination is characterised as a centralised or vertical information structure.

On the other hand, according to Aoki, the characteristics of work coordination in Japanese companies are the exact opposite of American firms. First, because the degree of job differentiation and specialisation are low in Japanese companies, coping with emergencies (workshop coordination) such as worker absenteeism, malfunctioning machines and the production of defective products tends 'to be entrusted to a team of operating workers' (p. 10). For instance, 'the J-firm (a Japanese company) does not have a specialised reliefman to cope with absenteeism. Instead, it relies on mass relief or the ad hoc reassignment of jobs at the discretion of the foreman. Inspection positions are also often rotated among operating workers on the shopfloor. When a high number of defective products are found, the cause of and solution to the problem are sought on the spot before calling in help from outside (p. 13–14).' Moreover, 'In fact, the J-firm has increasingly delegated work control to the shopfloor level since the mid-1960s and has encouraged workers to solve problems by themselves whenever possible. Individual workers are authorised to stop a production line when necessary. The number of specialists – such as repairmen, product inspectors and technicians – has been reduced as much as possible, and, when necessary, their expertise is used to help shopfloor workers solve a particular problem; thus they act as consultants rather than performing a special function exclusively (p. 16).' In other words, there is a tendency for the everyday tasks that operating workers perform (executive function) and the job of coping with emergencies (coordinated function) to be integrated (integrated system). What makes this possible is knowledge sharing amongst workers and individual workers acquiring wide-ranging skills (high information processing capability) due to job rotation.

Second, at the J-firm, the phenomenon on the shopfloor – the ambiguity and fluidity of jurisdiction – also appears in the sphere of intershop coordination. An example of this is Toyota's just-in-time (*kanban*) system.[1] Under the just-in-time system, the fine-tuning of production is performed in coping with evolving market conditions not through the administrative offices above the operating units but by the interconnected workshops, which maintain direct, horizontal contacts through the *kanban*. In other words, 'the centralized scheduling of production for a certain period of time only provides a general framework. As a supplement to the centralized plan, horizontal and direct dealing between interconnected shops for the actual transfer of materials, parts, and in-process products takes place within the period of implementation in order to fine-tune actual final output production to changing market conditions and in-process emergencies. The lack of a central office to control and expedite the flow of materials among shops is a conspicuous feature of the assembly factory of the J-firm (p. 22).'

In short, coordination within and between workshops in Japanese companies is not conducted through specialisation and upper management, as is the case with American companies. Instead, workers and workshops that are of equal status conduct this in the form of horizontal communication (information sharing). This method of work coordination is characterised as a de-centralised or horizontal information structure. It is considered to be efficient in assembly industries such as automobile, electric and electronic machinery industry for the following reasons. Markets and technology are constantly changing in these industries. These changes increase the occurrence of emergencies in companies such as fluctuations in production quantities, the production of defective products and malfunctioning machines. Coping with these emergencies, that is, work coordination in companies, is not left to specialists such as repairmen and inspectors or instructions by upper management, but is entrusted to the autonomous problem solving capabilities of the various workshops and communication channels among themselves (information sharing). They can therefore coordinate their works in a swift and flexible manner.

In this way, Aoki's model sharply contrasted the features of the information structure in Japanese companies with those in America. The model is not only concise, but because of its consistency in delineating the same characteristics of coordination within and between workshops, it appears to capture superbly the distinctive features of Japanese companies. It also appears to explain the high productivity of Japanese companies in the assembly industry. Certainly, Aoki's 'theory of horizontal information structure' captures one aspect of work coordination in Japanese companies (especially automobile assembly manufacturers represented by Toyota). However, this theory does not explain the total picture – just one aspect of coordination in Japanese companies. This chapter highlights the problems associated with the 'theory of horizontal information organization,' which sees the manner in which work is coordinated in Japanese companies as decentralised, horizontal coordination based on knowledge sharing (integrated system). Because Aoki's theory posits that automobile assembly manufacturers are, in effect, a typical example of Japanese companies, the argument put forward in this chapter focuses on them.

How work is coordinated

As discussed above, according to the 'theory of horizontal information organization,' coping with emergencies such as worker absenteeism, malfunctioning machines and the production of defective products (workshop coordination), and fine-tuning of production plans in coping with market changes (intershop coordination) are similarly seen as 'decentralised,' 'horizontal' coordination based on 'knowledge sharing (integrated system).' However, as will be discussed below, the way in which work is coordinated within and between workshops differs according to their particular characteristics. It is incorrect to make similar distinctions and identify features that differ to reality, while ignoring these differences.

Coordination in the workshop

I will first scrutinise coordination in the workshop. Although different companies may call it a 'group' (*kumi*) or a 'team' (*han*), the term 'workshop' in this context refers to the most basic work organisation in a factory under the jurisdiction of a foreman (group leader or *kumichō*).

1. I will consider coping with worker absenteeism. According to Aoki, there are no reliefmen for absent workers in Japanese automobile manufacturers. Coping with absenteeism is left to a work group (workshop) in which absent workers are covered through mass relief or the ad hoc reassignment of jobs at the foreman's discretion. In other words, the function of coordinating in response to circumstances involving absenteeism is not 'separated' from workers' everyday work (executive function), but integrated with it, or the knowledge required to respond to absenteeism is shared in the workshop. Therefore, it is called 'decentralised,' 'horizontal' co-ordination based on 'knowledge sharing.' However, there are problems associated with such an understanding.

First, if production goals are set per unit of time, in order to coordinate within the work group (workshop) to cover for absent workers, there are cases when the foreman – the person responsible for the work group and who is not normally engaged in operating work (line work) – and the team leader etc., who serves under him, are able to take on the work in place of the absent worker. When this is impossible, 'assistance' must be sought from another group (workshop).

In the case of the former, while the task of 'coping with absenteeism' (coordination function) is 'integrated' with the team leader and the foreman, it is not 'integrated' with other group members. In other words, in this case, coping with absenteeism is not left to the work group, but specific workers such as the team leader and foreman (it is a section of workers and not the workshop as a whole who share the knowledge to cope with absenteeism).

According to Aoki, coping with absenteeism in the Japanese work organisation is also seen as decentralised coordination, in other words, the transferring of authority to the superintendent and leaders on the shopfloor such as the foreman and team leader. But this task is their duty. Therefore, making the distinction that the duty is a delegation of authority greatly distorts reality. The superintendent and leaders on the shopfloor are forced to bear responsibility rather than having some of their superiors' authority transferred to them.

On the other hand, in case absent employees cannot be covered from within the same work group, it is necessary to seek 'assistance' from a separate group . In this case, it can no longer be said to be coordination in the workshop, but coordination beyond it. Therefore, it can only be deemed to be coordination between workshops. If this is the case, this type of coordination should be called 'vertical' and not 'horizontal' because personnel coordination (assistance) is performed based on the understanding of upper management, which has jurisdiction over several of the workshops in question.

Second, let us refer to the mass relief of absent workers, not as the filling in for specific workers within the group, but as the redistribution of the absent person's tasks among group members. In this case, the amount of work per person, and therefore the cycle time, increases. This is only made possible by reducing the production goals per unit of time. However, as is well known, because the greater part of the production process of automobile assembly manufacturers is closely linked with the production line, it is impossible for a single work group to extend the cycle time. In the event that it becomes necessary to change the cycle time, a decision at the section or factory level, beyond the work group, is necessary. In other words, this work coordination cannot be undertaken within the workshop and therefore must be done 'vertically.'

2. Let's examine coping with malfunctioning machines and defective products. According to Aoki, this task tends to be entrusted to a team of operating workers. Because the coordinating function that copes with such emergencies is 'integrated' with and not 'separated from' workers' everyday tasks, it is said that 'decentralised,' 'horizontal' coordination is undertaken. Certainly, there are cases in which tasks such as carrying out relatively simple visual inspections (check for defective products) and discovering machinery faults etc. are included among the responsibilities of operating workers (regular employees) other than the foreman and team leader. As so far as it goes, it can be said that very simple coordinating

functions are 'integrated with' workers' everyday tasks. As Aoki also notes, the fact that operating workers perform a very simple coordination function may indicate that the degree of specialisation in Japan is lower than in America. However, this does not mean that it is coordination in the sense of a devolution of authority from senior to junior workers, nor does it mean 'horizontal' coordination between equals in direct contact with one another.

Intershop coordination

Next I will examine intershop coordination. The scale of the workshop in this context, unlike the jurisdictional sphere of foremen assumed in the case of coordination within the workshop, includes assembly shops or processes (a workshop comprising several work groups) such as those for casting, forging, machine processing, presses, automobile bodies and painting up to external subcontractors (suppliers) for parts. A typical example of 'decentralised,' horizontal' intershop coordination is the just-in-time system. In this system, 'the shop that receives the *kanban* from the final assembly line in turn dispatches its own *kanban* order forms to shops located immediately upstream, and, through the circular flow of *kanban*, the chain of bilateral order-delivery links between directly interconnected shops extends to the outside suppliers who are involved in long-term transactions with the final assembly manufacturer' (Aoki 1988: 23).

The fine-tuning of production plans between the preceding process and following processes in the firm, and between an assembly maker and subcontractors in the just-in-time system takes place without any communications from the central production management department to the various processes and subcontractors – so long as directions are given to those working on the final assembly line. Therefore, it can be argued that, along with the flow of goods such as parts and materials between those workshops directly interconnected, to the extent that information pertaining to production directives is communicated between those workshops according to the *kanban*, the actual information flows are 'horizontal.' Nevertheless, in this case, information pertaining to production directives flows unilaterally from the downstream workshop to the one upstream. In other words, the downstream workshop only gives orders for production quantities to its counterpart upstream. No coordination whatsoever takes place between interconnected workshops based on this information. It is also not 'decentralisation' in the sense that a boss' authority is transferred to subordinates. There are two reasons that explain this. First, the fine-tuning of production plans between workshops is made possible by using the *kanban* as tool for production management in order to utilise the production information directed at (ordered to) the final assembly line by the central production management department. Second, each workshop and worker does not possess the authority to fine-tune production plans.

To sum up, part of the task of coping with worker absenteeism, malfunctioning machines and defective products (coordinating function) in the workshop is 'integrated' with the everyday tasks of a set range of operating workers. In other words, 'knowledge is shared' not between operating workers as a whole, but between a few workers. However, this is not 'horizontal' coordination in the sense that people of equal status maintain direct contact or 'decentralised' in the sense that boss' authority is transferred to subordinates. On the other hand, to the extent that the fine-tuning of production quantities between the interconnected workshops occurs through information methods for production directives (*kanban*), the actual information flows in this regard can be characterised as 'horizontal.' However, it is a unilateral flow of information (production directives) and no coordination whatsoever is conducted between workshops. The authority to fine-tune is not 'decentralised' to each workshop and workers. In this manner, one can only say that it is unreasonable to perceive the method of coordination within and between workshops in Japanese companies as 'decentralised,' 'horizontal' coordination based on 'knowledge sharing' (integrated system).

'Stylised facts'

The 'theory of horizontal information structure' is based on the 'stylised facts' of Japanese companies outlined above. However, these 'stylised facts' are not a true reflection of reality. First, the degree to which executive and coordinating functions are integrated in the workshop is greatly overestimated. Second, by characterising coordination between workshops as 'horizontal,' its 'vertical' aspects are essentially ignored.

Overestimating 'integration'

According to the aforementioned 'stylised facts,' coping with emergencies such as worker absenteeism, malfunctioning machines and defective products in Japanese companies tends 'to be entrusted to a team of operating workers.' As we know, this is based on the theory of 'intellectual skills' that was formulated by Koike Kazuo.

Koike's theory posits that many production workers in large Japanese companies possess the ability to deal with 'changes and problems' (intellectual skills) (Koike 1996: 63–74). However, Nomura Masami criticises this theory of 'intellectual skills' (refer to chapter six of this book). One of Nomura's criticisms of Koike is that 'coping with changes and problems' in mass production assembly plants for automobile, electric and electronic machinery is mainly the responsibility of manufacturing technicians, foremen, maintenance workers or the improvement team (*kaizen* team). As is the case with coping with machine stoppages caused by small problems (*chokotei*) and changes in assembling automobile models, 'coping with changes and problems' by many operating workers is extremely simple. In other words, either the 'integration' of executive and coordinating functions in the workshop only applies to a few workers such as the foreman, or the degree of 'integration' at the level of many operating workers remains extremely low.

If we were to make an assumption regarding such criticisms of Koike's theory of 'intellectual skills,' the 'stylised facts' – such as coping with emergencies such as worker absenteeism, malfunctioning machines and defective products etc. 'is entrusted to a team of operating workers' – overestimate one aspect of reality because they paint a picture – just as coping with all emergencies is entrusted to a team of operating workers.

The claim that 'inspection positions are also often rotated among operating workers on the shopfloor' is another example of this. While there are no limits whatsoever on 'inspection positions,' automobile assembly line inspections can be divided into two broad categories: relatively simple inspections such as visual inspections and technical inspections in which instruments are used. Inspections conducted by operating workers on a rotational basis are relatively simple such as visual inspections, while technical inspections are conducted by inspectors who belong to the inspection department (Asao et al. 1999: 149).

Moreover, the claim that 'the J-firm (a Japanese company) does not have a specialised reliefman to cope with absenteeism, instead, it relies on mass relief or the ad hoc reassignment of jobs at the discretion of the foreman,' is not only an exaggeration but is also inaccurate. Certainly, 'specialised reliefmen to cope with absenteeism' are not organised outside the work group (in other words, there is no group of specialists whose main task is to fill in for absent workers). However, there are 'specialised reliefmen' in the work group for whom coping with absenteeism is an important task. As discussed in the previous section, in order to coordinate within the work group to cover for absent workers, there are a specific number of group members who are not engaged in operating work (line work). They have to be able to perform any task within the group. Therefore, personnel who are able to fill in for absent workers are limited to the team leader and other leaders under the foreman. I will demonstrate this using several examples from automobile assembly manufacturers.

At Toyota, one of the roles of the team leader, who serves under the foreman (group leader) – the person responsible for the group – is to work on the production line when workers from within the group are absent. During busy periods when there are staff shortages, there are times when even the group leader must work on the line. At Nissan, support members (instructors), whose responsibility is to cover for absent workers, are reassigned to work under a foreman at the rate of one in 15–20 workers. Even at Mazda there are 1–2 relief staff (people who can fill in for absent workers) in the organisation, which comprises the foreman, the foreman's assistant, team leader and the worker. There are many cases in which the team leaders serve as relief staff. Similarly, at Mitsubishi among the work group consisting of the foreman, deputy foreman, leader (line keeper) and workers, the leader (one person) performs the role of relief staff. In other words, one to two 'specialised reliefmen' to cope with absenteeism are reassigned to each group. While the coordination function to cope with absenteeism is 'integrated' with a few workers within the group, it is not 'integrated' with the majority of workers.

In this manner, because there are no limits whatsoever to the type of emergency that is the responsibility of the operating work group and those in charge according to the 'stylised facts,' Aoki, who was influenced by Koike, reaches the following understanding. That is, in Japanese companies 'the number of specialists – such as repairmen, product inspectors and technicians – has been reduced as much as possible, and, when necessary, their expertise is used to help shopfloor workers solve a particular problem; thus they act as consultants rather than performing a special function exclusively.' When malfunctioning machines and defective products occur in the factory, the understanding that specialists' 'expertise is used to help shopfloor workers solve a particular problem; thus they act as consultants rather than performing a special function exclusively,' greatly overestimates the role of operating workers and, conversely, significantly underestimates the role of specialists. The problems with which operating workers are able to cope are relatively simple. Resolving problems that require technical knowledge must be entrusted to plant maintenance workers, manufacturing technicians or outside specialists.

Ignoring the 'vertical' aspect

As outlined in the first section, according to the 'theory of horizontal information organization,' the fine-tuning of production plans in coping with market changes is carried out by the interconnected workshops (bypassing central management), which maintain direct contact through the *kanban*. It is understood that this type of 'horizontal' coordination is performed not only among the various processes of the automobile assembly plants, but also between the assembly plants and subcontractors.

However, as discussed earlier, the 'horizontal' flow of information concerning production directives is only uni-directional from the downstream to the upstream workshop. There is no coordination among the interconnected workshops. When fine-tuning production plans, production directives (orders) from central management must be clearly given to the production processes. Even if these directives (orders) are only given to the final assembly line of an automobile plant, changes in 'vertical' production plans, which are directives from central management, exist as a starting point. Essentially ignoring this aspect and exclusively depicting the features of the fine-tuning of production plans as 'horizontal' is one-sided.

Moreover, Kaneko (1997) provides the following critique of the claim that order-delivery relations (bargaining relations) between assembly manufacturers (subcontractees) and parts manufacturers (subcontractors) are 'horizontal.' First, because of the 'just-in-time' system, subcontractees now mass-produce high value-added products in their own factories. On the premise that a (vertical) stratified division of labour is established whereby products in which economies of scale does not apply are produced by outside subcontractors, the just-in-time system serves to burden subcontractors with the costs of keeping products in stock. Second, subcontractees utilise this vertical division of labour and by demanding that subcontractors lower supply costs and reduce production volumes, they force subcontractors to serve as employment coordination buffers. Third, there are some subcontractors that receive technical and managerial advice from those who are dispatched from the subcontractees to the subcontractors. The relationship includes the vertical communication of information from the subcontractee (107–109).

What is missing in the 'theory of horizontal information structure'

In comparison with American companies, Aoki's model, which characterises work coordination in Japanese companies as something decentralised and horizontal based on the knowledge sharing, argues that these features are important factors that explain the high efficiency (strong competitiveness) in Japanese mass production assembly industries such as automobile, electric and electronic machinery industry. Markets and technology are constantly changing in these industries. Work coordination in companies, which these changes increase, is not left to directives from upper management and specialists such as repairmen and inspectors. By entrusting it to the autonomous problem solving capabilities of the various workshops, which maintain communication channels among themselves (information sharing), coordination is therefore conducted in a swift and flexible manner. This type of coordination is possible not because of the fragmented and specialised skills of work groups, but by workers being able to acquire wide-ranging skills (high-level information processing capability rather than routine work skills).

However, it was pointed out in the previous section that the 'theory of horizontal information structure' ignores the 'vertical' aspects of coordination between workshops. In addition, the high information processing capabilities that many operating workers, who share workshop knowledge, are claimed to possess (that is, the degree of 'integration' between executive functions and coordinating functions) is overestimated – at least in mass production factories such as automobile assembly plants. Instead, 'integration' is limited to a few workers such as the foreman. Moreover, even the foremen's knowledge has not reached a particularly high level. Therefore, one cannot distinguish work coordination in Japanese mass production assembly plants by only the horizontal flow of information and the partial integration of executive and coordinating functions.

Limiting the analysis to factory production systems, including the way work is coordinated in Toyota's automobile assembly plants, I will examine the important elements missing in the 'theory of horizontal information structure.'

A mechanism that steers supervisors into improvement activities

Toyota's factory production system is known as the Toyota production system. In this system, cost reductions are the biggest means by which it attains high earnings. Toyota, therefore, aims to drastically eliminate waste (*muda*). For Toyota, in order to eliminate waste, it is important to identify its causes and make improvements for the purpose of removing it. For instance, when waste such as defective products is produced, stopping the production line, ascertaining the causes and making improvements so the same defects do not occur again is one such method (Ōno 1978).

In this manner, the Toyota production system places emphasis on improvement activities in order to achieve high efficiency. Such improvement activities in the factory consist of significant improvements such as introducing automatic equipment and changing the production line, and minor improvements such as changing the combination of work elements, adding work carts and changing the width of shelving for parts. Among these, the superintendent (mainly the group and team leaders) is largely responsible for minor improvements.

Clearly, the superintendent plays an important role in minor improvement activities. First, among the 'important roles (guidelines) of the subsection managers, group and team leaders,' which Toyota's personnel division chiefly organised in the early 1980s, in addition to 'production,' 'quality' and 'health and safety,' 'costs and improvements' are specified (Tanaka 1982: 28).

Second, according to Ishida et al. (1997), while 'improvements' at the final assembly shop 'are the joint work of the section/subsection manager, technician, group leader, other operating worker and the *kaizen* team, items requiring significant improvement are created from above (it can be surmised that the section/subsection manager and the technicians create these items) and those below the group leader carry out minor improvements. In other words, 'minor improvements are basically the duty of the group and team leaders...The participation of rank and file workers is limited to "one second improvements"' (84–85).

At the same time, what is important is that in order for these improvement activities to be carried out routinely, waste is made tangible 'in a way that anyone can understand.' This is 'a mechanism that steers supervisors to make improvements.' Kaneda (1991) provides the following explanation of this point.

> The Toyota system has established the most rigid mechanism. The basic duty (responsibility) of managers and superintendents in the factory is the fulfilling of production plans. Nothing else matters. Therefore, if defects occur during the manufacturing process, workers temporarily stop their work. If it is a production line, they stop the line. While waste can be made tangible by stopping the line, further problems arise whereby factory managers and superintendents cannot fulfil the day's production plan. This is an extremely troublesome situation. In order to fulfil production plans, efforts must be made to ensure the line does not stop. In order to not stop the line, efforts must be made to remedy the problems causing the line-stoppage and ensure these problems do not arise again (145–146).

In short, the fact that workers stop the line means troubling the superintendents, in other words, the 'mechanism that steers improvement activities.' This is a factor that creates enormous tension for them. It certainly represents a type of 'management by stress' (Parker and Slaughter 1988). Moreover, management creates such a 'mechanism' in a centralised (vertical) manner. The 'theory of horizontal information structure' is completely non-cognisant of such a centralised 'mechanism' in the Toyota system. According to this argument, when problems such as defects occur, the fact the operating workers are able to stop the line is understood to be a transfer of 'authority' for the purpose of encouraging workers to cope with problems.

An excessive burden on workers

Another important feature lacking in 'the theory of horizontal information structure,' is that the Toyota production system, which possesses 'a mechanism that steers supervisors to make improvements,' has a negative influence on operating workers, including the superintendent on the shopfloor. In other words, it is an excessive burden on workers. In the production process, factory production systems that aim to thoroughly eliminate waste, from management's perspective, make all material and human waste tangible. In order to eliminate this waste, continuous improvements are carried out involving operating workers and superintendents. In particular, eliminating human waste, unless appropriate regulations are formulated, has a tendency to push the efficient use of labour to the extreme. Examples include the relocation of workers to cope with production changes, a lot of temporary transfers of workers to other shops or plants, long working hours, including constant overtime, the employment of the temporary workers and the determination of standard working hours that does not recognise normal allowance time, which inevitably results in high labour density.

Several surveys have already elucidated the reality surrounding the efficient use of labour (Oyama 1985; Nohara and Fujita 1988; Nomura 1993b; Saruta 1995 etc). However, it has also been argued that 'it is extremely difficult to believe that the large differences in efficiency can be explained by "long working hours and high labour density." Compared with the West, I do not think that Japanese production workshops are in operation for as long as they are said to be (Koike 1993: 7).' This is why I will briefly examine the actual situation surrounding the excessive burden on workers. I will do this by focusing on working hours, labour density and also issues related to superintendents (group leaders and team leaders), who play a key role in the production workshop, working on the production line.

First, concerning working hours, table 2-1 compares annual working hours per production worker at the major European and Japanese automobile manufacturers in 1990.

It is obvious that workers employed by Japanese automobile manufacturers work long hours. Apart from Honda, the gross working hours for the major Japanese automobile manufacturers is about 2 300 hours, while for automobile plants in Europe it is

Table 2-1 Comparison of annual working hours between major Japanese and European automobile manufacturers (production workers, 1990)

Firm/Plant	Country	Gross working hours	Collectively agreed standard working hours	Collective overtime worked by assembly workers
Mazda	Japan	2392	1800	496
Mitsubishi	Japan	2364	1800	513
Nissan	Japan	2357	1808	461
Toyota	Japan	2323	1808	457
Honda	Japan	1938	1800	112
Nissan Sunderland	UK	1911	1778	133 (In 1991)
Ford Dagenham	UK	1786	1778	8
GM Zaragoza	Spain	1773	1724	49
Peugeot Sochaux	France	1771	1725	46
SEAT Zona Franca	Spain	1768	1768	(20)
Ford Valencia	Spain	1751	1720	31
Vauxhall Luton	UK	1749	1688	61
Peugeot Poissy	France	1725	1725	(77)
Ford Genk (from 1993)	Belgium	1702	1702	(15)
Opel Rüsselsheim	Germany	1690	1635	54
Fiat Cassino	Italy	1680	1665	-
Fiat Mirafiori	Italy	1680	1665	15
Renault Flins (from 1993)	France	1658	1658	(30)
VW Wolfsburg	Germany	1648	1616	32
Mercedes Sindelfingen	Germany	1648	1624	24
BMW Munich	Germany	1630	1630	-
Opel Bochum	Germany	1628	1628	(15)
Ford Cologne	Germany	1628	1628	-
VW Brussels	Belgium	1625	1625	-
GM Antwerp	Belgium	1624	1624	-
Rover Longbridge	UK	1585	1585	-
BMW Regensburg	Germany	1548	1548	-

Source: Bosch and Lehndorff 1995: 6–8.

Notes:

1 Collectively agreed standard working hours does not include working hours during paid holidays (number of days allowed).

2 In the case of Japanese manufacturers, because workers do not receive 100% of their allotted annual leave, gross working hours are greater than the sum of collectively agreed standard working hours and overtime.

3 Nissan Sunderland's overtime (133 hours) is a 1991 figure.

4 Because the figures in parenthesis in the overtime column are not explained in the research material, the meanings are not clear. However, as the gross working hours and collectively agreed standard working hours are the same, it can possibly be surmised that holiday or time off, which are equivalent to the overtime, is given to workers.

between 1 500 and 1 900 hours. The difference ranges from between 400 to 800 hours. In particular, there is a notable difference in collective overtime performed by assembly workers. In this manner, the major Japanese manufacturers, apart from Honda, have extremely long overtime for the purpose of responding flexibly to production variations. 1990, the year that is the object of comparison in table 2-1, was the time of Japan's bubble economy (end of 1986 to early 1991), therefore overtime for Japanese automobile manufacturers were fairly lengthy compared to those before the bubble. However, it does not mean that they were exceptionally long. For instance, the average annual overtime for Toyota factories from 1981 to 1986 was 366 hours (Aichi Labour Institute 1990: 207). The difference between this and the 1990 figure was only 91 hours.

Second, regarding the degree of labour density at Toyota, an absence of suitable indices makes a careful comparison of labour density difficult. Nevertheless, I will examine the degree of labour density by concentrating on the method of determining standard time for operating work and the feature of job design on the final assembly line.

The method of determining standard time at Toyota differs from that which appears in a common industrial engineering text. Standard time at Toyota is determined based on the following thinking. First, standardise the minimum time for the most proficient workers (team leader). Second, apart from shop allowance, do not take into consideration allowance time such as fatigue allowance, personal allowance and process allowance. Third, the performance of the best workshop in the company becomes the standard time for other similar workshops (therefore, as efficiency improves, it can be said to be a mechanism that reduces standard time). As a result, Toyota's standard time is more stringent than normal standard times. Moreover, management holds the power to determine standard times, while the Toyota Motor Workers' Union has no say in this matter (Nomura 1993b: 60–71). In 1992, this stringent way of determining standard time included minor amendments such as not counting females, aged workers and trainees of workers temporarily transferred as the standard manpower (170). However, changes were not reflected in the aforementioned thinking.

The number of required workers is counted according to this type of standard time, which also determines the content and amount of work for each worker. In this case, the aim is the thorough elimination of workers' 'waiting time' (= waste). As a result, fragmented work elements are fully packed into a short work cycle time (1–2 minutes) for each worker, in other words, the job design on the final assembly line attaches importance to the line balancing. From the late 1980s to the early 1990s, an important amendment was added to this job design. A complete process that attached importance to quality was introduced in place of the job design that stressed line balancing. Due to this, some 'waiting time' was permitted compared with previous years (Asao et al. 1999: 140–151).

From the late 1980s to the early 1990s, the fact that certain amendments had to be added to the determination of former standard times and the job design stressing line balancing, on the contrary, reveals previously high labour density. Citing one example, in the standard time in the former General Motors' (GM) Freemont Plant, in the case where the cycle time was 60 seconds, apart from allowance time and waiting time, the net time was set at about 45 seconds, whereas at NUMMI (a joint venture between Toyota and GM) this was increased to about 57 seconds (Adler 1992: 145).

The final problem concerns superintendents (group and team leaders) working on the production line. The problem is that, because of shortages in required operating workers, super-intendents are forced to join in the line and work everyday. This makes it difficult for superintendents to deal in managerial tasks and for rank and file workers to take their annual leave (this is described below in Nomura 1993b: 84–87).

This problem became tangible at Toyota in the early 1970s. The Toyota Motor Workers' Union (TMWU) made an issue of this from 1973 and demanded that management should improve this problem. The situation surrounding superintendents working on the production line in 1973 was reflected in expressions such as '35 per cent mostly everyday,' '30 per cent occasionally,' 'an average of 16 per cent per month' and 'rarely join in 13 per cent.' Due to TMWU demands to remedy the situation, from 1982 to 1983, a labour-management agreement was reached which stipulated that 'joining in the line, which interferes with the group leaders' responsibilities, will be eliminated in principle,' and 'within his role as a playing leader, the team leader will, in principle, perform a relief function (substitute for the worker which takes his annual leave, is absent and is temporarily off the production line) on regular workdays.

However, this agreement was not strictly adhered to. This is evidenced by the fact that during labour shortages the frequency of superintendents working on the production line rose considerably. In the early 1990s, 56 per cent of the group leaders' and 70 per cent of the team leaders' working time was spent on the line. There are many reasons for this. For the group leader, these included 'covering during annual leaves – 48 per cent' and 'covering for absent workers – 17%.' For the team leader these included 'players – 58 per cent' and 'relief during annual leaves and for temporary off-the production line ' (the results of a survey of 1786 work groups conducted by TMWU . Saruta 1995: 271). As a result of the high frequency of team leaders joining in the line, group leaders spent more than half of their working time on the line. The scale of the burden on superintendents is obvious.

The 'theory of horizontal information structure,' characterises Japanese companies' work activities as decentralised, horizontal coordination based on knowledge sharing; as a result, Japanese companies have high efficiency. However, the theory completely ignores important aspects of Japanese human resource management such as 'the mechanism that steers supervisors to make improvements,' outlined above, and 'the excessive burden on operating workers' that results from this. That is, because the information flows in Aoki's model are mainly emphasised, the managerial aspect is inevitably ignored. It is the operating workers, including group leaders and team leaders that are mainly responsible for production activities on the shopfloor. One must say that the Japanese company model, which does not take into consideration the characteristics of the human resource management and its influence on workers, clearly takes a one-sided view of actual company activities.

3 People in Irregular Modes of Employment: Are They Really Not Subject to Discrimination?[1]

Mari Ōsawa

Including 'full-time and part-time workers'

Irregular modes of employment gathering speed

As Japan starts to become accustomed to rates of unemployment in the region of 5%, the casualisation of employment is steadily gathering speed. The number of people in various forms of more-or-less insecure employment outside the mainstream category of *seisha'in* ('full-time regular employee') has been rising for many years and, in the second half of the 1990s, that uptrend drastically accelerated (Rōdōshō [Ministry of Labour] 2000b: 109–111). According to the Special Labour Force Survey by the Management and Coordination Agency, in 1990 the total number of people in all the various forms of irregular employment stood at 8.81 million, of whom 6.46 million were women. Irregulars accounted for roughly 20% of all employees, and 38% of female employees. The corresponding survey for 2001 found 13.59 million people in irregular employment, of whom 9.93 million were women. Irregulars now accounted for some 27% of all employees and 48% of female employees. Among the various categories of irregular employment, *pāto* (the most widely used term for 'part-timer') accounted for 7.69 million people or 57.3% of the total figure for irregular employees (Kōsei-Rōdōshō 2003).

In Japan, it is considered a matter of course that irregular employees are treated differently from regulars. However, it is no easy matter to get a clear picture of the extent to which treatment varies between the two groups. The question of whether differences in treatment are justified – whether in terms of ability, contribution to the company or responsibility – is another highly debatable issue. Again, if those differences in treatment are not justifiable in reasonable terms, and are found to constitute discrimination, how is that discrimination to be eradicated? All these matters have long generated intense controversy, both on the shop floor and in academia.

Section 2 of this paper attempts to present a fairly accurate picture of the present situation of irregular workers, including the so-called 'full-time part-timers' or 'para-part-timers' (*giji-pāto*), who have the same scheduled working hours as full-time regular employees but are treated as part-timers. Section 3 looks at recent government policies and academic theories relating to part-timers, and Section 4 presents some fundamental challenges to those schools of thought that insist that differences in the treatment of regular and irregular workers do not constitute discrimination.

Defining 'part-timers'

Let me start, however, by explaining why it strikes me as important to include 'full-time part-timers' in my discussion. The apparently obvious distinction between full-time and part-time work is far from obvious in the Japanese context, and this presents any inquiry into labour conditions with some specific methodological problems. Official statistics show two different approaches to the definition of part-time work, and these differences naturally affect the numbers that emerge. The first approach is based simply on working hours. A representative example would be the Management and Coordination Agency's Labour Force Surveys, which define anyone working less than 35 hours as a 'short-hour employee' (*tanjikan koyōsha*). The figure for short-hour employees is often quoted as a measure of the part-time workforce in Japan. In 2002, the MCA counted 12.11 million people, including 8.35 million women, in this category, representing 23.2% of the overall employees and 39.7% of the female employees. Women thus accounted for about 69% of all 'short-hour employees' (Kōsei-Rōdōshō 2003).

On the other hand, the MCA uses a different set of terms in drawing up its 'Special Labour Force Surveys' (*Rōdōryoku Chōsa Tokubetsu Chōsa*) and its 'Basic Surveys of Employment Structure' (*Shūgyō Kōzō Kihon Chōsa*). Here, days per week or hours per day count for nothing. Instead, the MCA relies on job descriptors supplied by employers, on the strength of which it divides the work-force between 'regular staff/employees' (*seiki no shoku'in/ jugyo'in*) and four kinds of irregular worker: *pāto, arubaito, shokutaku* and *haken sha'in*.[2] There is also a section for 'others.' As I mentioned earlier, the 1999 edition of the Special Labour Force Survey found 6.86 million workers in the *pāto* category. This figure included 6.42 million women. The category thus accounted for 14% of all employees and 32% of female employees. This was the most predominantly female of any employment category, with women making up fully 94% of all *pāto*. Thus this definition of 'part-timer' showed a female proportion over 25 percentage points higher than the 68% proportion showing up using the 'short-hour employee' definition.

The proportion of 'full-time part-timers' and their wages

We shall now try to establish the proportion of 'part-timers' (*pāto*) who are really working full-time. Here we must turn to another statistical source, the 'General Surveys of the Conditions of Part-time Workers' (*Pāto-taimu Rōdōsha Sōgō Jittai Chōsa*), conducted three times, in 1990, 1995 and 2001. According to these surveys, in 1990 some 20% of 'so-called part-timers' (*iwayuru pāto*) were 'full-time part-timers' (*furu-taimu pāto*), in 1995 16.3% and in 2001 15.1% of 'part-time etc. workers' (*pāto-tō rōdōsha*) were full-time part-timers. The actual number of workers referred to in both surveys is of the order of 1.2–1.7 million. Recently, temporarily dispatched workers (*haken rōdōsha*) have become a hot topic of debate, but they are generally reckoned to account for only some 300,000 workers (Rōdōshō 2000c).

We shall now take a closer look at the figures for 'full-time part-timers'-a considerably larger category than dispatch workers. As I will presently demonstrate, the Ministry of Labour's Annual Report on the Basic Statistical Survey on Wages (*Chingin Kōzō Kihon Tōkei Chōsa Hōkoku*), published under the title 'Wage Census,' shows that for women, the hourly non-overtime wage for real (i.e. non-full-time) part-timers is less than 70% of the equivalent figure for general female workers, while for men the figure drops to just 50% (Table 3-2). To get an idea of the wage differential for full-time part-timers, it is worth consulting the work of Nagase Nobuko, an associate professor of Ochanomizu Women's University, who has conducted a rigorous econometric re-analysis using the raw data of the 1990 General Survey of the

Conditions of Part-time Workers. Nagase has convincingly demonstrated that for men and women alike, effective hourly wages for full-time part-timers are substantially lower than for regular employees, and differ little from those of real part-timers. In fact, in the case of male part-timers, the hourly pay for full-time part-timers was actually slightly lower than for real part-timers. Nagase also studied the marginal return accruing from continued service to the same employer, finding that part-timers benefit considerably less from extended tenure than do regular employees, and that full-time part-timers fare no better than real part-timers (Nagase 1995*b*: 168–171).

In short, it is perfectly clear that the wage rates for full-time part-timers are far closer to those paid to short-hour part-timers than to those of regular employees. The following section will show that there is no reason to suppose there has been any significant change in this state of affairs between 1995 and the present. It is the persistence of this phenomenon that prompts the discussion in this paper of the treatment of 'part-time' workers in the broad sense of the term, very much including full-time part-timers.

Treatment of 'part-time' workers during the 1990s

Classifying 'part-timers etc.'

As mentioned above, the two largest-scale surveys of part-time workers in recent years have been the General Surveys of the Conditions of Part-time Workers, conducted by the Ministry of Labour in October 1990 and October 1995 and by the Ministry of Health, Labour and Welfare in October 2001.[3] These surveys focused on 'part-time etc. workers' at work-places with five or more employees, outside the agriculture and forestry sectors. That 'etcetera' is important, for the three surveys go well beyond the conventional Japanese understanding of *pāto*, covering practically the entire spectrum of irregular modes of employment. In the case of the 1995 and 2001 surveys, the term covers all workers other than regular employees. The surveys then breaks down 'part-time etc. workers' into two categories: (1) those with fewer hours in the basic working week than regular employees ('part-timers'); and (2) those with as many or more hours as regular employees ('others'). This latter category, which corresponds closely to full-time part-timers, accounted for 16.3% of all workers surveyed-12.3% for women and

27.4% for men in 1995, and 15.1% of all workers-11.8% for women and 24.3% for men (Rōdōshō 1997a; Kōsei-Rōdōshō 2002.

The terminology and categorisation employed in the 1990 survey is somewhat different, making it impossible to compare the two with any great precision. Instead of 'part-time etc. workers', the 1990 survey refers to its subjects as 'so-called part-timers' (*iwayuru pāto*), defined as workers other than regular employees, excluding migrant and seasonal workers. Again there is a bipartite subdivision based on whether the scheduled working week is shorter than for regular employees or the same/longer, but this time the categories are called 'A part-timers' (A *pāto*) and 'B part-timers' (B *pāto*). The latter category, closely corresponding to full-time part-timers, accounted for some 20% of the total population surveyed – 15.7% for women and 32.4% for men (Rōdōshō 1992). The 1995 survey treated the A and B categories as corresponding to its own categories 'part-timers' and 'others' respectively, while admitting that the categories did not exactly correspond, thus precluding very precise comparative analysis. However, with this caveat in mind, this paper attempts some rough-and-ready comparative analysis.

Trends in part-time wages

On wages, the 1995 survey looks at remuneration systems-payment by the day, by the hour, etc. – and at levels of payment. In August 1997, a research group convened by the Director-General of the MOL Women's Bureau published a 'Report of the Research Group on Surveys Regarding Part-time Workers', which converted the daily and monthly remuneration data in the 1990 and 1995 surveys into comparable unified hourly figures (Rōdōshō 1997*b*: 17). Briefly, the report's findings were as follows:

1. For male real part-time workers, the practice of payment by the hour rose during the five years between the two surveys, while daily and monthly remuneration declined. The mean hourly wage rose from ¥957 in 1990 to ¥1,164 in 1995, an increase of 21.6%.
2. For female real part-timers, there was a slight increase in the use of hourly remuneration and a slight decrease in daily remuneration. The mean hourly wage rose from ¥707 in 1990 to ¥832 in 1995, for an increase of 17.7%.
3. For male full-time part-timers ('other'), there was a 9.7-point decline in the use of hourly remuneration, with both daily and

monthly remuneration showing increases. The mean hourly wage climbed from ¥943 in 1990 to ¥1,207 in 1995, a 28% increase that enabled male full-time part-timers to overtake male real part-timers.

4. For female full-time part-timers, hourly remuneration systems declined by 15.1 points, while monthly remuneration systems rose by 12 points. The mean hourly wage rose by 19.7%, from ¥735 in 1990 to ¥880 in 1995.

These figures show that for both real part-time and full-time part-time categories, men enjoyed higher rates of pay increase than women during the first half of the 1990s. It is also interesting to observe the sharp increase in the application of monthly payment systems to full-time part-time women, although wage increases for these women did not match those of their male counterparts.

As for the larger increase in wages for full-time part-timers relative to real part-timers for both genders, the Part-time Work Research Group speculated that one of the contributing factors could have been an increase in the number of specialist workers employed on a contract basis among the ranks of the full-time part-timers (Rōdōshō 1997b: 17–18). That may well be so, but as I have stressed elsewhere (Ōsawa 1997), it would be unwise to interpret this trend simply as a matter of 'full-time part-timer' gradually becoming a job classification for people with specialized skills. Other factors probably include changes in the distribution of part-time' workers in terms of employing industries, age composition etc.

Be that as it may, we now have to ask whether the relatively high rate of increase in full-time part-timer wages from 1990 to 1995, coupled with an increase in the application of monthly payment systems to female full-time part-timers, signifies an important shift in the treatment of full-time part-timers. Is it fair to conclude that full-time part-timers are gradually being treated less like ordinary part-timers and more like regular employees? Or to put it another way, when discussing part-time work in the 1990s, is it appropriate to limit the discussion to real part-timers, or short-hour workers, while excluding full-time part-timers from consideration? The very fact that full-time part-timers were included in the 1997 report from the Part-time Work Research Group (Rōdōshō 1997b) indicates the stance taken by that group, but a number of facts will clarify the issue further.

Differences between 'part-time workers' and regular employees in terms of working conditions

For a start, we find no reference to differences between 'part-time workers' and regular employees in terms of working conditions. We can get some idea of their significance from data in the three surveys on the application of various kinds of treatment to 'part-time' employees.

It should be pointed out in relation to the figures in Table 3-1 that they derive from somewhat different samples, since not all companies offer this kind of benefit to workers, not all companies employ either or both kinds of 'part-timer', and there is no one-to-one correspondence between the different groups. Even so, the trend is clear enough: benefits supplementary to the basic wage are being steadily withdrawn from 'part-time' workers and, moreover, they are being withdrawn from full-time part-timers faster than from real part-timers. We may infer that the overall trend in the remuneration of full-time part-timers from 1990 through 1995 to 2001 brought them closer to real part-timers, and further away from regular employees.

A little more light was cast on the issue of 'part-timer' bonuses in April 2000, with the release of a report from an MOL Research

Table 3-1 *Proportion of workplaces applying various kinds of treatment to 'part-time workers: 2001, 1995 and 1990 (where available)*

| | Number of workplaces applying treatment... | | | | | | | |
| | to real part-timers (%) | | | to full-time part-timers (%) | | | to regular employees (%) | |
Benefit	2001	1995	1990	2001	1995	1990	2001	1995
Bonus	45.5	56.4	60.5	53.7	66.7	78.3	88.1	91.9
Annual pay rises	14.3	30.7	35.1	20.9	33.5	44.1	43.4	59.5
Regular pay increments	20.8	29.4	40.4	22.5	33.4	54.3	67.4	78.7
Retirement benefit	8.3	9.0		14.2	21.3		77.8	78.6
Job transfers	9.2	14.5	9.3	13.0	21.0	20.9	49.6	49.5

Annual pay rises (*bĕsu-appu*) are rises, typically negotiated between management and unions, in which each rung on the pay scale rises by an agreed percentage. Regular pay increments (*teiki shokyū*) occur when an individual worker is moved to a higher ruing on the scale usually once a year.

Source: Rōdōshō (1992, 1997a); Kōsei-Rōdōshō (2002)

Group on Part-time Labour (Rōdōshō 2000a). This report, often referred to as the Monosashi Report, for reasons that will be explained later, found that, as of January 1999, 66.7% of workplaces were offering bonuses to real part-timers on entry to the company, compared with 85.5% offering bonuses to regular employees who were high-school graduates and 86.9% offering them to regular employees who were university graduates (Rōdōshō 2000a: 56). Unfortunately, this survey excluded full-time part-timers from its coverage. It purported to show that, compared with 1995, more workplaces were offering bonuses to real part-timers and fewer to regular employees. The amount of the bonus is another question, however. Workplaces that said they offered bonuses to real part-timers on entry to the company were further asked to state the size of the bonus for a first-year real part-timer. It is reported that as a percentage of the bonus paid to a first-year high-school-graduate regular employee, 37.8% of workplaces answered 'zero' for a first-year real part-timer, while 19.5% answered '1–20%', and a further 17.1% answered '21–40%.' The report concludes that '74.4% of workplaces pay part-timers 60% or less (of the amount paid in bonuses to regular employees)' (*ibid.*, 33). This is clearly an error-the correct figure is of course 40% or less.

Yet another statistical source is the MOL's Basic Statistical Survey on Wages. This includes a column for part-timers (*pāto-taimu rōdōsha*), who are defined as 'permanent workers whose scheduled working hours in the day, or working days in the week, are fewer than for general workers.' Figures for part-timers' scheduled wages per hour, calculated by MOL itself as a proportion of general workers' scheduled wages per hour, have shown a steady decline through the 1990s (Table 3-2).

Table 3-2 Scheduled wage per hour for part-timers as a percentage of full-time pay, 1990-2000 (at June in each year, for all industries, company-sizes and job descriptions)

Year	Male part-timers/male general workers	Female part-timers/male general workers
1990	57.8%	72.0%
1995	55.3%	70.4%
2000	51.6%	66.9%

Source: Danjo Kyōdō Sankaku Kaigi Eikyōchōsa Senmon Chōsakai (2002).

To sum up: the period from 1990 to 2001 saw an increase in wages for 'part-time' workers, with full-time part-timers showing a larger increase than real part-timers. However, this increase may be taken to reflect changes in the distribution of 'part-timers', in terms of industry, occupation and age composition, and should not be ascribed simplistically to improvements in management practices. Differences in management treatment of regular employees, on the one hand, and real part-timers and full-time part-timers on the other, remained large and indeed tended to widen during this period-whether viewed in terms of hourly rates of payor the application of remuneration systems such as bonuses and pay-rises. There is no solid evidence to suggest that full-time part-timers started to be treated more like regular employees and less like real part-timers during the first half of the 1990s, and at least in the case of real part-timers, there is evidence to show that the gap between their remuneration and that of regular employees continued to widen in the second half of the decade.

One further point should be made. The surveys mentioned above also furnish evidence that an increasing proportion of irregular workers are in that mode of employment involuntarily – because they cannot find more regular work, rather than because of the attractions of irregular work. The MOL general surveys of part-time work since 1990 show a marked decline in the number of workers citing positive reasons for choosing to work as 'part-timers', among full-time part-timers and real part-timers alike.

Table 3-3 Reasons given by 'part-timers for present mode of employment

	1990 survey		1995 survey		2001 survey	
	real part-time	full-time part-time	real part-time	full-time part-time	real part-time	full-time part-time
Voluntary reasons						
'I want to work hours that suit myself'	63.9	28.9	55.0	21.9	50.0	17.1
'I want to work shorter hours or fewer days'	31.7	12.9	24.0	8.8	31.2	8.9
Involuntary reason						
'I could not find a company to employ me as a regular'	13.4	31.7	13.7	32.9	21.1	38.0

Source: Rōdōshō (1997a); Kōsei-Rōdōshō (2002).

In addition, the 1999 survey of the MOL Research Group on Part-time Labour (Monosashi Group), using a different questionnaire from the two general surveys, shows fully 28.0% of real part-timers saying they wanted to work as regular workers (Rōdōshō 2000*a*: 25, 62) – more than double the figure in the general surveys.

Government policies and academic schools of thought on part-time employees

The 1993 Part-time Labour Law and its Theoretical Underpinning

Part-time employees are covered by general labour legislation such as the Labour Standards Law, the Minimum Wage Law, the Workplace Health and Safety Law and the Worker Disaster Compensation Insurance Law. In June 1993, moreover, a new law was passed specifically to improve their treatment: the Law Relating to the Improvement of Employment and Management of Short-Hour Employees (*Tanjikan Koyōsha no Koyō Kanri no Kaizen ni kan-suru Hōritsu*), usually referred to simply as the Part-time Labour Law (*Pāto-taimu Rōdō-hō*).

Article 3, paragraph 1 of this law obliges employers to make efforts to 'take necessary measures to establish appropriate working conditions in the actual employment circumstances of short-hour employees, taking into consideration balance etc. (*kinkō tō*) with regular employees.' The law defines regular employees (*tsūjō no rōdōsha*) as 'so-called regular-type personnel' (*iwayuru seiki-gata no jūgyō'in*). Hence full-time part-timers are left in limbo, since they are neither 'short-hour workers' nor 'regular employees.' An attempt was made to plug this loophole in December 1993, when the government promulgated a set of guidelines relating to the Part-time Labour Law, the 'Guidelines relating to measures that employers should adopt for the improvement etc. of employment management of short-hour workers.' Guideline No. 2, Part 3, states that in the case of 'short-hour workers whose scheduled working hours are almost the same as for regular workers', employers 'should make efforts to treat them in a suitable manner as regular workers.' With their vague exhortations to 'effort', and their total absence of penalties for non-compliance, these are about the weakest types of regulation imaginable.

Legal protection for part-time workers has long been a demand of labour unions and opposition parties, and in 1984 these demands bore fruit with the publication of a government directive (*tsūtatsu*) entitled 'An Outline of Part-time Labour Policy' (*Pāto-taimu Rōdō Taisaku Yōkō*). This was followed in 1989 by a government notice (*kokuji*) called 'Guidelines to be Taken into Consideration regarding the Treatment and Working Conditions of Part-time Workers' (*Pāto-taimu Rōdōsha no Shogū oyobi Rōdō Jōken ni tsuite Kōryo-subeki Shishin*). The 1993 Part-time Labour Law was basically designed to provide a firm legal foundation to the 1989 guideline, but in the meantime the first Part-time Labour Survey had been carried out in 1990, and in February 1992 a group of four opposition parties and one group-the Social Democratic Party of Japan, Kōmeitō, the Democratic Socialist Party, the Social Democratic Alliance and Rengō – had jointly proposed their own bill, entitled 'Bill relating to the Establishment of Equal Treatment with Regular Workers and Appropriate Working Conditions for Short-hour Workers' (*Tanjikan Rōdōsha no Tsūjō no Rōdōsha to no Kintō Taigū oyobi Tekisetsu-na Shūrō Jōken no Kakuho ni kan-suru Hōritsu-an*). The MOL responded to these developments by setting up a research group on part-time labour problems in July of 1992. The group's report, 'On the Future Form of Part-time Labour Policy' (*Kongo no Pāto-taimu Rōdō Seisaku no Arikata ni tsuite*) was the basis of the government bill presented to the Diet in March 1993.

How did these various reports and legislative items vary in their approach to the problem? The 1992 joint opposition party bill principally sought to outlaw discrimination against part-timers, and to establish equality of treatment between them and full-time workers. In November 1991, the directorate of the International Labour Organisation (ILO) had decided to put the issue of part-time labour on the agenda for the ILO's Annual General Conference. A draft article on the issue was being drawn up in preparation for initial deliberations at the June 1993 conference, and the key provisions were becoming apparent. Eventually, the article would be adopted at the June 1994 conference, as Convention No. 175 (1994). Article 5 of the Convention states the following: 'Measures appropriate to national law and practice shall be taken to ensure that part-time workers do not, solely because they work part time, receive a basic wage which, calculated proportionately on an hourly, performance-related, or piece-rate basis, is lower than the basic wage of comparable full-time workers, calculated according to the same method.'

Around the time when the 1993 Part-time Labour Act was being debated in the Diet, an influential feature article on 'The Present Circumstances and Issues of Part-time Labour' was published in the April 15 issue (No. 1021) of *Jurist,* a magazine widely read by lawyers and scholars of jurisprudence. The feature included a round-table discussion, in which Keio University professor Seike Atsushi argued that, since employers incur greater fixed costs per hour of labour in recruiting and training part-timers, it is reasonable to pay them lower wages than full-time workers even if they are doing the same work. This was a rebuttal to Ōwaki Masako, a lawyer and upper house Diet member (Social Democratic Party of Japan), who had been stressing the need for equality of treatment between full-time and part-time workers. Seike further argued that it was a mistake in the first place to discuss the issue of full-time part-timers as a problem of part-time labour (p. 22). Seike's contention regarding 'full-time part-timers' was reinforced by Nitta Michio's article in the issue of *Jurist*. In the article Nitta argued that wages and bonuses for female full-time part-timers are 'closer to general workers' than short-hour part-timers (Nitta 1993: 36).

In short, at the time when the 1993 legislation was drawn up, there was a debate going on at home and abroad on the issue of equality between full-time and part-time workers, focusing on prohibiting discrimination and ensuring equitable treatment in the workplace. Against this backdrop, Article 3 of the 1993 Part-time Labour Law stipulated that full-timer/part-timer balance (*kinkō*) was to be among the points of which employers should 'make efforts' to 'take account.'

The new law was soon put to the test. In October 1993, 28 female full-time part-timers employed by the Maruko Alarm Co. filed a suit demanding that the firm correct discrimination in its wage system between regular employees and 'temporary employees' (*rinji sha'in*), the category in which the plaintiffs were employed. Despite the title, the plaintiffs had been working for Maruko for periods ranging from six to 27 years; they were defined as 'temporary' simply because the company refused in principle to employ married women as regulars. This was a groundbreaking legal action-the first ever in Japan to address the issue of wage discrimination against part-timers.

The various academic theories justifying wage differentials

At this point, the various academic theories that have been advanced to justify wage differentials between regular and irregular workers should be considered. They can be broadly categorised according to whether they deal with the supply or the demand for labour. On the supply side, we find, among others, the 'human capital hypothesis' and the 'compensation wage hypothesis.' On the demand side, the differential is explained in terms of regional monopoly, the relationship between labour productivity and working hours, or the segmentation of the labour market (Furugori 1997: 82–83).

Looking first at theories based on labour productivity and working hours, we find a tendency to focus on non-wage costs, such as the (semi-) fixed costs of education, training etc. These theories state that employers choose to invest in training workers who can provide long hours of labour because they enable the firm to maximise the return on the fixed costs of training. This training in turn increases the marginal productivity of long-hour workers, and hence makes it appropriate to pay them higher wages. Seike's position in the *Jurist* round table approximates to this.

Turning now to the 'compensation wage hypothesis', this is an approach that became increasingly influential in the later 1990s. The theory goes that part-time workers supply their labour not so much in response to wage level and number of working hours as in response to the distribution of working hours and the convenience of commuting conditions. Part-timers are workers who wish to work on days and at times of day that suit them, and who wish to limit their working hours. In order to obtain jobs that fulfil these desirable conditions, they accept lower wages. Thus they are compensated for their low wages in the form of various non-financial benefits. Chūma Hiroyuki (Hitotsubashi University) and Nakamura Jirō (Tokyo Metropolitan University) are associated with this approach. Discussing Japan's female part-time workers, they have estimated hedonic wage functions in which the variables include commuting convenience and elasticity of working hours, in addition to human capital variables. They show how per-hour wages are higher where commuting time is longer, and lower where the number of workdays missed is larger (Chūma and Nakamura 1990; Nakamura and Chūma 1994).

Elsewhere, there are quite a few cases where analysts seek to combine segmentation or dual-market hypotheses with 'efficiency wage theories.' According to Ōsawa Machiko (Japan Women's University), the 'efficiency wage' (*kōritsu chingin*) is a system that has evolved in response to the problem of determining the productivity of individual workers in large organizations characterised by teamwork. Where the job requires a strong sense of responsibility or spontaneous effort on the part of the worker, the employer may pay a premium in excess of the prevalent market wage. From the worker's point of view, this is a systemically determined wage that increases the cost of dismissal and thereby acts as a deterrent to laziness (Ōsawa 1993: 116). By contrast, in situations where it is relatively easy to determine the productivity of individual workers, a market wage is paid that is determined by the labour market external to the company. This tends to apply to the jobs taken by part-time workers; hence full-timers are paid the efficiency wage while part-timers are paid the market wage, and this accounts for the gap between the two.

'The dilemma of industrial democracy?'

A more sophisticated approach to the wage differential issue may be found in the 'dilemma of industrial democracy' theory of Aoki Masahiko, a Stanford University professor who has been head of the Economy and Industry Institute since 1997. Aoki's 1988 book, *Information, Incentives, and Bargaining in the Japanese Economy,* was showered with prizes and translated into several languages. In that book, he develops the model of the 'J-firm'-a sort of ideal type of the big Japanese corporation-and argues that the J-firm will tend to seek a growth rate higher than the level required to maximise its stock value in the short term. This sought-after rate is defined by Aoki as a rate higher than that required to maximize-share price (1988: 166), i.e. an excessively high rate of growth. The motive for this, he says, is the company's drive to maximise promotion opportunities and retirement bonuses for its regular employees.

Aoki also argues that compared with a company that seeks to maximise its stock value, the J-firm will have a stronger tendency to adopt capital-intensive technologies. This is to restrict the recruitment of new regular employees, relative to the increase in the level of value added to products, thereby safeguarding the vested interests of existing regulars. Attaining the objective of excessively high growth entails sacrificing short-term income and retaining profits within the firm. These are the costs of excessive growth, and they are borne by serving regular employees. The improved promotion opportunities and retirement bonuses mentioned above are semi-monopolized by those regular employees in return for their bearing the costs of excessive growth (Aoki 1988: Chapter 5).

As the voices of these regular employees become more influential within the company, there is a negative effect on the company's demand for new labour power, and this is what Aoki calls 'a dilemma of industrial democracy' (Aoki 1988: 170–171). There were two reasons why these curbs on employment by big corporations did not result in large-scale unemployment. Firstly, the big corporations set up separate subsidiaries and made use of sub-contractors; secondly, they established 'differential employment status (such as that of part-time workers)' within the company (Aoki 1988: 204). In the 1960s, this was done mainly with temporary workers, with the focus shifting to middle-aged female part-timers in the 1970s. This 'differential employment' enabled big corporations to absorb extra employees into parts of the corporation that were not included in the redistribution of the profits accruing to growth.

In the case of subsidiaries and subcontractors, Aoki argues that profit arises that is proper to their relationship with the big corporation, and that these satellite companies and their employees also share in the redistribution of those profits. Hence, he argues, this is not a purely one-sided and exploitative relationship (Aoki 1988: Chapter 6). However, it is striking that Aoki offers no corresponding explanation to show how the part-timers and other irregular employees who are 'differentiated' from regular workers within the big corporation enjoy any privileges as a result of their characteristic relationship with the employer. We may, however, be able to infer Aoki's position on these workers from what he says about full-time, regular employees. Of these, he says that they engage in 'gift exchange' with the management. By this he means that compared with workers in a neo-classical labour relationship with management, workers in the J-firm exchange higher expenditure in effort (working hours) for higher levels of employment security. In the neo-classical relationship, the corporation aims simply at maximising profit, while workers seek to maximise the surplus wage left over after subtracting the disutility of having to work from the actual wage received. The corporation employs this kind of worker through the labour market, on market terms (Aoki 1988: 175–176).

To put it bluntly, Aoki seems to argue that irregular workers, recruited from the external labour market, are motivated by the desire to earn the highest possible wages with lowest possible expenditure of effort, whereas regular workers, who form the internal labour market, not only put up with postponement of wage increases under the seniority system, but also have to work long hours. In these ways the regular employees bear the costs incurred through excessive growth. When Aoki talks of irregular workers seeking to maximize income and minimize labour, one senses that he is not so very far away from the compensation wage hypothesis that I discussed above.

The Revision of the Part-time Labour Law and the Academic Response

In October 1995, the MOL carried out its second general survey of part-time workers. The 1993 Part-time Labour Law included a supplementary provision, added during Diet debate on the bill, stipulating that the law would be reviewed three years after coming into force. In October 1996, the MOL launched the research group whose deliberations led to the 1997 'Report of the Research Group on Surveys Regarding Part-time Workers' discussed near the beginning of Section 2 above, and in September 1997 the MOL's Council on Women and Youth Problems started its own investigation into part-time labour policy.

Meanwhile, March 1996 had brought a judgement by the first instance court in the Maruko Alarm case, with the plaintiffs being awarded a part of the redress sought on the basis of the equal treatment principle. The judgement included the following statement: 'The principle of equal treatment should be one of the important factors taken into account in determining whether wage differentials are illegal. Wage differentials that contravene that principle deviate from the limits of discretion permitted to the employer and as such may in some cases lead to breaches of law that offend against public order and public morality.' The judgement conceded, however, that 'the equality of treatment principle is an abstract thing, and hence there is some margin of discretion in assessing the various elements entailed in treating people with parity; where differences in treatment fall within the limits of that margin, the employer's discretion must be respected.' The judgement concluded that a fair place to draw that line would be at 80%. Where female part-timers were paid less than 80% on an hourly base of the salary paid to female full-timers, that differential should be regarded as illegal.

The Council on Women and Youth Problems came up with its own proposal in February 1998. In a document entitled 'On the Character of Policy Measures on Short-hour Labour' (*Tanjikan Rōdō Taisaku no Arikata ni tsuite*), the Council pointed out that it was very difficult to establish treatment and working conditions for part-timers that took account of balance between themselves and full-timers because there was no 'yardstick' (*monosashi*) by which the degree of equality might be measured. The Council therefore saw a need 'to set up a place for technical and professional investigation... to make it easier for workers and management to establish standards for comparison, and get to grips with establishing balanced or equal treatment.' Based on this proposal, a Research Group on Part-time Labour was set up at MOL, which has been referred to as the 'Monosashi group' ever since. The language used by the Council to discuss treatment of part-timers shows a slight terminological strengthening from 'balanced' (*kinkō*) to 'balanced or equal' (*kinkō mata wa kinto*), and this probably reflects the influence of the language used in the judgement by the first instance court in the Maruko Alarm case. However, it is also worth noting that the Council declines to discuss the problem of full-time part-timers because they are not in the category of 'short-hour workers' (Rōdōshō 2000*a*: 112).

In fact, however, this definition of the problem misses the point, since length of working hours is not a factor in the wage levels of real or full-time part-timers. There are cases revealed in the 1990 MOL survey where the hourly pay for male real part-timers is clearly higher than that for male full-time part-timers. Even where the distinction in hourly pay is less obvious, research by Nagase (Nagase 1994, 1995*a, b*) has shown that once the full range of factors affecting pay have been taken into account-years of service, educational background, job category, job title, etc.-real part-timers tend to get paid better per hour worked than full-time part-timers. Moreover, Nitta's argument that the wages and bonuses of female 'full-time part-timers' are closer to general workers than short-hour part-timers is based on careless research. Nitta compares the hourly take-home pay for 'full-time part-timers' in 1989 and 1990 bonuses with the hourly take-home pay for general workers in 1988 and 1987 bonuses (Osawa 1993, Osawa 1994).

Compensation wage hypothesis

Nagase also makes an important point with regard to the compensation wage hypothesis. She shows that while the hedonic wage hypothesis may succeed in explaining small wage differentials among fellow part-timers, they are inadequate in explaining the vast and growing differential between all part-timers, on the one hand, and all regular employees, on the other. Nagase finds that the average hourly wage differential between so-called 'part-timers' and regular employees, where personal factors are otherwise identical, is around 30%. 'It is hard to account for this simply as a compensatory differential reflecting the degree of ease with which the worker can cope with housekeeping and child-rearing', she says (Nagase 1995a: 99).

One legal scholar who clearly does not accept that view is Mizumachi Yū'ichirō, an associate professor at The University of Tokyo. He states that low wages for part-timers are the quid *pro quo* for the low level of restraint placed upon their activities by the corporation. This degree-of-restraint principle, he argues, 'can suffice as a theoretical basis to explain the low wages of part-time workers as reasonable in economic terms, and to justify them in legal terms' (Mizumachi 1997: 237).

Mizumachi claims to derive the degree-of-restraint principle from the economic theory of the compensation wage. In his view, the degree to which the corporation deprives the worker of personal freedom can be described in terms of forced overtime, forced transfers to other branches, restrictions on personal activities outside working hours, and the degree to which workers are obliged to accept working hours and holiday arrangements decided by the employer. Even in cases where full-time part-timers have turnover rates and scheduled working hours identical to those of regular employees – in short, where there is no evidence that their commitment to the company is any lower than among regular employees-full-time part-timers still enjoy a lower level of restraint on their personal freedom than do regular employees, and this is reflected in their lower wages. To support this variation on the theme of the compensation wage, he cites the empirical research of Chūma and Nakamura (Mizumachi 1997: 234–235).

If we compare Mizumachi's approach with that of Nagase, we find that there is a fundamental disagreement as to just what wages are supposed to compensate for. Where Mizumachi speaks of loss of freedom, Nagase's argument is couched in strictly materialist terms:

wages, she argues, should compensate for costs entailed in taking on a job, defined in terms of money (costs of clothing, child-care, commuting etc.) and in terms of time (such as commuting time). Suffice for now to say that Mizumachi's degree-of-restraint theory has yet to be adequately proved in economic terms.

Sugeno Kazuo's and Suwa Yasuo's criticism of the judgement by the first instance court in the Maruko Alarm case

This lack of academic validation has not prevented other academics from using Mizumachi's theory for their own purposes. In particular, University of Tokyo professor Sugeno Kazuo and Hosei University professor Suwa Yasuo have used it to criticize the judgement by the first instance court in the Maruko Alarm case.

Sugeno and Suwa are frequently to be found serving on MOL study groups and advisory councils. Their position is that the principle of equality of treatment – the same wage for the same work-is simply not workable in Japan, either as a tool for construing existing laws or as a principle for reforming those laws. Sugeno and Suwa view part-time workers in the context of the 'overall structure of the labour market' and divide them into three categories:

1. People whose current stage of life puts them either before or after the period of participation in the internal labour market: students doing spare-time jobs, retirees who stay on as part-timers etc.
2. 'People who for some reason deliberately avoid the internal labour market.' Sugeno and Suwa place the majority of irregular workers in this category.
3. Involuntary irregulars, who 'would like to enter the internal labour market but are unable to do so.' (Sugeno and Suwa 1998: 123–124)

The phrase, 'internal labour market', refers to the system of worker deployment, pay-rises and promotions within the company, expressed in terms of a market. Sugeno and Suwa describe the reasons why type 2 irregulars 'avoid' the internal labour market thus: 'Most long-term employment relationships demand that in exchange for stable employment and favourable economic treatment, the worker accept a high level of restraint, in terms of overtime, having to work on holidays, and job transfers to other branches or related companies.' The Maruko Alarm case, they argue, is 'a classic case' of problems that arise with type 2 part-timers (Sugeno and Suwa 1998: 124).

The Sugeno and Suwa paper cited here was actually presented in court by the team of lawyers representing Maruko Alarm at the hearing on the company's appeal against the original court judgement on its treatment of part-timers. In response, lawyers for the plaintiffs submitted a supplementary opinion written by Asakura Mutsuko, a professor at Tokyo Metropolitan University, which subjected the Sugeno/Suwa paper to detailed and careful criticism (Asakura 2000 [1998]). From my own point of view, Sugeno and Suwa appear to be labouring under the delusion that the labour market, including the internal labour market at major corporations, is formed entirely in accordance with the choices of workers. In particular, their argumentation ignores the insistence of the plaintiffs in the Maruko Alarm case that they worked as full-time part-timers because that was the only option the company would permit them-not out of their own volition. More generally, Sugeno and Suwa also ignore data such as those in Table 3-3, indicating that the number of involuntary 'part-timers' is on the rise. They dismiss the Maruko Alarm judgement, arguing that 'a judge cannot be expected to possess the specialized knowledge required to take the place of the parties directly concerned in fixing wage rates, which should be established through contract negotiations' (Sugeno and Suwa 1998: 133).

The reality of Aoki's theory

The economist Aoki Masahiko (see 192–193 above) has described the spread of part-time labour without benefits as 'one conspicuous manifestation of the dilemma of industrial democracy' (Aoki 1988: 174). From his 1980s work on the J-firm, Aoki progressed during the 1990s to comparative institutional analysis of economic development and the government's role in it. He emphasises that 'coordination failure' in the economy is likely to be broader and more generalized than predicted by theories of 'market failure' (Aoki et al. 1996: 33). In striking contrast, Sugeno and Suwa-influential scholars of jurisprudence-place an almost religious level of hope in the functions of the labour market, which they see as based on individual choice.

Aoki's account was a subtle combination between a form of labour market segmentation theory and elements of the efficiency wage hypothesis and the compensation wage hypothesis. However, in the case of the efficiency wage hypothesis, Furugōri Tomoko, a professor at Chūō University, has pointed out that in recent years the increased use of part-time workers, and progress in integrating them into companies' mainstay business, has led to a situation where sometimes part-timers actually have more appetite for the job, and higher productivity, than full-timers. This calls into question the efficiency wage hypothesis: 'Difficulties arise in explaining wage differentials and the segmentation of labour markets' (Furugōri 1997: 87). Seen in this light, Aoki's 'J-firm' does not seem particularly Japanese after all. Full-time part-timers who work as long hours as regular employees, stay with the company for just as many years as regulars, yet are paid much lower wages and hence pay the costs of growth? Real part-timers who work shorter hours than regular workers, but whose energy results in a bigger contribution to the firm's activities? Such people simply do not exist in the Aoki model. The model is an imaginary world, far removed from reality.

Settlement of the Maruko Alarm case and the Monosashi report

The Maruko Alarm case was finally settled out of court. On the final day of hearings on the appeal, in November 1998, the court issued a recommendation for informal settlement (*wakai kankoku*). Out-of-court negotiations lasted for another year, and were at last concluded in November 1999. The final settlement was more favourable to the plaintiffs than the original one handed down by the first court hearing (Iwashita *et al.* 2000)

On the government side, meanwhile, the 'Monosashi' research group mentioned above has been deliberating part-time labour issues since December 1998. Its chairman is University of Tokyo professor Satō Hiroki, while the group of academics that did the basic work for the group included Nagase and Mizumachi (see above). In February 1999, the Monosashi Group launched a 'Survey on the Actual Modes of Utilization of Various Kinds of Workers in the Workplace' (*Shokuba ni okeru Tayō-na Rōdōsha no Katsuyō Jittai ni kan-suru Chōsa*), submitting its report in April 2000.

The Monosashi group collected a considerable amount of data on the subject of full-time part-timers, but these data were excluded from the report, by a very simple procedure. The survey generated valid responses from 1,128 workplaces, but the report only covered those that described the hours of irregular workers as 'shorter than those of regular workers in all or most cases.' This accounted for 565 workplaces, 50.1 % of the total. The other 563 workplaces, 49.9% of the total, which had a majority of full-time part-timers, were excluded. The group also surveyed individual workers, and here there were 4,533 cases, of which the group only analysed the 2,521 (56%) who stated that their working hours were shorter than those of regular workers at their company. The other 2,012 (44%) were full-time part-timers, and they were not studied (Rōdōshō 2000a: 50–51,69,77).

The Monosashi Report also restricted its study of wage differentials between regular and irregular employees to a question asking employers about wages paid to the two types of employee immediately after they joined the firm (*ibid.*, 70). It is widely known that the differential widens with years of service, a point that is acknowledged in the report itself (*ibid.*, 37). The way the statistics are presented gives one the impression that the Monosashi Group did not really want to know the full details of wage differentials between regular and irregular workers.

Even so, the report did point to the necessity for employers to take measures to ensure 'balance' (*kinkō*) between part-timers and regular employees where the former were engaged in the same kind of work as the latter, and to take into account the principle of balance where job descriptions differed. The report also presented case studies to illustrate the kind of treatment it was talking about.

In July 2000, the MOL announced a new policy on measures to enhance gender equality of employment opportunity. The document included a passage on countermeasures for part-timers that discussed the establishment of treatment and working conditions for part-timers that took into account balance (*kinkō*) between them and regular employees. This was to be achieved 'by widely disseminating the gist (of the Monosashi Report), and encouraging workers and management to take up the issue autonomously' (Rōdōshō 2000c: 17). Given that the report has nothing to say about full-time part-timers, and given that there are no enforcement provisions but only an ineffectual call for workers and managers to somehow get together and sort it out, we may safely assume that the problem of full-time part-timers, as usual, is going to be quietly forgotten about.

The principle of equality of treatment also benefits regular employees

A gender-segmented labour market

Sugeno and Suwa (1998: 133–134) call for a stronger Employment Equal Opportunity Law (EEOL) and for policies to support those who combine child-rearing with employment, rather than to establish and enforce the principle of equality of treatment. From this set of policy recommendations, we can see that they take for granted the gendered division of homemaking, and view 'gendered employment management' (they would not say 'discrimination') at workplaces as some-how a subordinate variable of that domestic gender division. Yet Nakata Yoshifumi, an associate professor at Dōshisha University, has a different view of workplace gender discrimination. According to him, male/female wage discrimination can be perfectly well explained in terms of a gender-segmented labour market, and a seniority pay system based on the assumption of a gendered division of labour. There is no gender differentiation in the values attached to years of service or experience; in contrast, there is a large gender division in the value attached to a worker's simple age – irrespective of the amount of money invested by the company in training the worker. Such, at least, is the conclusion drawn by Nakata from econometric analysis (Nakata 1997b: 195).

According to Nakata's gendered labour market segmentation hypothesis, then, gender is an independent variable and not a subordinate variable. This, along with the clarification of the importance of simple age (as opposed to years of service) as a factor in employment conditions, constitutes the most noteworthy aspect of Nakata's work. Theories that treat gender as a subordinate variable see the segmentation of the labour market as deriving from a number of variables more or less independent of gender, such as whether each sector of the market is characterised by oligopoly or competition, the ease with which each individual worker's productivity can be controlled, whether a worker's skills and training are firm-specific or generally applicable, etc. The degree to which men and women respectively concentrate in that sector is seen as an outcome of those variables. Nakata, in contrast, sees gender as directly causing the segmentation of the labour market. Again, in his analysis of seniority-based remuneration, Nakata denies that this practice is a way of rewarding workers for their acquisition of firm-specific skills. Rather, he argues, it derives from 'the thought that male company employees must be paid enough to cover living costs' (Nakata 1997b: 200). When Nakata talks of 'living costs' (*seikei-hi*), moreover, he is careful to specify that this concept includes the cost of supporting a family (*ibid.*).

'Part-time' as a personal status

Nakata's research is concerned with wage differentials between men and women, but it also offers many useful suggestions regarding wage differentials between regular employees and part-timers. In this regard, Nagase and Furugōri have some interesting perspectives: 'the low wages (paid to so-called part-timers) derive from personal status (*mibun*), not from the number of hours worked' (Nagase 1995*a:* 10). 'So long as one is called a part-timer, and assuming that there is no difference in the hourly wage between part-timers who work long hours and those who work short hours, then one can see that the wage differential between full-timers and part-timers is an expression of a disparity in personal status (*mibunteki-na kakusa*)' (Furugōri 1997: 85).

The conclusive views based on quantitative analysis should not be skipped as a simple metaphor, even if the word 'status' is used without clarification. The most recent Japanese sociological research into class also notes that 'that gender (*seibetsu*) is status in the sense that it always acts as an important factor in society's opportunity structure' (Seiyama 2000: 24).

Article 3 of the Labour Standards Law on equal treatment stipulates that 'an employers shall not engage in discriminatory treatment with respect to wages, working hours or other working conditions by reason of the nationality, creed or social status of any worker.' Article 4 provides for the principle of equal wages for men and women. The established theory regarding 'social status' in article 3 focuses on aspects of public law purporting to the criminal laws and ordinances of the Labour Standards Law. The theory also refers to 'social classification that cannot be avoided by one's volition' and interprets the 'contractual status arising from the disparities in the employment contract terms' as not being applicable to this (this quote is from the judgement by the first instance court in the Maruko Alarm case). However, in recent years, the theory has recognised two aspects of article 3: necessary provisions that make up punishment and valid provisions of private law. The latter aspect presents an academic theory (dihedral interpretation) in which it is possible to broadly interpret 'social status' (Asakura and Kon'no 1997: 107; Wada 2000: 25).

Restrictions and treatment

It would remain possible to argue, as Mizumachi does (1997: 235), that regular employees are subject to heavy restrictions on their personal freedom, and that this sacrifice warrants reward in the form of higher wages. It might also be possible to argue, as Sugeno and Suwa do (1998: 133) that 'this is not a matter that courts can pass judgements on as a matter of rights and obligations.' Still, the fact remains that just because a worker is labelled 'part-time', that does not give the worker the right to ignore orders in the workplace. Obedience to orders is a matter of course, and many surveys have made it clear that part-timers are actually ordered to carry out overtime and holiday work.

Those who approve of differences in treatment between regular and irregular workers must first establish that there really is a clear substantial difference in the degree to which the two types of worker are constrained in their activities by the company. Is the loss of freedom suffered by regular workers really so much worse than for part-timers that it warrants compensation in the form of wages for regular working hours that are over 30% higher? Even if that really is the case, Nagase's research has already shown that the compensation wage hypothesis has only partial explanatory force.

Finally, supposing that it is true, as Mizumachi suggests, that regular company employees really are being deprived of their freedom to the extent of being treated like slaves, that in itself is a serious problem. The need to reduce the weigh of these corporate shackles to a level commensurate with a democratic civic society would surely b a further reason for confronting employers with the issue of equality of treatment between regular and 'part-time' workers as a matter of urgency.

4 Is Subcontracting Risk Sharing?

Hirofumi Ueda

Changing assessment of subcontracting and the emergence of a new debate

Subcontracting (*Shitauke*) generally refers to a relational and structural division of labour in which large companies place orders with small companies. However, the term subcontracting conveys a strong image of differences in working conditions, management details, productivity and technological standards, and harsh terms of business. Therefore, in order to sweep away this firmly entrenched image of subcontracting, there are many cases in recent years in which it has been consciously avoided and replaced by the term 'supplier.'

However, since the 1980s, attention has focused on the international competitiveness of manufacturers in industries such as automobiles, electronics and electric machinery and appliances, which often use subcontracting. This has led to changes in how subcontracting is perceived. Presently, even if the assessment of subcontracting differs, there is a common 'perception that a social division of labour in which there are many small- and medium-sized enterprises (SMEs) in the machine industry, and that both large companies and SMEs are linked by outsourcing is a contributing factor in the strong international competitiveness of the Japanese machine industry' (Watanabe 1997: 20).

This chapter examines the subcontracting system – a well-known form of inter-company relations in Japan. Focusing on the unique characteristics of subcontracting in Japan and the high efficiency of production systems to which it has contributed, this chapter criticises the argument emphasising that outsourcing companies and subcontractors are in an equal relationship in which both share risks. These arguments were put forward by Asanuma

Banri and Aoki Masahiko – two scholars whose work is fairly representative of Japanese research into subcontracting.

The term subcontracting employed in this chapter refers to a particular system, which features the sending and receiving of production orders from relatively large firms to small companies and the structural division of labour this creates. Therefore, the discussion is not premised on the assumption that subcontracting is a relationship between superiors and inferiors or based on control and dependence.

Subcontracting: the transition from 'problem' to 'key' of success

The issue of subcontracting for SMEs

Since the pre-war period, company personnel, researchers and policy-makers attached great importance to the issue of subcontracting in SMEs. During the war in particular, the large number of SMEs (factories) in Japan were mobilised as subcontractors for munitions production. Various issues such as how to efficiently utilise subcontracting factories, how to raise productivity and how to promote relations between those factories placing production orders and subcontractors, were addressed and attempts made to put theories into practice (Ueda 1998).

Even after the war subcontracting was considered to be a problem for SMEs. Subcontractors were generally recognised as being SMEs. Many of the first-tier subcontractors that have direct business dealings with manufacturers of finished parts for automobiles and electric machinery were in fact SMEs. It was easy to accept the view that subcontractors were SMEs because many of the new SMEs established during Japan's period of high economic growth since 1955 were incorporated into subcontracting relations. The elimination of a 'dual structure' in the Japanese economy was regarded as an important policy issue. The repressive circumstances associated with low levels of technology and productivity in subcontracting SMEs and business relations has often been raised as subcontracting issues. The 1956 Law on the Prevention of Delay in the Payment of Subcontracting Charges and Related Matters (*Shitauke Daikin Shiharai Chien-tō Bōshi-hō*) and the 1963 Small and Medium Size Enterprise Basic Law

(*Kyū Chūshō Kigyō Kihon-hō*) were undoubtedly behind these perceptions.

During the period of high economic growth from 1955 to 1973, automobile and electric machinery production rose rapidly. As a result, subcontracting, which included second-tier firms, expanded and many new subcontracting SMEs were established. However, among first-tier subcontractors there was an increase in the both the number of firms that grew beyond the scale of SMEs and 'middle-standing enterprises' (*chūken kigyō*), which developed original technology. Although there were disparities in wages and working conditions, the level of technology in SMEs on the whole rose steadily during the high growth period. According to Watanabe Yukio, 'As a continual problem associated with subcontracting, the problem of outdated technology in subcontracting SMEs has been resolved to such an extent that it will at least not hinder the international competitiveness of large companies' (Watanabe 1997: 16). This trend was further reinforced from the 1970s to the 1980s and the gap between traditional theories of subcontracting SMEs and reality came to be seen as problematic.

The turnaround in assessment of subcontracting

In the 1980s, the strong competitiveness of Japanese companies became the focus of international attention. Japan had overtaken America in terms of the number of automobiles produced and Japanese manufacturers had an overwhelming share of the market in VCRs. Emphasis was placed on the Japanese-style production system as a contributing factor in firms' competitiveness and subcontracting was considered to be an important element in an efficient production system. Japanese manufacturers produced high quality goods at low cost. Their ability to supply global markets was thought to be the result of a system that effectively utilised and improved the skills of subcontractors linked to manufacturers of finished parts and in which subcontractors were able to respond to various supply demands. The generalised image at present of subcontracting (or suppliers) comprised the following elements: 1. high external production rates for manufacturers of finished parts; 2. a substantively limited number of direct outside suppliers (subcontractors); 3. stable, long-term business relations or recurrent transactions; 4. a pyramid-like structure with clearly defined subcontracting layers (eg. first-tier, second-tier and third-tier etc.); and 5. close technology and production links.

Moreover, from the 1980s to the 1990s, the relationship between the capacity to develop goods and subcontracting became the focus of attention. A survey of the development conducted by automobile manufacturers and first-tier suppliers noted that cooperative relations between the two in Japan plays a significant role in the shortening of development periods, as well as appraising the efficiency of their relationship, which had been criticised for being closed (Fujimoto and Clark 1993). Subcontracting was transformed from being a 'problem' in the Japanese economy to a 'key' in strengthening the competitiveness in particular manufacturing sectors. Moreover, subcontracting was seen as an international model. Asanuma and Aoki's assessment of subcontracting, examined in the following section, idealised Japanese subcontracting as achieving high levels of efficiency, productivity and technology and argued that it was possible to introduce this model to other parts of the world. Many researchers and businesspeople within and outside Japan were interested in their views and understood Japanese subcontracting in this manner.

What should be considered when examining the theories of subcontracting

One of the reasons for the changing assessment was that past theories emphasised too strongly the control-dependency aspect of subcontracting and the subsequent technology lag, structural domination and dependency, as well as the subcontractors' role as a buffer, which forced them to bear the brunt of the impact of market shifts. As a result, researchers considered the technology lag and the control-dependency aspect of subcontracting to be set notions and were unable to fully grasp the changing reality that subcontractors raised their technological capacity, grew and otherwise played an important role in the production system.

However, the argument that turned existing theories of subcontracting on their head by claiming that relations between the prime manufacturer and subcontractors were equal, subcontracting contributes to the development of subcontractors' technology and companies that most effectively utilise Japanese-style subcontracting are able to raise their competitiveness was, not surprisingly, unconvincing. Before drawing a conclusion, the following problems should not be overlooked.

The first problem concerns the chaotic image of subcontracting. Since the pre-war period, subcontracting mainly involved SMEs. Even today the majority of subcontractors are SMEs. However, it should be noted that many large companies are also included among first-tier suppliers. Since the 1980s, the number of studies of finished goods manufacturers and first-tier suppliers has increased. They assumed tacitly that the relationship between final goods manufacturers and large first-tier suppliers must be the same as that between first-tier suppliers and second-tier suppliers which were often small or medium-sized firms. They made this assumption without conducting research on the latter. Without conducting research on the relations between first-tier suppliers and second-tier suppliers, we cannot speak of the whole structure of the subcontracting system in Japan.

The second problem relates to the period from which the images reflected in these arguments derived. Many studies that positively evaluated subcontracting since the 1980s can be divided into three categories: 1. those claiming that subcontracting has changed since Japan's period of high growth, while acknowledging that it was a social and economic problem before the high growth era; 2. those asserting that subcontracting from the beginning involves the development of subcontractors and efficiency of production systems and; 3. those that are completely disinterested in the historical development of subcontracting. The overwhelming majority of research falls into the third category. Ignoring the historical development, they are unable to grasp the dynamics of subcontracting.

The third problem concerns how we should evaluate the reality of subcontracting from the late 1990s to the early 21st century. Compared to a period in the 1980s, by the late 1990s, Japanese corporate practices and the production system had lost their former confidence. Subcontracting had also been rated lowly. In the automobile industry Mazda and Nissan developed closer relations with Ford and Renault. Under the banners of 'reconsidering *keiretsu*' (*keiretsu no minaoshi*) and 'the collapse of the *keiretsu*' (*keiretsu no hōkai*), moves were well underway to reconsider fundamentally established business dealings with parts suppliers.

In Europe and America, in response to modularisation, some big parts suppliers have become bigger, while others reorganised or dropped out of the supplier relationship (Ueda 2001). In Japan too, subcontracting relations experienced important changes in the past and will surely change in the future. Only adopting a positive view of the Japanese system makes it impossible to grasp the presently changing reality of subcontracting.

What are the defining characteristics of this research that became enormously influential from the 1980s to the 1990s and what are the problems associated with it? These questions are addressed in the following section.

Asanuma Banri's theory of subcontracting (suppliers)

Asanuma's research

Asanuma Banri (1935–1996) was a professor at Kyoto University. From the 1980s to the 1990s, he energetically conducted research into subcontracting (he avoided using the term 'subcontracting,' instead preferring 'supplier'), writing many articles. Asanuma addressed such questions as 'how do finished goods manufacturers and first-tier suppliers mutually share risks in long-term business relations?' 'how do first-tier suppliers obtain profits?' and 'what kind of incentives motivate first-tier suppliers in this process?' In a survey he conducted concerning business relations in the automobile and electronics/electric machine industries in the 1980s, Asanuma highlighted the characteristics of the contractual framework of long-term business relations and identified these as one of the important factors in Japanese companies' international competitiveness. As the Japanese economic system was the focus of international attention at that time, Asanuma attempted to theorise his findings by borrowing from microeconomics. Emphasising the technological innovations of first-tier suppliers, which existing research ignored, his theory gained a strong influence both domestically and abroad.

However, while Asanuma wrote several important articles concerning subcontracting, he passed away before he was able to publish these in a single book. His work, published after his death, was awarded the *Nikkei-Keizai Tosho* prize in 1997 – one of the most prestigious prizes in the social sciences in Japan. Kikutani Tatsuya – who conducted research jointly with Asanuma and is presently a professor at Kyoto University – published the existing articles in a book that was based on Asanuma's ideas. Though the book was edited by Kikutani and not by Asanuma himself, it is an especially well-ordered exploration of Asanuma's research and, as such, I would like to examine it here.

Is subcontracting based on negotiations between equal players?

Taking the dealings between a final assembler and its first-tier suppliers in the automobile industry as a case study, Asanuma tried to present a general theory of subcontracting relations. Focusing on how products are developed jointly by the final assembler and its suppliers and how the unit price is determined, Asanuma thought that there was a reasonable system for risk-sharing between the final assembler and its suppliers. Before examining his findings and his theory, I will comment critically on his assumptions about negotiations between a final goods manufacturer and its suppliers.

First, a premise of Asanuma's analysis is that automobile manufacturers and first-tier suppliers enter into negotiations as equal partners with equal power. When attempting to analyse the contractual framework, if one does not assume that power relations between the two are in balance, the actual meaning of the analysis of coordination becomes lost. However, it is very unreasonable to assume equality is a matter of course. In reality, power relations in business negotiations are not necessarily in balance, but are out of balance. Both the automobile manufacturers and first-tier suppliers strive to gain even the slightest degree of supremacy. Relations between the two are not preordained, but are established as a result of competition to gain the ascendency during negotiations. In order to understand the link between the two, it is necessary to explore the actual process of business relations.

Second, the relationship between final assemblers and first-tier suppliers is one of buying and selling. At the same time, from the perspective of the final assembler, it is natural that first-tier subcontractors are managed as external suppliers. It is a relationship between managers and the managed. Final assemblers try to purchase the best goods at the cheapest prices under regular delivery schedules from first-tier suppliers. They not only select the first-tier suppliers that meet their needs, but also cultivate them in a manner conducive to achieving this. Some automobile manufacturers have purchasing control departments that deal with the various problems of first-tier suppliers. In this way, two different types of relations – buying and selling and managing and being managed – coexist between final assemblers and first-tier suppliers. This complicates relations between the two and is the reason why both cannot simply be equal players and are not enmeshed in a relationship characterised by domination and dependency. However, Asanuma does not place any emphasis on the 'managing' behaviour of the firms that issue subcontracting work.

Needless to say, managing first-tier suppliers has consistently been an important issue for automobile manufacturers. Automobile manufacturers are faced with many tasks – from managing the unit price of parts to managing the production system for first-tier suppliers. Particularly from the 1970s to the 1980s, when the *kanban* system was introduced on a wide-scale, reforms to the production systems of first-tier suppliers became necessary. First-tier suppliers voluntarily initiated reforms to their production systems, *which brought these into line with those of the automobile manufacturers.*

Of course, the relationship between managers and the managed does not necessarily enmesh the two directly in a relationship of control and dependency. This is because it is possible for diverse types of management to exist and also the managed do not always remain so. Nevertheless, it is impossible to consider relations between the two while overlooking the issue of management.

Third, what Asanuma actually analysed was the relationship between final assemblers. He set himself the task of theorising about general inter-company business relations (including SMEs) and company networks. However, reading his remaining works, it is not necessarily clear how Asanuma linked the actual analysis with such a task. At present, I do not know what he thought of this problem. Asanuma was unable to complete his general theory of subcontracting. It is therefore important to consider if or to what extent the relationship between final assemblers and their suppliers can be generalized in the whole supplier system.

Problems associated with blueprints

1. Asanuma made a clear distinction between the different types of suppliers: between vendors to which blueprints are supplied and vendors who themselves handle design details. The parts involved are distinguished as 'drawings supplied (DS)' parts

Figure 4-1 Designs approved/Designs supplied system

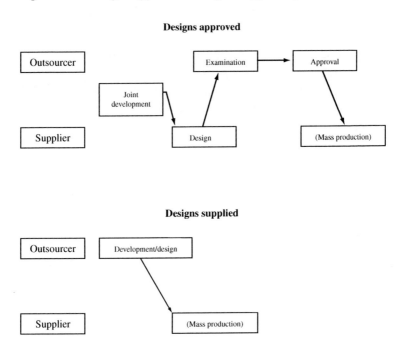

(*taiyozu*) and 'drawings approved (DA)' parts (*shōninzu*). According to Asanuma, For DS parts 'the assembler carries out the entire design process, with the vendor supplying only production services to the assembler.' For DA parts 'the detailed design is drawn up by the vendor and submitted to the assembler for testing and approval. Obtaining an order for a DA part is contingent upon final acceptance of the design, so that the vendor is supplying not only manufacturing but also design services' (Asanuma 1997: 187). The nature of business dealings involving DA and DS parts is illustrated in the diagram. Asanuma does not take this into consideration, but the same supplier is responsible for both the design and production of DA parts.

Asanuma also linked the type of supplier to its relational skills (skills used to supply parts efficiently in response to needs and demands of the outsourcing firm) and classified DA and DS vendors, as well as DA vendors internally, according to the differences in the vector of relational skills based on the amount of knowledge of the production process the outsourcing firm possesses. Asanuma's typology attaches importance to the technological and developmental strengths of parts manufacturers. Many researchers adopted this and from the 1980s, concentrated their analyses on product development and technological prowess in the automobile industry. Asanuma argued that middle-ranking suppliers are numerically most prevalent among the first-tier suppliers of automobile manufacturers than typical DS vendors and DA vendors that possess their own technology (193).

By classifying parts manufacturers, Asanuma sought to illustrate the following points. First, due to the balance between the technological prowess of suppliers and out-sourcing firms' understanding of the technology of their suppliers, every supplier is allocated an appropriate part to produce. This results in the effective application of these suppliers' relational skills. Second, the suppliers themselves develop from DS vendors into DA vendors (the evolution of suppliers). Third, the hierarchical structure of suppliers based on their technological prowess is effective also in terms of risk sharing (hierarchical nature and risk sharing). Asanuma believed that Japanese suppliers are incorporated effectively and efficiently into a division of labour. At the same time, because there is a trade-off between risk sharing and profit margins, suppliers have the incentive to strengthen their own technological prowess.

2. In this section I will examine Asanuma's views on whether automobile manufacturers absorb the risks borne by DS vendors. First, while DS vendors have low profit margins, automobile manufacturers bear a considerable portion of the risk for them. Asanuma was critical of the role played by subcontractors as buffers for automobile manufacturers. He emphasised that even in the event of fluctuating production, automobile manufacturers neither significantly reduce the amount of parts ordered nor harm first-tier suppliers' profit rates (Asanuma 1997: Chapter 8). However, a look at the facts reveals the following problems associated with this view. First, each automobile manufacturer has its own association of suppliers (*kyōryokukai*). Concerning the changes in the membership of the suppliers' association from 1975 to 1985,

while the percentage of suppliers that left the associations was certainly low for big manufacturers such as Toyota and Nissan, it was very high for the associations of the other manufacturers, in some cases nearly 40% (Ueda 1989). This is due to both the restructuring of parts manufacturers during this period and changes in subcontracting strategies of the automobile manufacturers. Whereas the relationship between the top automobile manufacturers and their first-tier suppliers is stable, ties between smaller manufacturers and their first-tier suppliers from the 1970s to the 1980s were unstable, which necessitated restructuring. This demonstrates the important influence of the strategies adopted by automobile manufacturers on the industry as a whole.

Second, it is believed that many of the manufacturers that left the suppliers' association as a result of this restructuring process were small DS firms that operated as first-tier suppliers. Under the conditions in which there has been a reorganisation of both automobile manufacturers' relations with first-tier suppliers and the division of labour, the impact on DS vendors is significant.

Third, does Asanuma's hypothesis also apply to second-tier suppliers and below? As Fujimoto (1997) points out, substantiated research based on solid data has not been conducted examining second-tier suppliers and below (179). Asanuma makes absolutely no mention of this. If his argument can also be applied to second-tier suppliers and below, then among the second-tier suppliers and below, where it is thought that the percentage of DS vendors is relatively high, the risk assumed by the outsourcing firm will be higher. This is highly unlikely when considering the instability associated with smaller suppliers.

3. The ambiguity of DA vendors' business dealings. The second point concerns business relations between DA vendors and automobile manufacturers. These relations feature the following characteristics. First, while DA vendors continually receive contracts for the development, design and production of parts (it is not a matter of course for European and American companies to do this continually), automobile manufacturers pay them only the basic unit price for each product. Development and design costs are only incorporated in some way into the unit price for finished products (Ueda

1995, 2000a). Second, it is difficult to know how much of the technological information concerning the relevant parts and products is shared between the outsourcing firm and suppliers. In addition to approving designs, the outsourcing firm attempts to examine the blueprint and obtain as much information as possible. However, because the parts manufacturer knows what to expect from the outsourcing firm, there are many cases in which the blueprint it submits for approval contains only the bare essentials. As a result, as the fire to the Aisin Seiki factory in January 1987 demonstrated, even if there are blueprints, it is impossible to simply switch production over to another parts manufacturer (Nishiguchi and Beaudet 2000). Third, it is unclear who owns the approved designs. Fujimoto argues that 'the supplier owns the designs – including the patent' (1997: 192). However, it has been noted that in many cases automobile manufacturers prohibit the supplier that developed the DA from selling them to other companies (Nihon Keizai Chōsa Kyōgikai 1993), further clouding the issue of ownership.

The reason why the approved designs are used, despite the ambiguity over their ownership, is because, based on the assumption that outsourcing firms and parts manufacturers are in a long-term business relationship, a system has been created in which this ambiguity ostensibly does not become a problem. In other words, while development and design costs are not clarified in the unit price of individual products, they are ultimately included in the gross sales from the supplier to the outsourcing firm. Concerning the issue of technology-related information, although the relationship between the outsourcing firm and parts manufacturer is usually tense, as long as a parts manufacturer responds to the outsourcing firm's needs, it is not necessarily important for the outsourcing firm to know all the design details. The situation surrounding ownership rights is that parts manufacturers only use the know-how included in blueprints in their business dealings with specific outsourcing firms and as long as these remain stable, ambiguity does not become a particular problem. This ambiguity allows firms in the automobile industry to reduce the amount of time spent developing products and is one of the contributing factors to the industry's international competitiveness. It also serves as a condition of the flexible and swift flow of information beyond the organisational structures of the outsourcing firm and the supplier.

However, when the conditions that support this ambiguity change, serious problems arise. The first problem is the expansion of production overseas. Local production results in a complex situation in which domestic parts manufacturers are responsible for product development, while production is entrusted to overseas manufacturers. It is the overseas affiliate of the automobile manufacturer that hands over the blueprints to the local manufacturer (see figure 4-2, Ueda 2000a). There are also issues related to parts manufacturers' intellectual property rights over the blueprints and whether it is possible to produce goods overseas at the intended cost, using blueprints developed in Japan. Second, while business relations have been developing beyond the scale of the previous *keiretsu* and foreign parts manufacturers have been entering the Japanese market (as has occurred in recent years), a possibility exists that business dealings premised on long-term relations will no longer be effective. Because it is very likely that there will be an increase in the number of cases whereby business relations develop intermittently, and not continually, investments will not be recouped in the long-term. Firms will seek to recoup their investments in the short-term and the previously ambiguous aspects of business relations will no longer function as such.

4. Concerning the evolution of suppliers, Asanuma argued that suppliers progress from the processing of simple parts to more complex parts – even if they are the same DS vendors. From here, DS vendors of complex parts develop into DA vendors. Among DA vendors there are those that proceed towards the production of parts that require developmental prowess, which few of their competitors possess. In the background of the evolution of suppliers is the trade off between high profit margins and the absorption of risks by outsourcing firms. Seeking high profit margins, suppliers minimise design details to the extent that outsourcing firms can understand them. To ensure the outsourcing firm assumes some of the risks, they, for instance, moderately weaken relations with specific outsourcing firms. The evolution of suppliers is a key point in understanding Japanese-style business relations and is an important source of their competitiveness.

Figure 4-2   Overseas production

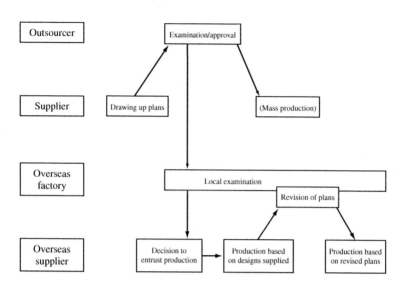

Certainly, as Asanuma noted, there are instances where suppliers became DA vendors after accumulating technology. However, as Asanuma himself recognises, in reality, many first-tier suppliers – even if they are DA or DS vendors of complex parts – are parts manufacturers that possess information concerning parts used by automobile manufacturers. Its solidity is a characteristic of this hierarchy. Even if SMEs were to expand in scale and possess an organisation allowing them to design and develop parts, further development, in technological terms, would be extremely difficult. As a result, there are limits to the evolution of suppliers.

Moreover, the evolution from DA to DS vendor must take into consideration not only the subjective conditions of the supplier but also the conditions of the outsourcing firm . Asanuma ignores the background of Japanese suppliers becoming DA vendors. In the late 1960s and the early 1970s, the number of DA vendors in the Toyota group increased rapidly. At that time, the variety of automobiles increased so rapidly that Toyota could not secure enough development engineers, which resulted in an increase of DA vendors

(Fujimoto 1997: 214). One cannot ignore the changing conditions in which outsourcing firms entrust the development of parts to suppliers.

How are unit prices coordinated?

Asanuma focused on how outsourcing firms and parts suppliers decide the unit price. In particular, he characterised the analysis of each item contained in the formula for calculating unit prices used by the automobile industry in the following manner: 'First, it can be predicted that the price does not show much responsiveness towards the rise in the yearly personnel costs to the degree that is usually estimated. Second, apart from periods in which there is an exceptionally sharp rise, it can be predicted that the price does not show much responsiveness towards rising energy prices. Third, the negotiating position of buyers, which is the basis of these two items, is used as pressure to prompt the rationalisation towards the reduction in working time, as well as energy consumption. Fourth, while buyers apply pressure in order to reduce the price of parts, from a long-term perspective, this, to a certain extent, works as a restraining force' (Asanuma 1997: 181). Among the items used to determine the unit price, Asanuma discusses the calculation of 'costs for specific dies and tools (*katashōkyakuhi*)' and 'remuneration for improvement proposals (*kaizen teian hōshū*)' and emphasised them as a means of risk absorption by automobile manufacturers and as an incentive to improvement activities by suppliers.

While Asanuma offered keen insights into the issue of unit prices and relations between outsourcing firms and suppliers, there are problems associated with the actual analysis. First, he attached importance to the process of deciding unit prices, but as a result, made absolutely no mention of unit price levels. Second, as an example of risk absorption by automobile manufacturers, Asanuma evaluated costs for specific dies and tools. However, as suppliers have to purchase expensive dies before producing parts for an automobile manufacturer, it is unreasonable to emphasise costs for specific dies and tools as an element of risk absorption by automobile manufacturers (Ueda 2000b). Third, concerning remuneration for improvement proposals, the claim that suppliers link the issue of forcing automobile manufacturers to acknowledge the results of improvement proposals to the potential for receiving future orders is more realistic than the argument that suppliers link improvement proposals to prime cost reductions through incentives such as remuneration. Fourth, Asanuma does not mention his views regarding the problem that suppliers' development costs are not paid by automobile manufacturers. Asanuma's method of calculating unit prices in the manufacturing process is extremely detailed, but he overlooked this important point. Fifth, the meaning differs depending on whether unit prices are evaluated in the context of long-term relations or short-term dealings. In other words, coordination is not carried out in a one-time process of determining unit prices, but within a long-term relationship premised on long-term business dealings. Therefore, assuming that economic growth is high, in a situation in which it is highly possible to maintain a long-term relationship it is also possible to prolong the problem – even if one-time units prices are not clearly coordinated – and settle it in a long-term relationship. In order to recover development costs, the supplier that developed the parts assumes the responsibility of mass producing them. Recovering development costs is ultimately possible in a long-term business relationship.

Evaluating Aoki's theory of subcontracting

Aoki Masahiko was fairly quick to evaluate Asanuma's research on subcontracting and suppliers, incorporating it into his own arguments. In chapter 6 'The changing nature of industrial organization,' section 1 'The subcontracting group,' Aoki 'describe[s] the generic mode of transactions within the subcontracting group, analyze[s] its sharing and incentive aspects from the viewpoint of contract theory, and identif[ies] factors that affect the efficiency of such subcontracting as well as the distribution of its outcome among the contracting partners. The traditional dual-structure hypothesis that has made the monopsonic power of the prime contracting firm a focal point is criticized for being at best one-sided' (Aoki 1988: 205, 1992: 210).[1]

Aoki argued that in 'subcontracting groups,' due to stratification based on long-term subcontracting contracts and the technological prowess of suppliers, the lower the position a company holds, the less it is allocated in terms of quasi-rent. However, because lower-tier companies function as an insurer of the outsourcing firm, the degree of risk-aversion rises. Moreover, concerning 'the insurance function of the subcontracting group,' 'The prime manufacturer absorbs a proportion of contract-specific risk, acting as a partial insurer for lower-tier risk-averse subcontractors, extracting a larger portion of the relational quasi-rent as a sort of insurance premium' (Aoki 1988: 222, 1992: 228).[2] Fewer quasi-rent allocations show up in wage-scales and welfare-related labour costs. Aoki claims he can explain rationally lower-tier companies gaining smaller proportions of quasi-rent in relation to risk aversion. The lower-tier companies that Aoki speaks of include SMEs below the second and third-tiers. It is clear that he attempts to theorise sub-contracting, expanding the argument put forward by Asanuma.

Because Aoki's arguments are based on Asanuma's work, most criticisms of the latter also apply to the former. The following point should also be added. Aoki claims that lower-tier companies receive smaller proportions of quasi-rent and that the outsourcing firm performs an insurance function. Is this a realistic assumption? As discussed previously, there is no data that indicates whether outsourcing firms absorb the risks for second-tier firms and below. However, the argument that the lower the level of a firm the smaller the proportion of quasi-rents is paid to subcontractors, whereas the share of risks assumed is alleviated, is unconvincing.

Subcontracting: past, present and future

What exactly is subcontracting (or the supplier system) in Japan? Asanuma and Aoki presented a new perspective of this. First, subcontracting is a relationship that links equal participants in a business relationship. Second, it is also a system, which contains incentives for parts manufacturers to develop technological prowess in a business relationship featuring a trade off between risk sharing and profit margins, as well as to encourage progressive responses from firms. However, when considering the issue of subcontracting in past and future contexts, it is important to be mindful of the following points.

First, outsourcing firms usually manage subcontractors (suppliers). There is considerable trial and error associated with subcontractors' attempts to maximise profits under management and gain the ascendency. Upon understanding both parties' positions in this manner, concrete power relations between the two should be thought of as differing according to the environment and conditions that occasionally develop. Certainly, the Japanese automobile industry in the 1980s was also supported by its international competitiveness and relations between outsourcing firms and suppliers appeared ostensibly to be in balance. However, it was the norm which developed under very special conditions whereby the Japanese automobile industry achieved high growth from the 1960s, that supported this. Norms, in this context, means that dealing with the various problems associated with business relations is based on the assumption of long-term dealings. Long-term business relations are a norm, although to what extent this functions in reality is a separate issue.

Second, in fact, outsourcing firms and subcontractors did not consciously seek to establish long-term business relations, as a norm, at first. Rather, the norm was created due to the special circumstances of the Japanese automobile industry, which basically continued to grow over a long period of time from the period of high economic growth. A relationship in which both parties attempt to deal with problems that arise in long-term dealings has left many grey areas. This ambiguity, in addition to raising international competitiveness, also had a positive connotation. However, on the contrary, if an environment that made long-term business relations possible were to disappear, there is strong possibility that problems would emerge.

Third, as we have entered the 21st century, the environment and time where the Japanese subcontracting system received high praise has changed (see Ueda 2001). The automobile industry is undergoing significant changes such as the reorganisation of international automobile and parts manufacturers and increasing modularisation. The domestic division of labour is also de-stabilising. The emergence of business dealings beyond the *keirestu* system, in particular, as well as increasing purchases from overseas and the gradual dismantling of traditional *keirestu* groupings are also evident. What should we think of the link between this period and the previously evaluated subcontracting system? The problems associated with the traditional system should be re-examined amid this changing environment.

5 Do Japanese Labour Unions Bargain?

Yoshihiko Kamii

Bargaining theories in the 1980s

Do Japanese labour unions perform a bargaining function? The established theory until the 1970s was that the organisational form that is based on the enterprise has limited this function. However, from the late 1970s, the notion that Japanese enterprise unions are indeed rational organisations that are congruent with internal labour markets was widely disseminated (see Kawanishi 1981: 4–6). A scholar whose work was representative of this notion was Koike Kazuo. Aoki Masahiko incorporated Koike's theories into a theory of companies. In his widely acclaimed book (Aoki 1988 – a Japanese translation was published in 1992), which explored Japanese companies in detail, Aoki presents a microanalysis of companies from the perspective of 'bargaining game' theory (*kōshō gēmu-ron*). Aoki discusses 'various behavioural characteristics of the J-firm as the bargaining outcome that is efficient, free of strategic disturbance, and fair to the constituent bodies' (Aoki 1988:154, 1992: 167).[1]

Koike and Aoki's bargaining theories posit that enterprise unions perform a bargaining function. Their theories were designed to portray Japanese companies, which were notable for their international competitiveness in the 1980s, and large enterprise unions, which cooperated with management, as being fair and just. These theories ignored inconvenient facts and, in terms of theory building, presented what 'ought to be' as being 'factual.' This bargaining theory was tarnished by the collapse of Japan's bubble economy. However, it does not mean that this theory was valid until the early 1990s and then lost relevancy with the burst of the bubble. Their bargaining theory was from the very beginning theoretically incorrect and was divorced from the reality of Japan in the 1980s. I will demonstrate this below.

Aoki Masahiko's 'bargaining game' theory

First, I would like to dissect Aoki's 'bargaining game' theory. However, because chapter 8 examines Aoki's theory of the J-firm, I will focus on the issue of bargaining and workers' bargaining strength, based mainly on Aoki's (1988) work.[2]

Bargaining as fiction

According to Aoki, 'the Japanese firm should be regarded as a *coalition* of the body of employees and the body of stockholders rather than the sole property of stockholders, as postulated in the neoclassical paradigm' (Aoki 1988: 4; Aoki 1992: 7). While he discusses the 'bargaining game' carried out between these two bodies, Aoki does not apply 'game' theory to the actual bargaining that takes place. In fact, Aoki lists 'a wide range of bargainable subjects' and 'implicit commitment' as characteristics of the 'bargaining game' in the J-firm. Concerning the former, he notes (Aoki 1988: 156; Aoki 1992:170):

> Bargainable subjects at the J-firm extend to a relatively wide range of issues beyond conventional collective bargaining subjects such as remuneration to the quasi-permanent employee and other conditions of employment. Strategic decision variables of high relevance to the welfare of quasi-permanent employees, as well as their standard effort level to accumulate and efficiently use contextual skills, are included (implicitly) as bargainable subjects.

Regarding the latter, Aoki states that 'The agreement regarding some variables defining a bargain outcome may not be written in an explicit and enforceable contract, but may be understood only as implicit commitment' (Aoki 1988: 156; Aoki 1992: 170). The terms 'implicitly' and 'implicit commitment' suggest that, in reality, bargaining does not take place.

Corresponding to the trichotomy of the bargaining game at the J-firm, Aoki claims that management plays three complementary roles (Aoki 1988: 181–182; Aoki 1992: 195):

1. *Bargaining agent vis-à-vis the enterprise-based union*: Management is engaged in collective bargaining vis-à-vis the enterprise-based union regarding the disposition of the organisational quasi rent to ensure a satisfactory return to stockholders, as well as an adequate addition to the physical assets of the company.
2. *Administrator in ranking hierarchy*: Management monitors quasi-permanent employees to ensure that they fulfil their commitments to exercise sufficient effort for the maximised organisational quasi rent net of the cost of their effort. It can do so by providing the quasi-permanent employee with the pay and promotional structure…as an incentive scheme and admistering [*sic*] it centrally.
3. *Arbitrative strategic managerial decision maker*: Management is engaged in making strategic managerial decisions so as to balance the interests of the constituent bodies of the firm by following the weighting rule.

Despite Aoki's claim, we cannot find evidence anywhere in the 'effort' and 'strategic managerial' variables that bargaining has actually been conducted.

The 'bargaining game' in game theory originally referred to hypothetical bargaining, which was used to explain various social phenomena. Moreover, game theory leaps towards an equilibrium solution at a stroke based on the assumption of a game characterised by the players' preferences, beliefs and rules of the game. Game theory, as Takeda Shigeo notes in chapter 8, is problematic in that it completely fails to resolve issues such as the course one should follow when the game becomes detached from an equilibrium solution and how a result is ultimately arrived at. In fact, it must be noted that the more a subject is unbargainable, the more these type of difficulties in game theory are avoided. The reason why is because equilibrium solutions are presented as reality while remaining unbargainable.

Workers' bargaining power

Aoki's 'bargaining game' theory has problems explaining the bargaining power of labour. Aoki cites labour unions and individual workers as the bargaining agents representing labour vis-à-vis management and states that 'individual bargaining complement[s] collective bargaining' (Aoki 1988: 94; Aoki 1992: 106). So what then is the source of the bargaining power of labour unions and individuals workers? In order to answer this question, Aoki introduces the concept of 'contextual skill,' which draws from and further refines Koike's notion of 'intellectual skill' outlined in his information theory. 'Contextual skill' refers to when:

> Those workers nurtured in a wide range of skills may be able to understand, as individuals or as a collective, why defective products have increased, and may be able to devise and implement measures to cope with the situation and thus prevent the problem from recurring. This can be done without much, if any, "outside" help from specially designated craft workers, reliefmen, repairmen, and other specialists...One may also say, from the perspective of the information system, that collective learning enhances workers' capacities for processing information relevant to shopfloor efficiency (Aoki 1988: 15 16; Aoki 1992: 19).

Moreover, Aoki claims that 'since contextual skill is to be specific to the organization, each individual may be considered to have potential bargaining power over the evaluation through the potential threat of non-cooperation' (Aoki 1988: 94; Aoki 1992: 106). He also states that 'employees' "threats" to withhold cooperation collectively over information processing and mutual communication are credible' (Aoki 1989: 94). While it can be said that strikes and sabotage, which are normally thought of as bargaining power, are included in acts of 'non-cooperation' and 'collectively refraining from cooperation,' the main point of Aoki's 'bargaining game' theory is that such 'potential threats' and 'intimidation,' which do not extend to the exercise of power, are transformed into bargaining power.

However, this type of bargaining power does not actually exist. First, if we examine individual workers' bargaining power, 'intellectual skill,' as analysed in chapter 6, is a fictional creation of Koike's. Therefore, it goes without saying that Aoki's 'contextual skill,' which is based on this, also does not exist. Second, Aoki's argument contradicts or negates what he calls bargaining power. Concerning the 'ranking hierarchy', which relies on personnel assessments, Aoki claims that 'merit assessment (*satei*) by supervisors is an important determinant of an employee's earnings as it is the basis for promotion...'(Aoki 1988: 56; Aoki 1992:65). He also notes that 'The J-firm has evolved a system of individual incentive schemes...Under such schemes, the firm can identify slow learning, low productivity, low motivation, and uncooperative workers by actual observation and differentiate them in pay and status over the long run...'(Aoki 1988: 50; Aoki 1992: 59). In this way, it is hardly possible that workers who are enmeshed in the 'ranking hierarchy...have potential bargaining power...through the potential threat of non-cooperation.'

The same can be said of the bargaining power of labour unions. First, Aoki characterised the information structure of the J-firm as a 'horizontal information structure.' Under this structure, coping with emergencies in the workshop and the fine-tuning of production plans between workshops are carried out in a decentralised and horizontal fashion based on 'information sharing.' A premise of this argument is the high information processing capabilities of production workers, in other words, 'contextual skill.' As discussed above, because this type of 'contextual skill' was fictitious, the core elements of Aoki's labour union bargaining power do not hold true. Second, as Asao Uichi (chapter 2) observes in his criticism of the one-sided nature of Aoki's 'theory of horizontal information structure,' it should have seen that horizontal information processing and communication by work groups in the workshop is integrated by centralised 'vertical' information processing. In other words, work groups do not possess information processing and communication capabilities. An 'intimidation' strategy, which uses this type of information processing and communication as a weapon, is unlikely to translate into bargaining power.

Koike Kazuo's theory of bargaining function

The autonomy of workshop collectives and the bargaining function of labour unions

In 1977, Koike declared that 'one has to say that labour-management relations in our country are the most "advanced" at present' (Koike 1977a: 240). In this section I would like to examine Koike's research, which was representative of those works praising Japan.

In the early 1970s, Koike, with the aim of comparing the situation with that in America and focusing on 'career regulations,' conducted interviews of 13 unions in the steel, chemical and machinery industries and sought to ascertain the real situation surrounding union regulations concerning promotions, relocation, short-term replacement for production adjustment, overtime and related output. He discovered the following three 'facts' about large Japanese companies: 1. transfers occur frequently between 'distant workplaces,' which are loosely linked in terms of skills; 2. transfers also occur frequently within the workplace, as well as between 'close workplaces'; and 3. the workplace has a 'flexible structure.' The claim about the 'broad experience' of Japanese workers derives from this research.

As Nomura (2003) points out, it is very doubtful if these 'facts' are really substantiated by his research. The point is, however, Koike leapt from these 'facts' to an imaginary world. As regards the mechanism whereby 'movement is frequent and flexible, according to changing circumstances within workshops, as well as between close workshops,' Koike notes that 'this is an area in which unions do not intervene, and is a recognised semi-autonomous rule that makes up for this deficiency.' In other words, he notes that based on 'workplace practices,' the foreman carries out transfers and selects suitable people for a post in 'egalitarian' fashion (Koike 1977a: 205, 215, 218). From here, he stipulates that workplace workgroups are 'semi-autonomous collectives in the workplace' and later claims 'this is different to a labour union, it might be a type of industrial democracy' (Koike 1983: 236). He then went so far as to present a non-union model of industrial democracy.

Is Koike's claim about 'semi-autonomous workshop collective' regulations correct? Definitely not. First, it should be noted that it does not stand up based on his arguments. According to Koike, there are two aspects to the foreman: 1. for the foreman, who is at the lower levels of formal management, 'ascertaining how to make workers work more in order to maximise profits is the most urgent requisite.' As a result, the foreman uses his discretion to conduct 'arbitrary' transfers and promote competition among workers through per-formance reviews. On the other hand, since his chances of further promotion are poor, he acts as a representative of the workgroup; 2. in the case of the latter, Koike states that 'the discretion of the foreman brings about flexibility in transfers...[The flexibility of these transfers] largely reduces the cost of adapting to changes. This is a plus for management. Therefore, the firm tacitly approves so-called "autonomous" movements based on the practice of work collectives under the leadership of a foreman;' 3. He also states that 'the critical turning point [between the former and the latter paths] perhaps depends on the extent to which the amount of work performed by a workshop collective as a group is regulated by labour unions' (Koike 1977a: 203–205); However, 4. as a result of examining the output regulations of labour unions in the machine industry, 'generally, labour unions and workshop collectives do not speak out strongly against output itself...At the most, they have some say regarding overtime regulations' (Ibid., 208–209).

Second, while Koike arrived at the notion of 'semi-autonomous work collective' regulations by way of 'egalitarian' transfers and personnel selection, a look at the facts reveals that this is an erroneous claim. 'Flexible transfers' are a strong request relayed from management to the foreman – who is at the lower levels of management. In particular, from the late 1970s to the 1980s, in order to carry out flexible production with fewer personnel, management aimed to establish a system in which personnel coordination between workshops, through overtime and transfers, could be conducted flexibly. Mass and frequent transfers went beyond the bounds of what the foreman considered in terms of raising the skill levels of individual workers and using his discretion to put the right people in the right place. According to an empirical study of a Toyota assembly plant in the mid-1980s, 108 workers from the auto body section (from a total of 565) moved to other factories and other divisions within this plant for production adjustment. In addition, there were many workers who moved to other sections within the same division for the same purpose (Kamii 1994: 204). These movements are repeated every month and, in some cases, everyday. Under this system, the foreman has no means of responding to requests for short-term transfers other than carrying out 'egalitarian' transfers and personnel selection. Under conditions whereby transfers are frequently carried out at the request of management, egalitarianism – contrary to Koike's argument – as a distributive rule of work, is an expression of a lack of 'autonomy.'

However, Koike, in fact, offered important perspectives on the issue. The first is that the foreman has a dual character. In the words of the late Professor Ujihara Shōjirō, this refers to a supervisor's character and a labourer's character (1953). Koike termed these the lower levels of formal management and the most senior member of the workgroup. As Koike states, the foreman determines the degree of 'autonomy' from the management of the workshop collective, depending on which of the two characters he reinforces. If the foreman becomes a union official, this also extends to the union character. Second, such independence by the foreman from management and 'autonomy' of the workshop collective first became possible due to the existence of union regulations.

It is understandable that Koike (1977a) made no mention at all of the bargaining power of labour unions, which made these type of regulations possible. The labour movement once tried to obtain bargaining power at the workplace. As the slogan 'from a leadership struggle to a mass struggle' (*kanbu tōsō kara taishū tōsō e*) (Uchiyama 1954) reveals, Sōhyō, the largest national centre of labour unions, adopted a policy in the 1950s to mobilise rank and file members for workplace-centred activities, aiming to narrow 'management prerogatives' at the workplace.

However, in large enterprises in the 1960s, foremen became the pillar of enterprise unions and the rank and file employees were excluded from administration of enterprise unions. And thus bargaining at the workplace diminished. The bargaining unit was no more the workplace level but the whole enterprise level.

'The risk sharing model' and the bargaining function of labour unions

In the 1980s, Koike jettisoned both of the two points mentioned above. Koike only brought up the aspect of the workshop collective's 'autonomy.' He cited workers' 'wide ranging skills' as the basis of this autonomy and the source of labour unions' bargaining power. Koike explained that 'if labour unions and workers decreased their contribution to the expanding pie, it would be a significant blow to management' (Koike 1983: 235). However, considering that the wide range of skills alone is a weak basis for workshop collective's 'autonomy' and labour unions' bargaining power, Koike claimed that production-line workers possess 'trouble-shooting skills' similar to engineers' knowledge (Koike and Inoki 1987: 187) and created the concept of deep skill, namely, 'intellectual skill.' As discussed previously, Aoki's concept of 'contextual skill' is a refined version of this notion of 'intellectual skill.'

As demonstrated in chapter 6, the theory of 'intellectual skill' is based on fictitious evidence. Therefore, a bargaining theory that is based on this is meaningless. Nevertheless, Koike's bargaining theory had many followers. Therefore, I will comment on his arguments. Koike attempts to reinforce the concept of 'intellectual skill' by superimposing the firm-specific skills' (*kigyō tokushu jukuren*) hypothesis, which is a theoretical manipulation of the theory of human capital. From the viewpoint of 'intellectual skill,' he insists that the enterprise union is the most advanced organisational form in the modern economy and highly appraises their bargaining function.

That is not all. Koike further claims that individual companies certainly negotiate wages with enterprise unions. However, due to industry-level coordination within labour unions as well as within personnel managers of leading companies, wages are in fact negotiated at the industry-level. In addition, Koike emphasises that the principal difference between Japanese and American unions is 'The extension of a consultative labour management system in the company and plant levels...In Japan, enterprise unions have a say regarding plans for product sales etc. and, generally, management conditions and policy.'

Why, Koike asks, do enterprise unions speak out regarding management and production problems? His answer is that 'when there are some firm-specific skills, the suffering caused by retrenchment is great and workers attempt to avoid this as much as possible. This not only applies to retrenchment. A company's rise and decline largely depends on the skills of its workers.' Thus, Koike proposed a 'risk sharing model' (*kiken buntan moderu*) for labour-management relations.

In this manner, concerning a sphere that was only at the most assessed as 'implicit' bargaining in Aoki's 'bargaining game' theory, Koike gave high praise to labour unions speaking out without providing corroborative evidence. However, if we look at the failures of Japanese companies, which were at the centre of many scandals in the late 1980s following the rise and subsequent collapse of Japan's bubble economy, it is clear that enterprise unions cannot monitor or check 'strategic management' decisions and 'management policy.' Moreover, as can be easily surmised from the long working hours, frequent occurrence of overtime, death from overwork (*karōshi*) and increasing employee layoffs in Japan, labour unions do not have bargaining power over work conditions. It is important to note that layoffs target mainly middle-aged and old employees. This contradicts the notion of 'intellectual skill,' which ought to rise in level as workers continue to work for a company.

Regarding the realities of labour union bargaining power, from the mid-1970s to the 1980s – the period Aoki and Koike's research covered – a slightly more thorough observation is necessary. In the following section I would like to offer a new perspective of union bargaining power, focusing on the three variables – 'distribution,' 'effort' and 'managerial strategy' – in Aoki's 'bargaining game' theory.

Labour unions' bargaining power over 'distribution'

The bargaining power of labour unions during the spring labour offensive

The first issue I will examine is 'distribution,' or in other words, the bargaining power of labour unions regarding wages and work conditions. Interestingly, an investigative report headed by Tachibanaki Toshiaki (Tachibanaki et al., 1993) and conducted for the Research Institute for the Advancement of Living Standards (*Rengō Sōken*) passed harsh judgement, noting that:

> wages were not necessarily higher for male workers in companies that had unions, whereas they were higher for female workers in companies that had unions. Strictly speaking, there is no meaningful, statistical difference in wage levels between unionised and non-unionised companies (244).

Satō Hiroki and others, who sympathise with Koike's theory, arrive at a similar conclusion (Nakamura, Satō and Kamiya 1988: 43–45). Because Koike's concept of 'intellectual skill' and Aoki's notion of 'contextual skill' refer to regular male employees, the fact that the presence of unions has no bearing on the wages of male workers is an important point.

Nevertheless, the difference in wage levels between unionised and non-unionised companies, apart from in America, is not evident in any advanced industrialised country. This is due to a spill-over effect. The report conducted for the Research Institute for the Advancement of Living Standards noted that regarding the wages of male workers, 'there is a possibility of a spill-over effect from wages in unionised companies to wages in non-unionised companies' (214). Therefore, in this section I would like to focus on the spring labour offensive (*shuntō*) in order to examine whether labour unions really had bargaining power.

Concerning the *shuntō* led by the General Council of Trade Unions of Japan (*Sōhyō*) during the period of high economic growth, wage increases from the 1960s to the early 1970s exceeded 10% every year (apart from 1963). However, consumer prices continued to rise. To examine if wage increases were the main reason for inflation, the government set up two research committees in the late 1960s and the early 1970s. One committee chaired by Kumagai Hisao presented a report in 1968 and the other chaired by Sumiya Mikio released a report in 1972. Both reports reached the same conclusion regarding the bargaining power of unions over wage increases, namely, labour unions did not have bargaining power sufficiently strong enough to cause inflation. (Kōshiro, Research Institute for the Advancement of Living Standards eds., 1995: 388–389).

After the end of the period of high economic growth, the wage increase rate plummeted. The wage increases achieved by the *shuntō* from 1960 to 1974 averaged 14.8%. However, this figure dropped to 5.7% from 1975 to 1990. During this time, Japan became the country with the least number of strikes. A comparison with the percentage labour productivity increases reveals that while the percentage wage increases achieved by the *shuntō* surpassed the percentage labour productivity increases until 1975, from 1976 to 1990, it fell below the average (a little more than 6%) percentage labour productivity increases. The *shuntō* has remained completely within the framework of the 'Productivity Standard Principle' (*seisansei kijun genri*), the principle that wage percentage increases should be within productivity increases, emphasised by the Japan Federation of Employers' Associations (*Nikkeiren*).

Trends in labour share

When examining 'distribution,' it is necessary to discuss labour share – labour's portion of added value. Yoshikawa (1994: 119–20) calculated the labour share of large companies using the Financial Statements Statistics of Corporations by Industry base (FSSCI). To examine the bargaining power of labour unions, I cite here the labour share of the manufacturing sector. This is because the manufacturing sector has traditionally been the heart of the labour movement.

According to Yoshikawa's study, the labour share averaged 60.5% from 1966 to 1970. It increased rapidly in the first half of the 1970s and posted a record-high 75.5% in 1975. It then stagnated. It averaged 70.7% from 1976–1980, 71.4% from 1981 to 1985 and 70.5% from 1986 to1990.

How should we interpret these trends in labour share? Generally, Japan's labour share is relatively low compared to America and the U.K. Moreover, it is said to fluctuate significantly, falling when the economy is robust and rising when the economy weakens. Of course, there are business cycle factors such as production, sales and capacity operating rates that influence these movements in labour share. However, within the parameters of labour share fluctuations, labour unions' thought and behaviour patterns and bargaining power in the *shuntō* naturally also have an impact. In short, that large companies kept a lid on wage increase demands, beginning with the 'economy-compatible theory' (*keizai seigōsei-ron*), following the oil shock, was nothing other than a policy of not raising the labour share. This is diametrically opposite to the case of the German metal union, IG Metall, which, from the perspective of 'distributive fairness' (*bunpai kōsei*), made calculations of labour share improvements (= increases), inflation and productivity growth rates and decided to make concrete wage demands against the industry based on these (Nihon Rōdō Kenkyū Kikō 1994: 182–183). In this way, Japanese labour unions, which even restricted their own wage increase demands, did not achieve this.

The result is evident in the changes in the labour share. Even Chiba Toshio, who played a leading role in the Japan Federation of Steel Workers' Unions' (*tekkō rōren*) 'economy-compatible' policy after the first oil shock, analysed the long-term trends in the macro- and micro-labour share in 1990 (he was an advisor to the union at the time). His following comments deserve close attention. 'Conditions in recent years have even been worse than during the period of high growth in the first half of the 1970s, falling to the lowest level in the past 20 years. This is a terrible situation...What is important for labour unions is that one of the major factors contributing to such absurdity under free collective bargaining is labour unions' lack of power, or the fact that there are repeated minimum wage increases that derive from the tendency of unions themselves to over-prioritise companies' economic success' (Chiba 1990: 18–19).

As demonstrated above, large, private sector unions do not demonstrate any bargaining power in the *shuntō*. Indeed, it is appropriate to view them as having surrendered their bargaining power over wage increases.

Fixing wage disparities by company size

Because of Koike's aforementioned claim that the *shuntō* in large companies in major industries such as steel, electric machinery and automobiles 'is essentially carried out at the industry level,' I would like to examine this point. Koike's (1991) statement about 'bargaining at the industry level' rests on the claim that the amount or the percentage of wage increases to which major companies will agree is either the same or is only slightly different. Therefore, it is necessary to examine the issue pertaining to the differences in the amount or percentage of agreed wage increases.

First, the same or very similar amount or percentage of wage increase among major companies in an industry does not mean that bargaining 'is essentially carried out at the industry level.' For example, in the electric and electronic industry, similar wage increases were agreed upon among only 14 large companies such as Matsushita, Hitachi and Toshiba, even though there are numerous companies in the industry. Why can wage increase coordination among 14 big companies be called industry-wide bargaining?

Second, regarding wage disparity by company size, enterprise unions play a problematic role. As is well known, there is a clear wage disparity according to company size. The smaller the company, the lower the wage. Labour unions were expected to even out wage disparity by company size. However, recent research has found that labour unions have maintained wage disparity by company size, not narrowed it. Analysing the process and results of wage negotiations in the automobile industry, Nakata Yoshifumi concluded, 'From 1980 to 1994, the difference in percentage wage increases in the automobile industry was reduced considerably, thus fixing pre-existing wage disparities by company size in the industry. The various confederations of enterprise unions contributed much to this fixing of the wage disparity by company size' (Nakata 1997a: 25–26).

Other research on wage bargaining in the automobile industry found a clear hierarchy among enterprise unions in All Toyota Unions in the late 1970s and 1980s. The Toyota Union – the enterprise union of the Toyota Motor Company, enjoyed the highest wage increase rate. The wage increase rate of the other enterprise unions varied according to the principle of 'the smaller, the less" (Ueda1992). In this case, enterprise unions contributed to a further widening of the wage disparity by company size.

Labour union bargaining over 'effort'

Enterprise unions' say in personnel assessments

In the previous section, it was noted that large, private sector unions had ineffectual bargaining power over 'distribution.' In fact, this bargaining power has been further restricted. Whether the wages decided in the *shuntō* are standard workers' wages or whatever, they are the average workers' wages. Labour unions' bargaining power does not extend to deciding individual wages. In Japan individual workers' wages and promotions are decided on the basis of personnel assessments. Labour unions generally do not intervene in this process.

How do large, private sector unions deal with personnel assessments? A report entitled 'The Realities of Management Participation Among 84 Private Sector Unions' (*Minkan 84 Rōso no Keiei Sanka no Jittai*) which contained the results of a questionnaire published in the spring edition of *Kikan Chūō Kōron* (special focus on management problems) uncovered the true thoughts of union officials in large, private companies regarding personnel assessments. Concerning personnel assessments, which prescribe employees' 'effort' (= how they acquit themselves), unions officials stated that the right to speak among workers at the workshop level in regards to individual assessments is extremely limited. Officials also replied that in the present circumstances 'it is OK that workers have little say [in personnel assessments]' (*hatsugenken wa sukunakute yoi*). While this was the response by union officials to a question about the right to speak, it was also the same in regards to labour unions' influence. One of the reasons why unions do not have a say in individual personnel assessments is because union leaders do not like to define fairness among individual employees. Large, private sector unions continued to hold this view throughout the 1980s (Kamii 1993: 85–86).

Accepting discriminatory assessments

As Endō Kōshi discusses, the most serious problem associated with the Japanese system of personnel assessments is discrimination based on gender and political beliefs (Endō 1999). Aoki's notions of 'morale' and 'cooperativeness' equate with the 'morale and attitude appraisal' (*jōi kōka*) item in personnel assessments. However, because these concepts can be broadly interpreted, employees who are critical of companies receive low evaluations and are discriminated against in terms of wages and promotions. The position of union officials not to intervene in individual personnel assessments is tantamount to accepting such discrimination. There have been not a few court cases and appeals to the Labour Relations Commission from employees claiming discrimination in their personnel assessments. However, it is mostly left wing activists critical of management who have launched these appeals. To enterprise unions that pursue cooperative policies with their companies, they are an opposition faction within the union or members of an opposing union. By making an example of them, management and the unions expect to have an impact on employees/union members.

In this way, personnel assessments are completely confined to the world of management. Indeed, large enterprise unions understand that the avoidance of bargaining on personnel assessments serves their interests. Thus, labour unions relinquish their bargaining power at a critical stage in which wages and promotions are fleshed out for individual workers.

According to various opinion surveys of union members conducted by labour unions in the late 1970s and 1980s, about half had strong aspirations for promotion in companies (Inoue 1997: 292). The way in which Japanese workers throw themselves at their work, which manifests itself in the extreme as death from overwork (*karōshi*), demonstrates their competitive spirit. This should be seen as the result of personnel assessments. This is the reality of what Aoki refers to as 'incentive.'

Labour unions' bargaining power over 'strategic management' decisions

The labour-management consultation system

Pointing out the fact that a labour-management consultation system has been established in most companies and that management policies too are consulted between labour and management, Koike insists, 'workers have a say in business conditions and management policies, including basic policy, production and sales plans' (Koike 1991, 210).

Certainly, a labour-management consultation system has been established in most companies. According to the Ministry of

Labour's '1984 Survey of Labour-Management Communication' (*Rōshi Komyunikēshon Chōsa*), 72% of all business establishments have established labour-management consultative mechanisms. Among businesses that have more than 5000 employees, this figure is 94.2%, while for firms that have between 1000–4999 employees it is 83.6%. However, the point is how the important items are consulted. Companies that have a labour-management consultation system gave the following responses regarding 'basic business policies': explanation or briefing 78.9%, hearing opinions 7.3%, discussion 10.1%, need approval 3.7%, unknown 3.1%. For 'basic plans for production and sales' the following answers were given: explanation or briefing 66.8%, hearing opinions 14.0%, discussion 15.9%, need approval 3.3%, unknown 4.1%. On very important items such as 'basic business policies' and 'basic plans for production and sales', most 'consultation' is 'explanation or briefing' or 'hearing opinions.' Does this mean, 'workers have a say in business conditions and management policies, including basic policy, production and sales plans'?

Strong voice of unions in consultations?

Though exceptional, there are enterprise unions that seem to have a strong say in the management decision-making process. I will focus on two particular enterprise unions in order to ascertain whether they really do have a strong say in such matters.

One of the unions is the Union of Nippon Steel, the biggest steel maker in Japan. Nitta Michio investigated labour-management consultation in the Union of Nippon Steel in regards to the problems of personnel relocation, necessary personnel and factory stoppages that arose following the first oil shock. Focusing on 'the procedural aspects of statements and regulations,' he reported mainly from the perspective that the union had a say in the consultations. Nitta concluded that Japanese labour unions 'speak out and involve themselves more positively and substantially than is generally assumed' (Nitta 1988). However, this is a reference to procedural aspects. For instance, Nitta puts forward the following argument regarding necessary personnel:

> It cannot be said that enhancing consultative procedures has a strong preventative effect on the rationalisation of necessary personnel (161)...In fact, the union has been admissive and cooperative towards

rationalisation. Tacitly expecting reasonable union behaviour, companies responded to [union] requests for prior consultations (162).

If unions are only permitted to make statements in acceptance of strategic management decisions, to what extent can they be said to have influence or bargaining power?

The limits of union bargaining power

Another example is the Nissan Motor Company, whose union expressed opposition to the company's overseas expansion strategy. As it is very rare for unions in large companies to oppose 'strategic management' decisions, I would like to explore this case in greater detail (for the account below, see Kamii 1994: 138–141).

In the early 1970s, Nissan had already established an elaborate labour-management consultation system, which extended from the company level to the workshop. The Nissan Union was deeply involved in most aspects of the company, ranging from strategic management decisions to production problems in the workshop, and essentially secured for itself the right to have a voice in matters that was so strong it could be called 'consent' procedure. Such a consultative mechanism came to embody relations of 'mutual trust' (*sōgo shinrai*) between labour and management.

However, by aiming to create a flexible production system (as Toyota had done) that did not require it to undertake burdensome procedures with the union, the president of Nissan Motor, who was appointed in 1977, quickly exacerbated tensions between labour and management. Amid these tensions, a problem arose concerning investing in the U.K. The problem's origin lies in a request made by the U.K. government for cooperation in rebuilding the national passenger vehicle manufacturer. Nissan, looking to export to the European market, adopted a positive stance on investing in the U.K. However, the union, from the perspective of dealing with the problem of export restrictions into America, which was the largest market, and securing a share of this market, emphasised that if the company was to invest, it should produce passenger vehicles in America. Moreover, according to the company's initial estimates, investing in the U.K. was a big project that required 150 billion yen. The union adopted a basic stance of 'protecting our company' as well as 'the jobs and livelihoods of the workers' and conducted feasibility studies in the U.K. The union compiled the results of the survey and sought a response from the president, who refused their requests.

After a long absence, consultative meetings were finally held at the central level in 1983. However, the company refused substantive consultations on this issue. Anticipating that the company would decide finally in autumn 1983, the union decided to formally oppose this and on 1 August, issued a written statement to this effect. The four reasons behind union opposition to investing in the U.K. were:

1. The company must realise that if it were to build a factory in the U.K., it would be in substantial debt for a long period of time.
2. The most important task for the company is to restore its gradually decreasing domestic sales.
3. There is a fear that producing passenger vehicles in the U.K. will result in a decline in car exports to the U.K., as well as the EC countries.
4. The union is vehemently opposed to having private companies' autonomy and safety undermined as a result of political pressure.

However, while the union was voicing its opposition to the plan, it was unlikely the company would accept union demands and change its negative stance towards consultations. As a result, the union decided to adopt the extraordinary measure of conducting a press conference at the same time as it notified the company of its opposition. As far as the issue of investing in the U.K. was concerned, the press conference was certainly effective. This is because the company agreed to the union's requests for consultations, which after several rounds, led to the decision to reduce the size of the initial planned investment.

Thus, in this case, the union was able to curb the company's plans. However, the company's management, believing that the press conference was an intervention in its affairs and also exposed what it considered to be an internal company problem, publicly criticised the union. This led to further tension in labour-management relations. Criticisms of white-collar workers from the company's head office, who supported management's stance, and top union officials, comprising workshop foremen, who were the main pillar of the union, began to surface. In 1986, leading officials were expelled from the union and labour-management relations were reorganised. The labour-management consultative mechanism was completely overhauled and union influence dramatically declined. A totally new agreement reached in October 1986 specified that labour-management meetings would serve as 'a mechanism for explanation or discussion', not a mechanism for consensus-building any more.

The case of Nissan certainly underscored the limits of union bargaining power over 'strategic management' decisions. Based on an exceptionally strong organisation, the union tried to influence management decisions. It partly succeeded before finally collapsing.

Aoki Masahiko's 'bargaining game' theory avoids these problems. However, as this is due to hypothetical bargaining enacted in the minds of company managers, it is, in reality, meaningless.

Problems with enterprise unions

As discussed above, Aoki and Koike's notions of bargaining are theoretically wrong and erroneous in light of the realities. Inoue observes that 'The decline of collective labour-management relations, the development of individual personnel management, diminishing labour union functions and the expansion of labour and personnel control are the basic trends in Japanese management today [in the 1990s]' (2000: 1). However, these trends had already emerged in the 1980s.

Why has unions' bargaining power been limited? Undoubtedly, it is difficult for enterprise unions to maintain solidarity beyond their companies. While companies compete with each other, how can enterprise unions show solidarity at the industry-level? However, this is not the sole problem faced by enterprise unions.

Nearly all enterprise unions have agreements with companies, according to which all regular employees automatically become union members, while denying membership to non-regular employees such as part-timers. According to this principle, the sphere over which unions are able to extend their bargaining power within the company has always been narrow. In the 1990s, the tendency among companies to retrench regular employees and increase the number of irregular employees to work in their place has further reduced unions' bargaining power.

The automatic membership principle has also contributed to the decline in the current rates of union membership. In 1970, the percentage of workers, who were union members, was 35.4%. In

2003, this percentage has fallen to 19.6%. The growth of the service economy, the increase in white-collar jobs, as well as job cuts and other considerations, are believed to be significant factors in the declining rates of union membership. In relation to this point, Takahashi (1998) makes the following comment about what he sees as an insufficient sense of crisis among union leaders:

> Why are union leaders not seriously alarmed at the decline in union membership rates? This is because, although rates have declined at the macro-level, there is a perception that under the union-shop agreement at the individual (micro) company level, a 100% membership rate is being maintained and unionisation is already complete. Although union membership was originally said to be 100%, it was not exactly 100%. This is because management level employees and non-regular employees were not targets of the union recruiting-drive. In other words, union membership was 100% within dual limits. However, in reality, since the numbers of non-unionised workers in the company – such as those in management positions or irregular employees – are increasing, the unionisation rate of all employees of the company will clearly decline unless they can be unionised. (21–22).

Generally speaking, an enterprise union mirrors its company. For example, since the company discriminates against non-regular employees, enterprise unions deny them union membership. As foremen supervise rank-and-file workers in workplace, they become union officers and control union members. Because this limits bargaining power, both within and beyond the company, if labour unions were to attempt to restore their bargaining power while continuing to be based on enterprise lines, they would have little choice but to establish a new order based on workers' own unity and a behaviour pattern distinct from the company. For instance, regarding wages, whether it concerns the amount or the way they are decided, it is necessary to reconstruct a theory of wages, from the perspective of wages for 'unity', in which workers who work in the same workshop will not be discriminated against on the basis of gender or employment status and in which fellow workers will not become rivals.

Since it is unable to avoid a head-on clash with the prevailing corporate order, it is important to accept the challenge of establishing a new theory of companies and then translating this into reality.

6 A Critical Analysis of Koike Kazuo's Skill Theory

Masami Nomura

The theory of intellectual skill

This chapter critically examines Koike Kazuo's research about labour. From the mid-1980s, Koike called his theory the theory of intellectual skill. This theory became an important pillar of Aoki Masahiko's theory of Japanese companies.

The development of Koike's theory of skill

Koike came to be seen as a pioneer in labour research following the publication of his book entitled *Participation of Labour Unions in Management at the Workplace: A Comparison of Industrial Relations in Japan and the U.S.* (*Shokuba no Rōdō Kumiai to Sanka: Rōshi Kankei no Nichibei Hikaku*) in 1977. Following this, he poured his energies into writing. A majority of the books Koike wrote dealt with the issue of skill formation. Koike's argument underwent a theoretical transformation on four occasions following the publication of the aforementioned book. Therefore, this section divides Koike's theory of skill formation into five periods (for details see Nomura 2001).

The first period is from 1977 to 1984. The depth of workers' skill is important. However, as there was no way of measuring this, Koike only discussed the breadth of skills, which he claims can be measured according to a worker's career in terms of transfers and promotions. Koike examined the careers of workers in Japan and the United States directly involved in production and concluded that Japanese workers have broader and more flexible skills. Koike's ideas, which centred on this notion of careers, can be described as a theory of career skill formation. *Participation of*

Labour Unions in Management at the Workplace was representative of his works in this period.

The second period is from 1985 to 1988. Koike claimed that the ability to 'deal with changes and problems' represents the skill depth of workers and he termed this capability intellectual skill. In his theory of career skills developed in the first period, Koike declared that while the depth of workers' skills was certainly important, because this cannot be measured, he would only discuss workers' skill breadth (Koike 1977b: 34). In the second period, the depth of workers' skills referred to their ability 'to deal with changes and problems.' This notion of intellectual skills implied that the depth of workers' skills could be measured. However, at this stage, Koike did not describe how he would be able to do this. Moreover, in this period Koike only stated that intellectual skill was the ability to 'deal with changes and problems' and did not develop theories of wages or labour unions based on this. His discussion of the theory of intellectual skill was extremely limited. I will refer to the theory Koike expounded during this stage as the limited edition theory of intellectual skill. Two books – one he co-authored with Inoki Takenori (1987) entitled *An International Comparison of Skill Formation* (*Jinzai Keisei no Kokusai Hikaku*), and the other entitled *The Formation of Intellectual Skills* (*Chiteki Jukuren no Keisei* – Aichi Prefecture 1987) were representative of this period.

The third period is from 1989 to 1992. During this period, Koike claimed that companies were measuring the depth of workers' skills by means of a pair of job matrix charts and were paying wages based on this. He also attempted to explain wages and labour unions in an integrated fashion based on intellectual skill. Koike developed a general theory of intellectual skill. I will call the theory Koike promulgated during this stage the complete version of the theory of intellectual skill. Koike's *Intellectual Skills and Long-term Competition* (*Chiteki Jukuren to Chōki no Kyōsō*, 1989) and *The Economics of Work in Japan* (*Shigoto no Keizaigaku*, 1991) were representative of this particular period.

The fourth period is from 1993 to 1999. Koike considerably revised his complete edition theory of intellectual skill. The reason he was forced to do this was because of criticisms I levelled at the main points of his argument in *The Economics of Work* (Nomura 1993). In his reply to my critique of his work, Koike wrote that 'I cannot possibly think Nomura understands my argument. I do not even think he attempted to understand it' (Koike 1993:2). If this were the case, it would be absolutely unnecessary for Koike to concern himself with my criticisms. He should have ignored them or he was forced to ignore them. Nevertheless, a completely revised (2nd) edition of *The Economics of Work* was published eight years after the original version was first released. Though Koike made no reference at all to my criticisms of his theory in the 2nd edition, he deleted, rewrote and made additions to all the points at which I directed my criticisms. The most important criticism then was that Koike had ignored highly skilled specialists such as maintenance workers in his theory of intellectual skills and that he had declared the skills of production-line workers in mass production workplaces to be as high as specialists. In the second edition he admitted the existence of specialists for the first time. This means that Koike admitted that my criticisms of his theory were on the mark. Because Koike made the necessary additions and revisions to his book without completely repudiating his complete edition theory of intellectual skill, the narrative in the 2nd edition is confused and lacks theoretical consistency. I will refer to the theory of this period as the revised edition of the theory of intellectual skill. *Skill Formation in Japanese Companies* (*Nihon Kigyō no Jinzai Keisei*, 1997) and *The Economics of Work in Japan* (2nd edition) were representative of Koike's work in this period.

The fifth period is from 2000 onwards. Koike radically reformed the theoretical arguments underpinning his notion of intellectual skill. In the complete version, as well as the revised edition of the theory of intellectual skill, Koike claimed that companies were measuring the breadth and depth of individual workers' skills according to a pair of job matrix charts, one concerning breadth and the other depth. Endō (1999), however, was highly sceptical that a pair of job matrix charts really existed in Japanese companies. He noted that Koike had possibly made it up. Following Endō's comments, Koike withdrew his claim that companies measure skills by means of a pair of job matrix charts. Koike now argues that the breadth and depth of workers' skills can be measured using a 'skill level chart' he conceived. Because this argument is fundamentally different to the previous theory of intellectual skill, I will call the theory from this period the revamped version of the theory of intellectual skill. Representative of his research in this period is a book he co-authored with Chūma

Hiroyuki and Ōta Sōichi (2001) entitled *Manufacturing Skills* (*Monozukuri no Ginō*).

In the 'development' of Koike's theory of skill formation outlined above, the point of contention as to whether it is possible to measure the depth of workers' skills is of pivotal importance. In each of the five periods Koike made the following claims:

1. The first period. The depth of workers' skills cannot be measured.
2. The second period. It is expected that the depth of workers' skills can be measured.
3. The third period. The depth of workers' skills is being measured by management using a pair of 'job matrix charts,' which is in turn reflected in remuneration.
4. The fourth period. The depth of workers' skills is being measured by management using a pair of 'job matrix charts,' which is in turn reflected in remuneration.
5. The fifth period. The depth of workers' skills can be measured by the 'skill level chart' Koike invented.

Koike's works, which Aoki Masahiko cites in his *Information, Incentives and Bargaining in the Japanese Economy*, as well as the book he co-authored with Okuno Masahiro (1996) entitled *Comparative Institutional Analysis of Economic Systems* (*Keizai Shisutemu no Hikaku Seido Bunseki*), are from the first, second and third periods. However, Aoki was unaware of the changes that Koike's theory underwent from the first period to the third. Moreover, on the whole, Aoki understood the complete version of the theory of intellectual skill to be Koike's only argument and treated both the theory of career skill formation and the limited edition theory of intellectual skill as being the same as the complete version when citing them. This, of course, amounts to a misreading of Koike's work on the part of Aoki. Since Aoki misunderstood Koike's theory – a theory that was a major pillar of his own research – Koike's theory of skill formation can generally be considered to be consistent in terms of a complete version of the theory of intellectual skill. Therefore, this chapter also concentrates on this complete version of the theory of intellectual skill and, in particular, examines the problems associated with it.

Koike did not always make the same assertions in each of these five periods. Koike's expressions differ subtly throughout his works and a close theoretical examination of these subtle differences will lead to significant theoretical variations. Therefore, while there is a problem concerning which of his works (on the complete version of the theory of intellectual skill) to analyse, this chapter examines Koike's *The Economics of Work in Japan*, which is the most comprehensive discussion of the theory of intellectual skill.

The theory of intellectual skill

The essence of Koike's theory of intellectual skill is as follows.

There are two types of jobs in the workshop: 'usual operations' (*fudan no sagyō*) and 'unusual operations' (*fudan to chigatta sagyō*). 'Unusual operations' deal with changes or problems. Change occurs in five areas: product mix, output, new products, production methods and workforce composition. The types of problems that may occur in the workshop are machinery breakdowns and defective products. In order to deal with changes and problems, it is necessary for workers to fully understand both production methods and machinery. This type of knowledge is common to that possessed by engineers, and it is therefore appropriate to call it intellectual skill.

There are two forms of division of labour in a workshop. One is a separated system in which 'production workers' are in charge of 'usual operations,' while 'engineers' are responsible for 'unusual operations.' The other is an integrated system that puts 'production workers' in charge of both operations. Because the integrated system is widespread in Japan, the Japanese manufacturing industry displays high efficiency.

'Production workers' attain intellectual skills by remaining in a company for a long period of time. Therefore, long-term employment is a precondition of intellectual skill formation. Moreover, under the seniority wage system, wages appear to rise automatically together with workers' ages. But in reality, wages rise not because of age increases, but as a result of the intellectual skills that 'production workers' accumulate after years of continuous employment in a company.

Employees are employed in a company for a long period of time. Because they subsequently acquire firm-specific skills, solidarity among workers and labour unions takes the form of an enterprise union and not an industrial union. Thus, lifetime employment, seniority wages and enterprise unions are all consistently explained by the theory of intellectual skill.

An absence of definition

At a glance, the theory of intellectual skill is quite easy to understand. One of the important reasons Koike's theory was so widely accepted lies in its simplicity. However, the theory is only easy to understand on the surface. When one attempts to grasp Koike's argument, he/she is constantly confronted with ambiguity and impreciseness. These two characteristics derive from the fact that Koike has not defined his key terms.

The classification of workshop skills into 'usual operations' and 'unusual operations,' which is the starting point of the theory of intellectual skill, is a case in point. Koike writes as follows:

> Workshop jobs include usual and unusual operations. Work on mass-production assembly lines does not appear to be dependent on skills and seems entirely repetitive. Only speed seems to affect efficiency. This is a usual operation. However, observe the line closely, and you surprisingly see frequent changes and problems in just two or three hours. Dealing with these situations constitutes unusual operations (Koike 1991: 65).[1]

According to this, 'usual operations' are evident in mass-production assembly lines and appear to refer to 'entirely repetitive operations.' However, what precisely are 'entirely repetitive operations'? Operations repeated every 15–20 seconds, such as those seen in assembly plants in the electronics industry and every 60 seconds in assembly plants in the automobile industry appear to be 'entirely repetitive operations.' What about when operations are repeated every five or ten minutes? Moreover, speaking of automobile assembly plants, do those operations that are repeated every few hours, such as that which occurred in the Volvo factory in Uddevalla, equate to what Koike calls 'entirely repetitive operations'? Because he fails to clarify where he draws the line at what falls under this category and also to adequately define 'entirely repetitive operations,' the concept is vague.

While 'entirely repetitive operations' could be evident in mass-production assembly plants, is this also the case for non-mass-production assembly lines in the shipbuilding and machine tool manufacturing industries? Are there 'entirely repetitive operations' in non-mass-production assembly lines? Even if many of the operations in non-mass-production assembly lines are repetitive, they are not based on a short time scale such as seconds and minutes, but a long time scale in terms of hours. Is this included in 'entirely repetitive operations'? What about in the process industry?

That the concept 'usual operations' is imprecise also means that so is the term 'unusual operations.' The above quote is from the first edition of *The Economics of Work in Japan*. I have been critical of this passage, noting that 'if "changes and problems" occur "surprisingly frequently in just two or three hours" these cannot be deemed "changes and problems." It must be "usual operations" that deal with these situations' (Nomura 1993a: 111). Koike made the following revisions to this passage in response to my criticism in the second edition of *The Economics of Work in Japan*: 'Work on mass-production assembly lines does not appear to be dependent on skills and seems entirely repetitive. Observe the line closely for at least half a day, and you can clearly recognise two operations: Usual operations and unusual operations' (Koike 1999: 12).

Now, changes and problems no longer occur 'surprisingly frequently in just two or three hours.' Koike was able to alter this passage because he did not define the term 'unusual operations.'

Koike's approach is not to provide clear definitions to his concepts. In writing for readers who lack knowledge about the production process, Koike leads them to believe that clear concepts exist by basing his arguments on vague impressions these readers have, such as, for instance, on the final assembly line in the automobile industry.

Moreover, Koike only discusses intellectual skills. Intellectual skill is the ability 'to deal with changes and problems.' He also argues that intellectual skills determine workers' wages. If this is the case, how does Koike's theory treat skills that are unrelated to 'dealing with changes and problems'? Koike makes absolutely no mention of these types of skills in his work. For instance, skills used in assembling ultra-precision machinery and high-level welding skills etc., which are only possessed by those workers who are often called 'workplace gods' (*genba no kamisama*), do not equate to the ability to deal with 'changes and problems,' and are therefore not what Koike refers to as intellectual skills. However, these are without doubt extremely high skills. These are also the skills that the Law for the Promotion of Basic Manufacturing Skills (*Monozukuri Kiban Gijutsu Shinkō Kihon-hō*) is promoting to hand down to the next generation. Koike's theory of intellectual skill excludes these types of skills from his theory. According to Koike, wages reflect the skills workers' possess. However, what he is in fact asserting is that wages reflect intellectual skills. Are skills other than intellectual skills reflected in workers' wages? If they are not, why is it that although intellectual skills are reflected in wages, other skills are not? Koike should explain this, but makes no mention of it at all.

Specialists and Productivity

Ignoring specialists

Koike often uses the term 'production worker' (*seisan rōdōsha*) in his research. He also claims that Japanese 'production workers' possess intellectual skills. To whom is Koike referring when he speaks of 'production workers'?

Employees involved in production are engineers, specialists and production-line workers. Engineers are white-collar workers, while specialists and production-line workers are blue-collar workers. In the mass production industries, such as automobiles and electric machinery, a standard time is set for production-line workers and the speed of the production line is imperative. Specialists are responsible for tasks requiring high skill levels such as maintaining equipment, inspections, die production, prototype production and so on. Their skills are formed mainly by off-the-job training. The production worker concept includes both specialists and production-line workers, according to ordinary terminology.

When speaking of production workers' skills, it is important to clearly distinguish between mass-production workshops, such as those typically seen on automobile final assembly lines, and non-mass productions workshops, such as ship building and machine tool manufacturing. It is common for production-line workers in non-mass production workshops to be highly skilled. It is mass production workshops that have become a hot issue in industrial sociology and labour studies. In Europe and the United States from the late 1960s to the 1970s, it was in an industry featuring mass-production workshops – especially the automobile industry – that labour problems such as strikes and the high rate of worker absenteeism gained considerable attention at the social level. The fact that production-line workers in mass-production workshops are engaged in simple, repetitive operations results in dissatisfaction and anger among them. Thus, one can ask how a division of labour between highly skilled specialists and production-line workers who perform simple tasks can be changed toward the re-skilling of the latter. The 'humanisation of work' program in Germany and the 'quality of working life' project launched by automobile companies in the United States have tackled this problem. Koike's theory of intellectual skill has become the focus of international attention because of its link with this point.

Koike discusses the skills of 'production workers.' According to ordinary terminology, both specialists and production-line workers are included among production workers. However, Koike uses the term 'production worker' interchangeably with production-line worker. If this is the case, what are specialists called in the theory of intellectual skill? In fact, there is no reference at all to specialists in this theory. The only employees to which the theory of intellectual skill refers are engineers and 'production workers,' that is, production-line workers.

Koike makes the following statement regarding the intellectual skills of production-line workers: 'These are rightly called intellectual skills. A knowledge of production and production machinery has much in common with the expertise of engineers' (Koike 1991: 68). If one intends to discuss the strong expertise of production-line workers, one should mention the degree to which they have acquired the skills and knowledge of specialists. However, because Koike ignores specialists, he skips the issue of the expertise they possess and concludes that the skills of production-line workers 'have much in common' with the knowledge of engineers. This gives readers the surprising impression that the skills of production-line workers in mass production workshops are equivalent to those possessed by specialists. For instance, Aoki Masahiko makes the following statement based on Koike's theory:

the J-firm...has encouraged workers to solve problems by themselves whenever possible...The number of specialists – such as repairmen, product inspectors, and technicians – has been reduced as much as possible, and, when necessary, their expertise is used to help shopfloor workers solve a particular problem; thus they act as consultants rather than performing a special function exclusively (Aoki 1992: 19; 1988: 16).

In other words, according to Koike, the strict division of labour between specialists and production-line workers, who were commonplace in mass production industries in the United States and Europe, or 'Taylorism,' is unrelated to Japan. He argues that not only have production-line workers acquired skills to the level of specialists, but they also have skills 'much in common' with the expertise of engineers. It is only possible to make such assertions by ignoring specialists.

It is not true that Koike is totally unaware that specialists such as maintenance workers exist. In fact, he uses such terms as 'maintenance person' (*hozen no hito*) and 'repair specialist' (*shūri no senmonka*) in his empirical research reports. Koike also knows that 'maintenance people' and 'repair specialists' are far more highly qualified than production-line workers. However, he simply ignores 'maintenance people' and 'repair specialists' when theorising about workers' skills. The debate in Europe and the United States over 'Taylorism' concerns what the division of labour between production-line workers and specialists ought to be. However, Koike ignores specialists and discusses 'production workers' (production-line workers) as though they are the only blue-collar workers. He therefore propagates the image that Japanese companies are not based on the principle of 'Taylorism,' which is not the case in Japan.

OJT and Off-JT

In regards to on-the-job training (OJT) and off-the-job training (Off-JT) in education and training, Koike claims that Japanese companies concentrate on OJT. He also argues that Off-JT is only conducted for a short period of time as a supplement to OJT. Such an evaluation of OJT is possible because Koike's theory excludes specialists as an object of analysis. Koike knows that specialists are trained by long-term Off-JT. Koike writes that 'Longer training periods of up to a year can be found, but are limited to exceptional workshops (*tokushuna shokuba*), such as maintenance. Most blue-collar workers enter workshops without skills and depend on OJT for skill formation' (Koike 1991: 55–56).

This claim clearly demonstrates the shortcomings of Koike's theory, which ignores specialists. Koike sees maintenance and other supporting sectors, which are very important workshops for the manufacturing industry. Although he knows 'long-term Off-JT' is conducted for specialists, Koike, who calls workshops for specialists 'exceptional workshops,' ignores this fact in his theory. In addition, he asserts that production-line workers possess high intellectual skills, that is, skills formed that have 'much in common' with engineers in OJT. Ignoring specialists and the long-term Off-JT intended for them, Koike quite wrongly insists that OJT for production-line workers can form skills nearly as high as engineers who have graduated from university.

Intellectual skills and productivity

The reason Koike places importance on the concept of intellectual skills is because he considers it to be critically important for productivity. He states that 'The efficiency of the Japanese workplace is founded on intellectual skills – large Japanese companies are highly efficient because many of their production workers possess intellectual skills' (Koike 1991: 68).

Concerning the issue of how much intellectual skills bring about differences in productivity, Koike makes the following statement in reference to Thai, Malaysian and Japanese companies:

> Due to the broad applicability of skill formation systems, a large discrepancy in the extent of implementation of such systems is sufficient to explain the ample variance in productivity observed between the three countries. Among the cases surveyed, two kinds of workshops utilize similar machinery: the main workshops in the cement industry and the pasting-machine shops in the battery industry...Japanese labor productivity is three times or more than that of the other two. If we look at pasting-machine shops in the battery industry, Japanese firms are four times more productive than those in the other two countries...(Koike and Inoki: 1987: 28–29).[2]...It is safe to say...that a large part of the gap originates from workers' skill.

Despite this claim, Koike fails to explain why it is appropriate to consider that the large part of the ample variance in productivity originates from workers' skill. Koike's theory comprises the following elements: The machines are similar. The skill formations are different. Therefore, skill formation is a critically important factor in the ample variance of productivity.

Productivity depends largely on design technology, production technology, production management, engineers' knowledge and the quality of parts and raw materials. This is common knowledge among those involved in production and researchers. Koike's theory, which posits that the skills of production-line workers are the most significant factor in productivity differences, contradicts such commonly held perceptions. However, Koike must do two things in order to refute such orthodoxy: ascertain that there is no disparity between Thai and Japanese companies in terms of design technology, production technology, production management, engineers' knowledge and the quality of parts and raw materials; or substantiate what cannot be substantiated – that these factors only have a minor influence on productivity variations. Koike, of course, fails to do this.

Moreover, in the *Economics of Work* (2nd edition, 1999: 42) Koike presents data that appears to prove that intellectual skills do have a major influence on productivity. However, Koike inserted data unrelated to intellectual skills and attempted to pass this off as evidence that intellectual skills have a significant influence on productivity (for details see Nomura 2001: ch. 4).

Koike's internal labour markets theory

Seniority wages

According to Koike, age does not have a significant impact on wages. Instead, skills are accumulated in accordance with length of service, which are in turn reflected in wages. However, there is no basis to the claim that skills determine wages.

If we examine the method for determining wages in large companies, it is evident that these firms do not take skill differences into consideration. Among production workers in mass production workshops, there are highly skilled specialists, such as maintenance workers, and production-line workers, who are not highly skilled. However, under the wage system in large Japanese companies, there is absolutely no difference in wages between the two types of workers. In the case of regular production workers who join a company at the same age and receive the same personnel assessment results every year, the basic portion of their wages, apart from additional wages such as the family allowance etc., irrespective of whether they are specialists or production-line workers, remains the same.

Even Koike's theory tacitly acknowledges that specialists ('maintenance people' and 'repair specialists') are more highly skilled than direct workers. If we accept Koike's theory that skills determine wages, there should be a wage disparity between the two. However, Japan's wage system is structured so that such disparities do not arise.

Koike's theory that the so-called seniority wage curve derives from the accumulation of intra-company skills can be criticised if we look at it from another angle. According to Koike, a seniority wage curve is established as a result of workers accumulating skills by remaining in a company for a long period of time. However, in South Korea a seniority curve, the same as or more pronounced than the one in Japan, exists, despite the high mobility of labour. Ono Akira (1989) – the scholar who pointed out this fact – calls the seniority wage curve the 'age-specific guaranteed living expenses model' (*nenreibetsu seikatsuhi hoshōgata*).

Moreover, Koike makes absolutely no mention of skills other than intellectual skills. If he claims that skills determine wages, it is necessary for Koike to discuss how these other skills are reflected in wages. However, according to the theory of intellectual skill, Japanese companies only consider workers' intellectual skills when determining wages.

Long-term employment

Koike explains long-term employment based on the theory of human capital and the theory of internal labour markets. Company-specific skills are formed in internal labour markets. Training expenses are required to form company-specific skills. If training expenses are divided among the company and the worker, in the event the worker leaves the company, both sides are unable to recoup the costs. As a result, both the company and the worker desire long-term employment (Koike 1991: 79–82).

However, Koike claims that '...enterprise-specific skills are thought to constitute about 10 to 20 percent of a worker's skills' (Koike 1991: 88).[3] In other words, he is saying that general skills that are applicable beyond a particular company comprise 80 to 90% of a worker's skills. As Ono (1989: 138) and Inoue (1992:

135–136) note, Koike cannot explain why companies and workers seek long-term employment for the sake of forming company-specific skills that only 'constitute about 10 to 20 percent of a worker's skills.'

Moreover, in regards to the historical development of long-term employment in Japan, Koike completely ignores factors related to labour-management relations. The practice of employing blue-collar workers on a long-term basis in large Japanese companies began in the 1920s. After the First World War, major disputes occurred, mainly in the Kansai region. Large companies, which were alarmed by these disputes, employed young workers straight out of school and in addition to training them within the company, employed them long-term (Hyōdō 1971: ch. 3; Nakanishi 1982: appendix 2). The practice of employing workers on a long-term basis was disrupted by the wartime economy. While it was restarted after the Second World War, a series of major disputes around 1950 gave crucial momentum to long-term employment. It was not only companies such as Toyota, which experienced first-hand these disputes, but a wide-range of Japanese companies that became keenly aware that employment was the major issue in labour-management relations. The training of employees, who had a sense of loyalty to the company, was also recognised as being important. Without this experience, long-term employment in post-war Japan would have been impossible (Nomura 1994).

Enterprise unions

Koike makes two basic claims regarding enterprise unions. The first is that labour union organisations developed into enterprise unions as a result of the establishment of internal labour markets. The second of Koike's claims is that Japanese enterprise unions 'bear close resemblance' to German works councils (*Betriebsrat*) in terms of 'labour's voice in various matters.'

Denying the widely-shared view that enterprise unions have been established as a result of internal labour markets, Nimura (1984) persuasively argues that enterprise unions have been established regardless of internal labour markets. It is natural that solidarity among workers is created at the workplace and just as the workplace is the company, labour unions are enterprise-based. Therefore, the question is not why enterprise unions have been established in Japan, but rather why craft unions and industry-based unions extending beyond the scope of individual companies have been formed in the other industrial countries? As Nimura notes, the tradition of medieval guilds helped to establish craft unions and industry-based unions in Western countries. The lack of guilds in Japan inevitably resulted in the establishment of enterprise unions.

Koike claims that Japanese enterprise unions 'bear close resemblance' to German works councils in terms of 'labour's voice in various matters.' For instance, he insists in the case of dismissal, both have not created 'clear rules.' However, it is hardly possible that the 'close resemblance' between the two can be explained by only lacking 'clear rules.'

At the time of the first oil shock, Japanese enterprise unions and German works councils 'had a voice' in various matters, both initially dismissing peripheral workers. However, when it became necessary to cut jobs from among core employees, companies in Japan were inclined to mostly dismiss middle-aged and older employees. In Germany, on the other hand, company managements' proposal to cut middle-aged and older employees was not put into effect because of works council opposition. Young employees were dismissed instead.

This is not an isolated example. Even though 'clear rules' such as seniority rights are not established, there is still the problem associated with the range of selection criteria. Moreover, even if unions 'had a voice' or decided on consultative meetings, an evaluation of the substance of the decision ought to be the exact opposite depending on whether it suited management's convenience or restricted it. An evaluation of labour unions that does not make such an inquiry is incorrect.

An unsubstantiated theory

Making up the job matrix

In the complete version of the theory of intellectual skill Koike claims that companies remunerate workers by fairly evaluating their depth of skills. He states that:

> ...evaluation would be simple and based on current job – someone doing a difficult job would receive a high rating and a high salary...Among workers doing the same job, the ability to deal with change and problems varies. If differences are not properly evaluated, why learn to do different

jobs? The other reason is previous experience...If this experience is not evaluated, why learn to do different jobs? (Koike 1991: 72–73).[4]

So how do companies measure the depth of workers' skills and have this reflected in remuneration? Koike states that:

> Assessment ultimately depends on the judgement of a veteran worker. A worker's skill in dealing with changes or problems cannot simply be measured in output, as with repetitive work; evaluation must be by a veteran worker well versed in the job – the foreman. This, however, opens evaluation to subjective opinion and possible bias. Bias on a foreman's part can shift emphasis from skills so that workers do not make the effort to upgrade them. To minimize bias, Japanese workplaces use a job matrix (Koike 1991: 73).[5]

In other words, according to Koike, the 'foreman' measures the skill depth of individual workers. In addition, a job matrix is used to minimise bias on the part of the 'foreman.' A job matrix consists of two charts: one indicating 'breadth of experience' and the other citing 'depth' of experience. The job matrix is revised periodically every three months and 'is an important factor in determining compensation' (Koike 1991: 73–74).[6] In a word, the job matrix is material that substantiates the theory of intellectual skill magnificently.

However, the job matrix is something that Koike has made up. It was Endō (1999: 22–27) who first raised doubts about the actual existence of the job matrix. Taking this one step further, Nomura (2001: ch. 1) proved that the job matrix actually does not exist. This section briefly examines the specific doubts surrounding the job matrix.

Every time Koike presents the job matrix, he rewrites it. The first job matrix that Koike presented was in 1989. This is the only one that is in a concrete form. All the job matrices presented since this time have been abstract and without empirical values. Therefore, I will examine the 1989 job matrix (table 6-1).

It is hardly possible that the chart indicating 'breadth of experience,' which lists the positions workers have experienced, exists in a workshop that is expected to use the job matrix Koike presents. Koike fails to cite the chart's source. There is absolutely no explanation regarding the kind of workshop from which the chart derives. However, he does list the name of the type of machine

Table 6-1 Job Matrix

	13.1 a certain job matrix – breadth of experience			
Name	Cutting machine	NC lathe	Horizontal milling machine	Cylindrical grinder
Abe	4	1	2	4
Itō		2	4	
UKAI	4	4	1	3
Etō	1	4		
Ogata	2	2		

Note: This is a somewhat simplified version of an actual job matrix.
1 – initial training received
2 – can do the job alone
3 – can do setup
4 – can teach others

	13.2 a certain job matrix – depth of experience			
Name	Can reprogram	Can deal with defects	Can make repairs – machinery	Can make repairs – electrics
Abe		4	4	3
Itō			4	3
UKAI	4	3		
Etō	3	3	3	
Ogata		3		

Note: This is a simplified version of the actual job matrix.
3 – can do the job alone
4 – can teach others

Source: Koike (1989) pp.331–32.

tool such as the NC lathe and the horizontal milling machine in the chart demonstrating 'breadth of experience,' which tells us that the workplace in question is a machining workshop. According to Koike, 'there is no doubt that "the nature of the job" in an automated machining workshop can only be "unusual operations." "Usual operations," or repetitive operations are continually carried out by machinery' (Aichi Prefecture 1987: 9). In other words, it is not likely that 'usual operations' exist in a machining workshop. Why is there a chart indicating 'breadth of experience,' which evaluates 'usual operations,' despite the fact that 'usual operations' do not exist?

This chart comprises a four-stage grading system: stage 1 – initial training received; stage 2 – can do the job alone; stage 3 – can do set up; and stage 4 – can teach others. Stage 3, in particular, deserves closer attention. Koike writes that 'To accommodate diverse products, workers must replace tools and jigs in a process that alters the previous setup' (Koike 1991: 66).[7] In other words, 'setting up' is important 'to accommodate diverse products' and it is a matter of course that it be included in the chart citing 'depth of experience,' which evaluates 'accommodating diverse products.' Why then does 'setting up' appear in the chart that indicates 'breadth of experience'?

The job chart citing 'depth of experience' used to evaluate workers' ability to deal with changes and problems contains such assessment items as: can reprogram; can deal with defects; can make repairs – machinery; and can make repairs – electrics. These are certainly marvellous skills. Nevertheless, I am still sceptical. Koike writes that there is one chart that cites 'depth of experience.' The machines listed on the chart in this workshop alone include a cutting machine, NC lathe, a horizontal milling machine and a cylindrical grinder. Each of these machines differs in terms of structure and function. Even if a worker is able to repair a NC lathe, this does not mean that he will be able to repair a horizontal milling machine. If the chart citing 'depth of experience' really does exist, one would expect there to be one for each of these machines. In other words, there should be at least four charts in this workshop. Why is there only one chart that indicates depth?

There are several other dubious aspects of the 1989 job matrix. The chart, theoretically, cannot exist. For those interested in the process Koike undertook to make up the job matrix, please refer to chapter one of Nomura's book (2001). Koike has been silent in the face of criticism that the job matrix charts he presented do not really exist but were made up by him. Koike had to make up the job matrix in order to give the appearance that his theory of intellectual skill, which posited that companies fairly evaluate workers' skills and have this reflected in remuneration, could be substantiated. This means that the theory is fundamentally flawed.

Evaluating the theory of intellectual skill

What is characteristic of Koike's approach is the absence of definitions. Beginning with concepts such as 'usual operations and 'unusual operations' – the starting point of the theory of intellectual skill – Koike does not present clear definitions of any of his original terms. Despite this, scholars and students believed the theory of intellectual skill to be an accurate explanation of reality. This is because Koike provided his readers, many of who are unfamiliar with what actually happens on the shop floor, with a description based on vague and popular images.

Koike's theory of intellectual skill is not a refinement of ideas deriving from research conducted into the actual conditions of the workplace in Japan. The theory was initially a casual idea. The survey was conducted in order to provide this idea with a veneer of legitimacy. As a result, the research findings lack credibility. Not only does the narrative of Koike's research report contain many questionable points, but it also self-contradictory. It therefore has no value as factual evidence of the theory. Moreover, since his research report alone was unable sufficiently to serve as proof of the theory of intellectual skill, Koike was forced to make up the job matrix. The theory of intellectual skill is theoretically erroneous and lacks empirical evidence.

7 Aoki's Theory and the Reality of Japanese Companies

Masaru Kaneko

Why question Aoki's theory now?

Aoki Masahiko's analysis of Japanese companies has been rapidly losing its explanatory power since the 1990s. Above all, this is because the performance of the J-firm (a Japanese company) greatly deteriorated following the collapse of the bubble economy. In addition, the introduction of both Japan's 'big bang' financial reforms and international accounting standards from 1999 to 2002 led Aoki (1989) and Koike (1991) themselves to 'dismantle' the distinctive systems of the J-firm they claimed were sources of its international competitiveness.

The J-firm's evaluation completely changed during this process. Japanese company management was once hailed as the major contributing factor behind Japan's rise to number one. Aoki naturally attempted to trace this superiority to game theory based on a contractual approach. However, Japanese company management is now generally considered to be significantly behind its American counterpart. The more genuine neo-classical economists call for an end to employment mobility and corporate governance based on control by shareholders, as well as the dismantling of the 'convoy system' (*gosō sendan hōshiki*). The practical policy proposals put forward by Aoki and his adherents in response have been noticeably impoverished.

At a glance, it appears that Aoki's theory and the views held by the neo-classical economists were in conflict. Aoki claimed that the characteristics of the J-firm were the source of its international competitiveness, whereas the neo-classical school believed these were the cause of its declining international strength. Aoki also claimed that while the J-firm was suited to continual systemic changes and high-mix low-volume production, this was not the case with sudden environmental changes. Genuine neo-classical economists, on the other hand, argued that due to the demise of Japan's catch-up economy, the J-firm must catch-up to the improved A-firm (American company). They contradicted themselves.

What we need to be wary of is that Aoki and the neo-classical school, in fact, shared an identical image of Japanese companies and were also both in agreement that the J-firm had lost its effectiveness as a result of a changing external environment. Both merely reversed their evaluations of the J-firm following the rise and subsequent collapse of Japan's bubble economy. In this sense, they are on two sides of the same coin. Aoki's theory had the effect of engendering a popular image of the J-firm and it is precisely because of this that the significance of questioning Aoki's theory has been obscured today.

First, above all, we must question the inaccurate image of the J-firm. The reason why this image of the J-firm, which has been systematised by Aoki, is inaccurate is because it forced policy-makers to lose sight of the direction of necessary reforms and proceed along the path of misdirected 'reforms.' Because the neo-classical school basically inherited this popular image of the J-firm and forcedly carried out not entirely necessary 'reforms,' it has brought on a severe deflationary economic slump. We must once again re-examine this image of the J-firm from its starting point in accordance with Aoki's theoretical framework.

There are several levels of this framework that need to be considered. The first level relates to those problems inherent in the contractual approach or the theoretical framework of game theory which forms the basis of Aoki's theory. The second level relates to those problems associated with an understanding of the facts in Aoki's theory concerning Japanese companies or inter-firm relations in Japan. The third level concerns those problems caused when Aoki's theoretical framework is extended to other areas. Specifically, this is a problem concerning the extent to which a micro-analysis of corporate structures is able to explain macro-economic performance in Japan. It also relates to whether this framework can be extended to Japan's entire social system.

Because Takeda Shigeo examines the first problem in this book, I will focus on the second and third issues. I have already critically examined Aoki Masahiko and Koike Kazuo's theoretical frame-work (Kaneko 1997) based on Nomura Masami's critique of Koike's research. Continuing with this critical approach, I attempt to once again underscore the disjuncture between the theoretical propositions put forward by Aoki in his analysis of Japanese companies and the realities, based on the arguments made in each of this book's chapters.

The principle of duality: the backbone of Aoki's theory

The 'characteristics' of Japanese companies

As is commonly known, Aoki's theory cites the duality principle as a pervading principle of the internal structure of Japanese companies and inter-firm relations (Aoki 1989; 1992). Aoki refers to a system in which a 'horizontal information network' and a 'hierarchical incentive system' interact with each other in repressed equilibrium as the duality principle.

First, Aoki regards 'workshop autonomy' in regards to the theory of 'contextual skill' or work duties based on on-the-job training (OJT) and job rotation – in other words, the mobile and flexible demarcation of jobs and coordination – as a rent-producing 'horizontal information network.' This theory of 'horizontal information networks' has also been applied to transactions conducted with *keiretsu*-affiliated companies. In other words, unlike theories emphasising the traditional control by parent companies over subcontractors, Aoki, upon evaluating the technological prowess of first tier subcontractors, also considers both the just-in-time (JIT) and the *kanban* systems as a 'horizontal information network.' That is, Aoki perceives those aspects ranging from the autonomy of workshop groups in the company to inter-company *keiretsu* transactions to be a coherent 'horizontal information network.' Aoki's theory of 'horizontal information networks' evaluates the role of *collective* networks that cannot be dissolved by the relationship between individual employment contracts and emphasises the *role of organisational coordination* both within and outside the company which has been neglected by economic studies of transaction costs.

Second, Aoki believes the 'rank hierarchy' of the J-firm as an incentive scheme combines with this 'horizontal information network' to serve as a counterbalance. In other words, he believes that under the internal promotion system within the company, competition over job rotation among operating workers on the shopfloor (cumulative learning on the shopfloor) and rankings (promotions) are hierarchically organised as a form of counterpoise against the 'autonomy' of workshop groups. This is because it is precisely the 'autonomy' of workshop groups regarding work duties that gives rise to opportunistic behaviour on their part. While Aoki's framework for analysis basically inherits the contractual approach, it replaces *the individual with the group* as the subject of this opportunistic behaviour and further weakens the relationship with the neo-classical economists.

Moreover, this leads Aoki to a discussion of the organisational symmetry between Japanese and American companies. According to Aoki, Japanese companies maintain a horizontal information network and hierarchical personnel administration, whereas the hierarchical information structure and employment relations/ personnel administration in American companies features de-centralised and market-orientated decision-making. In other words, based on a dual structure comprising 'vertical' and 'horizontal' elements (concerning information structure and employment system), Aoki considers Japanese and American companies to be symmetrical. He also argues that the Japanese company system is suited to continual changes and high-mix low volume production, whereas American companies have adapted fully to mass production and violent shocks under a stable environment.

Third, Aoki claims that Japanese corporate groups, which have been formed as a result of cross-shareholding centred around banks, have the following characteristics: 1. managerial autonomy; 2. information sharing; 3. internal selection regarding intra-company work duties; and 4. competition for company rankings. In terms of their decentralised decision-making and the organised (centralised) incentive structure, the internal organisation of Japanese companies is homogenous. Therefore, Japanese companies operate under the dual, isomorphic organisational principles of intra-company organisation and bank-centred *keiretsu* groups.

The mechanism for distributing company profits

Based on the aforementioned organisational principles, Aoki's analysis features a mechanism for distributing corporate profits in Japanese companies. First, due to its swift response to stock reductions and local shocks such as machinery breakdowns, defective products and worker absenteeism etc, the horizontal information network produces network rents ('organisational quasi-rent'). However, the distribution of these rents and managerial decisions, are influenced reciprocally by financial and employment considerations. In other words, Japanese companies pursue the dual aims of maximising both shareholders' benefits (stock prices and corporate value) and the welfare of employees. In financial terms, shareholders centred around a bank exercise exclusive control over a company when its debts exceed its liquidation value. On the one hand, the company's management, which assumes the risks of bankruptcy and takeover, attempts to control the company in order to raise share prices, which will in turn reduce the ratio of liabilities to their own net worth. On the other hand, rents depend critically on workers' collective capabilities and become company-specific assets that cannot be placed on the market. That is why, as a collective, workers are able to exercise effective bargaining power over the distribution of rents. Therefore, Japanese companies differ from neo-classical type firms, which aim to maximise profits based on shareholder control, and are also not 'firms controlled by and managed on the behalf of their workers' (*rōdōsha kanri kigyō*), as claimed by Komiya and Itami (Imai Ken'ichi and Komiya Ryūtarō 1989). The Japanese corporate system is described as a world of 'cooperative games,' which takes reciprocal control of the financial and employment aspects of the company.

Aoki's theory and reality

The reality of the 'horizontal information network'

As discussed above, Aoki describes the Japanese corporate system, from shopfloor workers to business transactions between *keiretsu*-affiliated companies, as a cross between a 'horizontal information network' and rank hierarchy (hierarchical incentive system).' However, he persistently seeks its prototype in the 'horizontal information network' on the shopfloor and regards the JIT as extensions of this. This is because Aoki's arguments are ultimately based on the idea that workers' collective capabilities in coping with local problems produce network rents and that this has a decisive impact on inter-company competition.

Forming such an argument requires several conditions. First, above all, in comparison with the other factors contributing to rising productivity, unless there is an increase in company-specific skills formed as a result of OJT carried out in workshop groups, and rents produced by networks maintained in the workshop groups, Aoki's theory will be unable to explain the competitiveness of Japanese companies. In developing this argument, first, shopfloor employees' skills and expertise must be at a level sufficiently high enough to produce rents. Second, the coordination carried out by workshop groups must similarly play a decidedly important role in the production process. Moreover, since it has been named the 'horizontal information network,' information must be 'shared' based not on specific individuals, but cooperative relations among the workshop group. However, it requires more than this.

Third, coordination both within and between workshop groups must have a certain degree of 'autonomy' from managerial control. If this does not happen, then employees (or workshop groups) will not become an independent entity that bargains over the distribution of rents.

However, in reality, Japanese companies cannot necessarily be said to have fulfilled these conditions. Koike Kazuo claims that 'usual operations' and 'unusual operations,' which refer to coping with changes and problems, are a feature of mass production assembly plants. He also notes that because 'production workers' are also responsible for 'unusual operations,' which were originally the task of engineers, they possess a high degree of 'intellectual skill.' However, as Nomura Masami notes in chapter 6, Koike's theory of 'intellectual skills,' which informed Aoki's notion of 'contextual skill,' posits that among engineers, specialists and production line workers engaged in production, production line workers possess skills and expertise equivalent to engineers. Koike makes this claim by intentionally omitting specialists from his analysis. Moreover, specialists are responsible for high-level tasks such as equipment maintenance, producing metallic moulds, and experimental production and their skills are formed through long-term off-the-job training (Off-JT). It is obvious that Koike intentionally overestimates the skills possessed by 'production line workers.'

Nomura's observations in this context are linked to the argument Asao Uichi puts forward in chapter 2. In regards to the discussion about 'coping with changes and problems,' production line workers are basically responsible for minor operations. Moreover, these operations are not necessarily based on coordination among the workshop groups. For instance, in regards to inspecting products, production line workers only conduct simple inspections such as visual inspections, whereas specialist inspectors are responsible for carrying out inspections requiring the use of instruments. In addition, factory workers do not cope with absenteeism by rotating positions on the shopfloor. Instead, this is the responsibility of a specialised reliefman who normally does not work in the work team. This task is limited to the team leader and other leaders who serve under the foreman. Moreover, improvements (*kaizen*) are carried out jointly between the factory and the *kaizen* teams. During this time, large-scale modifications are decided from above and carried out by the section head, the foreman and engineers. Minor modifications are also the task of the group and team leaders, while general workers are restricted to extremely minor operations.

Even from the perspective of 'unusual operations' or coping with changes and problems, the role performed by 'production line workers' is not as important as Koike and Aoki claim. Moreover, 'unusual operations' are not necessarily coordinated within and between workshops in an 'autonomous manner.' Of course, information relating to production volumes flows from management to the workers in the form of orders. Each workshop and factory worker is not given the right to 'fine tune' production volumes. The *kanban* system is merely a means of production management in which production information flows vertically from the central production control department to the final assembly line – from the top to the bottom of a company.

Even when a worker stops the line, this is not for the purpose of sharing information within and between workshops and 'autonomously' fine tuning production volumes. Workers stop the line first and foremost as a result of being unable to achieve production targets assigned from above. This means exposing waste, which becomes an obstacle to achieving production targets. It is the duty of the supervisor to ensure that this waste is reduced and that the line does not stop. As Asao remarks, this type of mechanism is not based on a horizontal information network within the workshop. Instead, it works as an incentive for the supervisor to continually engage in modification (*kaizen*) in order to fulfil vertically flowing production orders.

Hierarchical incentives and power

Establishing the rank hierarchy, which equates with the vertical axis of the duality principle, requires at a bare minimum the following conditions. First, an evaluation system should be put in place that can objectively recognise 'contextual skill' or 'intellectual skill' and that anyone can understand. Second, in order for the incentive system to function fairly, employees should have the right to know their assessment results. Third, a system of wages and promotions should be constructed based on evaluated 'contextual skill' and 'intellectual skill.' Meeting these conditions gives employees, for the first time, the motivation to raise their own 'contextual skill' or 'intellectual skill' levels.

But unfortunately, these conditions have not been created. First, Koike (1991) cites the two published job matrices as factual evidence of the existence of a system to evaluate 'intellectual skill.' This, however, has been revealed by Endō to be a fabrication (Endō 1999; Nomura 2001). Even if we concede that 'intellectual skill' and 'contextual skill' exist, unless there is an open evaluation system that everyone can recognise, the incentive system will not function.

However, as Endō notes, employees in most Japanese companies do not have the right to know the results of their personnel assessments (Endō 1999). Rather, unpublished assessments of 'loyalty to management' serve as a means of monitoring employees. This contributes to frequent wage discrimination based on the beliefs and gender of long-serving employees. Looking at the situation today, it is precisely the conformist social structure of 'groupism' in Japan brought about by these unpublished assessments of 'loyalty to management' that ought to be re-examined (Kaneko 2001).

Finally, it certainly cannot be said that the wage system reflects 'intellectual skill' or 'contextual skill.' As Nomura discusses, the wage differential between highly skilled specialists and production line workers is not that significant. Although the situation is slowly changing at present, it is natural to consider that many Japanese companies still provided subsistence wages based on a seniority wage curve – at least during the period from the second-half of the 1980s to early 1990s during which Aoki's and Koike's theory was complete.

If we do not think in this light, we cannot comprehend the fact that it is middle-aged and elderly workers who are the initial targets of employment restructuring (retrenchment/redundancy). The reason is because as long as one accepts Aoki and Koike's theoretical assumptions, if redundancies affect the middle-aged and elderly workers, who have high levels of 'contextual' and intellectual' skills, then that would mean that Japanese companies are acting 'irrationally' by throwing away the source of their competitiveness.

Does the bargaining game exist?

As we have seen, the framework of Aoki's 'bargaining game' theoretic, comprises the mutually opposing elements of 'horizontal' and 'hierarchical,' and 'network' and 'incentives.' The framework arrives at a Nash equilibrium whereby labour unions (as well as individual employees) and management bargain. The object of bargaining between unions and management is not only the distribution of organisational quasi-rents produced by workshop groups. Aoki argues that under the internal promotion system, because it is not only wage increases, but long-term employment that becomes a problem, managerial decisions, whether unofficial or tacit, are, along with wages, the object of bargaining. The fact that both sides take into consideration the trade-off between losses and gains during labour-management bargaining is important for effective bargaining (Aoki 1989).

However, as Kamii Yoshihiko highlights in chapter 5, it is difficult to argue that Japanese enterprise unions bargain sufficiently over wages, employment and the intensification of labour etc. In the end, because bargaining does not actually exist in Japanese companies, Aoki frequently uses the expression 'implicit commitment.' Despite the fact labour and management are not bargaining with or talking to one another on equal terms, if the concept of an 'implicit contract' is used, *the researcher does not have to demonstrate who has agreed implicitly with who and about what*. If nothing else, the researcher assumes a priori that the end result is one in which the aims of labour and management are congruent. In other words, Aoki introduces the notion of hypothetical contractual relations, which are assumed by the observer, in order to explain this congruity. This is a 'thesis' that is impossible to disprove. Instead, the emphasis here should have been placed on *the fact that it has not taken the form of an equitable agreement, bargaining formally over rules*. To express this is a more forceful way, it is precisely *the fact that bargaining and contracts are not equitable* that represents the system adopted by Japanese companies. Therefore, this should be re-examined.

In this regard, it is important to note that unlike in America, the foreman is still a union member in Japanese companies. The foreman and the team leader, who are exceptional workers, are union representatives on the shopfloor and, at the same time, are also at the lower levels of management, deciding issues pertaining to personnel management, operational procedures and production volumes. In many Japanese companies, these shopfloor leaders are forced to assume a *double identity*, comprising their positions as both union representatives and lower-level management. These foremen are forced to stand at the point at which Aoki's horizontal information network and hierarchical incentive structure intersect. Therefore, under conditions in which standard working hours, assessment rules, small group activities, skill formation and rules regarding dismissal are not the object of bargaining/contracts, if the foreman and team leader are forced to assume such a dual personality, the balance between the horizontal information network and the hierarchical incentive system is only achieved in the individual hearts and minds of these shopfloor leaders.

According to Aoki's model, the horizontal information network is based on the *group unit*, whereas the rank hierarchy comprises *individual units*. The foreman and the group leader, on the one hand, represent the 'autonomy' of the workshop group and must bargain with management over the distribution of network rent (organizational quasi-rent) on equal terms. However, on the other hand, they must also achieve productivity targets and carry out the individual workers' assessments set by management. If the 'cooperative game' were to exist, because the subject and object contained in the two coordinate axes (ie. the horizontal information network and the rank hierarchy), which should offset each other in Aoki's model, are asymmetrical, it could only *develop conflictingly in the hearts and minds of the shopfloor leaders* who occupy the middle point between the horizontal information network and the hierarchical incentive system. The preceding discussion represents the reality of Aoki's model.

Moreover, these shopfloor leaders are also the *subjects of individual assessments* set by management. The matter of how they coordinate their own workshop groups and are able to come close to achieving the targets set by management is continually assessed in a 'closed' manner. Needless to say, this influences their own prospects of promotion, as well as their lifetime income, including pensions. Moreover, in Japan, even if they hypothetically possess a certain degree of skill and expertise, these are not tied to job security based on the seniority principle. Beyond this, it is difficult for them to demonstrate bargaining power, which is 'autonomous' to a certain degree from management. It is natural to think that they would limit the 'autonomy' of the workplace from management.

Is industrial democracy in a dilemma?

Thus, it is difficult to make the claim that labour unions or workshop groups bargain with management on an equal footing. As might be expected, long working hours and high labour density are one of the competitive strengths of Japanese companies on an international basis.

As Kamii states, since the oil shock, the spring labour offensive has been reduced to a shell and labour unions have been unable to obtain sufficient wage increases. In fact, while wage increases that outstripped labour productivity were evident until the 1960s, since the oil shock, wages were suppressed within the limits of the productivity standards principle in order to maintain Japanese companies' international competitiveness. Of course, as will be discussed later, it is difficult to argue that the *upward* rigidity of wages was rational at the macro-level, let alone at the micro-level of the company. This is because this wage 'flexibility' brought about an increase in Japanese exports, creating a vicious cycle, which led to a rise in the exchange rate and further demands for wage elasticity. Despite the fact that the necessity of stimulating domestic demand was extolled, the restraint on wage increases hindered it.

It is doubtful that the underlying trend of wage restraint since the oil shock was a necessary trade off for long-term employment. This is because it is not necessarily considered that the employment adjustment capabilities of Japanese companies are inferior to firms in other countries. While Aoki claims that long-term employment has been secured as a result of 'implicit contracts' in the J-firm, his model is inconsistent with the facts.

Since the principle of the selected few was promulgated in the mid-1960s, with the increasing automation and introduction of mechanical engineering in Japanese companies, the areas in which the principle 'long-term employment' were applied had a tendency to contract. In fact, even in the periods following the two oil shocks, the high-yen recession and the collapse of the bubble economy, Japanese companies carried out considerable adjustments to employment practices. Moreover, as discussed previously, it was customary for middle-aged and elderly workers, who were 'employed on a long-term basis' and received relatively high wages, to become the targets for redundancy in the J-firm during that time. In other words, unlike the A-firm, a characteristic of the J-firm is that staff cuts are not carried out according to the seniority principle. In addition, the practice of rotating personnel and the system of individual assessments serves to smoke out those targeted for redundancies.

If we argue that labour unions do not exercise bargaining power over employment and wage standards, what Aoki refers to as the industrial democracy model will then lack relevance. This is because, while the J-firm increased its casual workforce, including female part-timers and immigrant workers, it cannot be claimed it did this to boost 'long-term employment' for full-time workers or to increase wage distribution.

Rather, there are an enormous number of people in irregular modes of employment in large companies and the peripheral labour market. As Ōsawa Mari demonstrates, the simple reality is that these workers are discriminated against both within and outside the company. In fact, the number of female part-timers and casual employees increase the further down the subcontracting chain we go. Adjusting for economic fluctuations is carried out through reducing working hours for casual employees and personnel downsizing. Employment adjustments are also carried out for employees in parent companies by dispatching them to subsidiaries and related firms. One certainly cannot make the claim that there is a trade off between long-term employment and wages in Japanese companies, even in those in the *keiretsu* system. Thus, by increasing the 'flexibility' of wages and employment, Japanese companies have been able to maintain their international competitiveness in the face of repeated rises in the value of the yen.

Understandings of the main bank and keiretsu-affiliated companies

Finally, I wish to raise the issue of whether the duality principle can be applied to banks and companies (main bank system), as well as inter-company relations (*keiretsu*), as Aoki claims. From the perspective of the relationship between theory and reality, it must be noted above all that Aoki's description of the main banking system does not accord with the facts. There is no basis to the claim that the bank serves as the principle agent for individual shareholders and monitors companies on their behalf (see Kaneko 1997: 106–107).

Aoki makes an abstraction of Japanese-style financial contracts based on the matrix-model corporate groups that have been formed as a result of cross-shareholding centred around banks. On the one hand, the features of employment contacts cited by Aoki are typically evident in the machine assembly industry such as automobiles and electric machinery etc., which boast considerable export competitiveness. However, *both are not necessarily cross-linked*. This is because, in reality, large companies in this industry did not originally belong to matrix-model corporate groups centred around banks, but to independent companies that had weak links with banks. One would expect it to be a well-known fact that in order to streamline management and alleviate the burden of paying interest on loans *at a time when performances were poor* following the oil shock, these large companies *became less dependent on bank loans for financing*. In addition, also at a time when they were expected to have increased their export competitiveness and enjoyed the 'network rents' produced by workshop groups, these large companies (there was also the development of the euro-market) raised funds by issuing shares and low interest corporate bonds, as well as positively managing surplus funds. As a result, in 1984 – just before the rapid yen appreciation – the top four companies in terms of surplus amounts in financial account balances were (in order of ranking) Toyota (833 million yen), Nissan (613 million yen), Matsushita Denki (577 million yen) and Hitachi (283 million yen). Moreover, eight of the top ten companies were in the automobile and electric machinery industries. Even in this context, Aoki's cooperative game model does not accord with reality.

What is the situation regarding inter-company relations within the *keiretsu* structure? Aoki's argument that relations between a parent company and its affiliates amount to a 'horizontal information network' is an over-exaggeration.

First, finished car manufacturers act as outsourcing companies in their relations with first-tier subcontractors. Following the oil shock, in the course of fully introducing the *kanban* system in finished car manufacturers, first-tier suppliers received guidance from these manufacturers concerning the administration of the manufacturing process. First-tier suppliers in turn pass on this technical advice to second-tier suppliers. This is a relationship between firms that manage and firms that are managed. Information clearly flows, not horizontally, but vertically (Kaneko 1989: 109).

Second, while Aoki emphasises the risk-sharing assumed by the manufacturer placing the order during its long-term relationship with parts manufacturers, it is doubtful he examined this closely. Certainly, the ambiguity surrounding the ownership of the drawings for design-approved parts reduces the time spent on research and development and is one of the sources of the international competitiveness of the Japanese automobile industry. However, as Ueda Hirofumi notes in chapter 4, this type of relationship was initially created on the assumption of steady economic growth. Asanuma Banri, who analysed the decision-making process for model service costs and remuneration for improvement suggestions, also did not dwell on the issue of standard units costs nor did he incorporate development costs into unit costs. This problem surfaced as Japanese automobile manufacturers shifted their manufacturing operations overseas.

More problematic are the drawings supplied by parts manufacturers. Aoki argues that while the lower placed suppliers are in the subcontracting hierarchy, the smaller their share of quasi-rent, their degree of risk aversion rises as a result of serving as insurers for the outsourcing firms. However, as Ueda demonstrates, apart from Toyota, there is a high membership turnover in the Japan Automobile Manufacturers Association among small- and medium-sized automobile manufacturers. It cannot necessarily be said that such a relationship between low-tier suppliers and outsourcing firms has been formed. Moreover, there has been a further restructuring of parts suppliers in recent times. It is unreasonable to apply Aoki's theory of 'horizontal information networks' to what actually occurs in relations between *keiretsu*-affiliated companies.

As the preceding discussion suggests, the major elements of Aoki's theories concerning the horizontal information network, the rank hierarchy, the contractual approach and bargaining game theory, the dilemma of industrial democracy, the main bank system and risk sharing among *keiretsu*-affiliated companies comprise a model that is divorced from the reality of Japanese companies.

Is company rationality macro-economic rationality?

The bubble economy and Japanese companies

Another problem with Aoki's theory relates to his claim that company 'micro-economic rationality' explains macro-economic 'rationality.' His company model has been employed as a framework for explaining the entire social system and is self-containing. Therefore, Aoki seeks the causes of the changing social system, not in its internal features, but in the outside environment. He also claims that since the social system, as a whole, features institutional complementarity, changes to it are historically path-dependent. As a result of adopting this approach, Aoki et al. employ an evolutionary game analysis (Aoki 1995; Aoki and Fujiwara Masahiro eds., 1996). Setting aside the claim that changes appear as a result of sudden problems, as well as the propriety of a social dynamism approach that explains these changes in terms of survival of the fittest and natural selection, the failure to seek the cause of these changes from within the system is clearly problematic. It serves to prevent a critical analysis of Japanese companies' internal deficiencies.

Specifically, looking back, there are two reasons why many people felt Aoki's theory lacked explanatory power. First, since the latter half of the 1980s, the strong performance of the J-firm appeared to result from the bubble economy. Second, it could not necessarily be said that the generation of quasi-rent due to contextual skill was significant. Despite this, Aoki failed to address head-on important issues such as why the Japanese economy (the J-firm and J-bank) became so seriously overheated and why it has taken so long to recover from the collapse of the bubble. The causes certainly cannot only be attributed to changes in the external environment. It is not that the J-firm and J-bank failed to cope well with changes in the external environment, but simply that they are inherently flawed.

Needless to say, this does not refer to claims made by neo-classical economists such as 'if only shareholders had gained control, this would have prevented a bubble economy from developing in Japan,' and 'Japan has successfully dealt with the collapse of the bubble economy.' This is because if such a huge quantity of shares were to be traded and, moreover, the economy thrown into disorder by speculative money that can move in an instant, it is obvious that shareholder capitalism would not function. A look at present-day America where speculative money flooded into venture capital (especially into the American telecommunications industry and dot-com companies), which is representative of shareholder capitalism, leading to the Nasdac bubble and its subsequent collapse, is sufficient to understand this.

The problem is that not only were the characteristics of the J-firm Aoki cites as the source of its international competitiveness unable to curb the emergence of Japan's bubble economy, but they also became a mechanism that led to the failure to respond to the bubble's collapse. Cross-shareholding, which forms the basis of *keiretsu* company groups, makes an expansive managerial policy based on unrealised share profits/capital gains 'possible.' In fact, the main bank does not act as a monitoring agent of corporate management. Banks carelessly increased the amount of loans in which land was put up for collateral without conducting thorough examinations of loan applications.

Of course, there are several politico-institutional factors linked to the J-firm and bank's decision to purchase land. The first of these factors is the Japanese corporate tax system, which is based on the assumption that companies themselves are entities that cannot be divided among shareholders. This is because of the occurrence of unrealised capital gains from including the interest on loans for land purchases in expenses and the principle of acquisition costs, which allows companies to put a squeeze on profits and avoid corporation tax. In addition, if companies establish loss-making subsidiaries, they can even avoid heavy taxes on short-term capital gains. Treating transfer costs derived from redeemable and conditional land transfers between companies as debts payable, as well as advanced depreciation and lease write-offs, have a similar effect.

The next point is related to the fact that the weakness of Japanese urban planning and land-use regulations, in comparison with Europe and America, over-inflates the final demand for land. While land-use regulations have been distorted – as the tax exemption on farm land in suburban areas demonstrates – a situation has now developed in which residents are opposed to weak land-use regulations because of falling asset prices. Because of the pursuit of 'property possession democracy' (*shisan shoyū minshushugi*) under Japan's post-war welfare state system, final demand for home ownership was both long-term and steady. As a result, the risk of falling prices was relatively small.

However, it cannot be forgotten that the myth surrounding land has been formed in conjunction with the mechanism of the J-firm. First, in the case of companies that are fixated on growth, even if they put a squeeze on short-term profits, it is more advantageous for them to obtain assets that will strengthen the company's viability. In that respect, in relation to the aforementioned tax system, land assets are excellent purchases. Second, in the case of companies that maintain relatively long-term business relationships due to cross-shareholding centred around the bank and loans to affiliated companies, even if capital investments drop, rather than putting a squeeze on borrowing and placing emphasis on maintaining profit rates in the short-term, from a long-term perspective, it is more 'economically rational' to maintain relatively long-term business relations while purchasing the most beneficial assets through borrowing. Third, in addition to casually observing each other, *keiretsu*-affiliated companies also share managerial risks. In this case, while measures such as buying increased capital, additional finance and extending the credit period are adopted, if the companies wish to maintain managerial autonomy, it is naturally better to be backed by assets that have collateral value. Therefore, the company's managerial base will become unstable and asset purchasing will increase during periods of structural change, when predictions of economic growth will become unclear. Land assets have now become the safest precaution against risk. This not only extends to the bank, but also to non-banking enterprises in the *keiretsu*, real estate companies and even as far as subsidiaries in the manufacturing industry. The buffer role of relations among *keiretsu*-affiliated companies is not only limited to making employment adjustments.

In fact, looking at developments since the 1970s, the *period during which there was an increase in land purchases by incorporated enterprises accords with the period in which the Japanese economy underwent structural changes* following the Nixon shock in 1971, the two oil shocks in 1974 and 1979 and the high-yen recession in 1985. This period was one in which the rate of increase in capital investment plummeted (and therefore, the rate of increase in GNP). Because of uncertainty and a restrictive interest rate policy linked with controlling inflation and exchange rate adjustments, it was also a period in which the trends in land prices did not necessarily accord with movements in real interest rates.

This fact is closely linked with corporate capital accumulation in the 1970s and the changing circumstances surrounding this. Specifically:

1. In the event of a rising trade surplus and an absence of favourable investment destinations domestically and abroad, a situation is created in which surplus funds are continually produced.
2. The rate of increase in capital investment resulting from the oil shock is significantly revised downwards.
3. Due to companies being able to raise funds cheaply from the Euro-market etc. since the 1980s, banks' lending margins and companies' ability to raise funds surpassing the amount necessary for capital investment has emerged.

Under such conditions, if there is uncertainty surrounding a company's future, it will be forced to manage assets such as land and shares, which are profitable and stable, in order to prepare for future risks. First and foremost, the bubble economy arose as a result of the close link between changes in the external environment and endogenous factors.

Moreover, the isomorphic nature of the government and companies and the close institutional and complementary relationship between the two emphasised by Aoki obfuscates the issue of responsibility and plays a critical role in hindering the management of the bubble's collapse. Bank managers' fraudulent assessments of non-performing loans, shuffling and hiding stock in subsidiaries and *keiretsu*-affiliated firms, Financial Supervisory Agency officials' rubber-stamping of these fraudulent assessments, chartered accounts' breach of trust and the rubber-stamping of creative accounting practices are cases in point. The fundamental cause of the turmoil since the collapse of the bubble economy results from the fact that the Japanese economy represents a style of capitalism in which there are no referees who represent public needs. This is clearly an internal flaw in the social system.

Can enterprise unions bring the bubble into check?

The problem not only concerns the main banking system and *keiretsu* corporate groups. This is because there is also an issue concerning enterprise unions in the J-firm. As will be discussed later, since the oil shock, a number of factors including inflation control and companies' regaining international competitiveness, *Nikkeiren*'s proposal of a theory of 'economic compatibility,' which called for restricting wage increase rates to within the limits of the percentage rise in labour productivity, and the acceptance of this by large enterprise unions centred around the IMF & JC, have led to a situation in the manufacturing industry in which the nominal wage rate index corresponded for the most part with the nominal productivity growth index. Once labour unions agree to voluntary restraint on wage increases based on the notion of prioritising company growth, it will become difficult for a wage-price spiral to occur.

A wage-price spiral refers to a vicious cycle whereby if many labour unions attempt to recoup lost wages caused by price rises and increase nominal wages, it will rebound on manufacturing prices and cause further prices rises, as well as ultimately a decline in real wages. In other words, while each union demand is rational, they are a type of 'fallacy of composition' (*gōsei no gobyū*) in that the overall result brought about is irrational. Certainly, in the event that industry-based unions have weak bargaining power or labour unions are organised horizontally across companies and several of them are in competition within the same company, such is the case in Europe and America, it cannot be denied that such a possibility will arise. This is because if many unions do not strive for wage increases, it will threaten the existence of union organisations. However, the situation arising in Japan following the oil shock was a completely opposite 'fallacy of composition.' In the case of labour unions that have been organised along company lines, as they come to accept voluntary restraints on wage increases in the name of securing future employment, company-based unions get caught up in the logic of inter-company competition and, even if the Japanese economy as a whole seeks wage increases, it becomes difficult to make such strong demands for it. If only one company were to take the lead in reducing working hours, because it would lose its competitiveness, a similar situation would arise. Thus, a completely opposite 'fallacy of composition' to that in the West will arise.

The problem lies in the fact that the principle of labour productivity standards promotes the purchasing of land assets by companies. First, while services related to the buying and selling of land are included in GNP, the capital gains from land are not included in value-added production (and GNP). In addition, when purchasing land with borrowed money, depending on the interest payments in terms of GNP, corporate income and operating surpluses will decline.

As a result, from the labour productivity standards, which divided 'value-added' by 'employment numbers x working hours,' the capital gains on land will be omitted and wage levels will be overestimated. The value of company-owned land in 1988 on an acquisition cost basis was 110.5 trillion yen, while capital gains reached 342 trillion yen. The value of these capital gains had swelled to approximately the same amount as the total GNP. Based on this, the rise in labour's relative share in the national income in terms of the flow level, following the oil shock is meaningless. This is because if we were to hypothetically add the hidden capital gains on land and shares to the denominator, labour's relative share in the national income would decline drastically.

The problem remains the same even if each company was to take ordinary profit rates as the basis for determining wage increases. This is because corporate income declines as a result of the interest payments made when purchasing land. Ultimately, while the rules governing wage increases based on the principle of labour productivity standards caused consumer prices to cool, they also brought about an imbalance in the form of stock inflation.

It can be said that such a method of determining wages was the most adaptable framework for export industries such as the electric machinery and automobile industries. This is because it was necessary for companies in this industry to maintain export competitiveness by suppressing wages, while avoiding the risks associated with fluctuating exchange rates. Enterprise unions were also unable to check business activity during the bubble economy.

What is the real issue?

As we have seen, the explanatory power of Aoki's theory has been seriously undermined. The reason behind his theory's loss of explanatory power is that the images he portrays of the J-firm and corporate groups in terms of the duality principle have clearly lost touch with reality. In addition, the framework Aoki employs, which extends the image of the J-firm to the entire social system, is unable to explain the workings of Japan's bubble economy and its subsequent collapse. This is because, in addition to concocting a false image of the J-firm, there are errors in the methodology itself, which seeks the causes of 'evolution' in changes in the external environment, premised on the self-containment of the system.

Amidst the advance of globalisation, Japan's 'big bang' financial and accounting reforms have led scholars to attempt to 'dismantle' one by one the systems Aoki cited as characteristics of Japanese companies (Kaneko 2001). Of course, it cannot be said that what is known as 'global standards' is necessarily correct. However, in accordance with Aoki's erroneous theory, it is not sufficient to simply defend the 'good points' of Japanese corporate organisation. What is required now is a critical analysis of the nature of the impact of institutional pressure on the J-firm resulting from the introduction of 'global standards.' The task is to find a new framework that can explain such changes.

8 The Failure of J-Firm Theory

Shigeo Takeda

'Comparative Institutional Analysis' and the Theory of the Japanese Firm

In the 1980s, Aoki Masahiko analysed the Japanese firm using micro-economics. His research was published in *Information, Incentives, and Bargaining in the Japanese Economy* in 1988. Following this, he broadened the focus of his research to the Japanese corporate system. Aoki termed his approach CIA or 'Comparative Institutional Analysis,' and this recently has been used to analyse economic development in East Asia. CIA has been constructed as a general theory to be used in coming to grips with the structure of and historical changes in the economic system (Aoki et al. [1995, 1996, 1999]).

However, despite these grand intentions, CIA contains inherent difficulties that emerge from micro-economic theory. There are also debatable points in its analysis. Furthermore, CIA cannot explain the failures of Japanese governance in the management of firms and government administration, which were revealed one after another as the Bubble Economy emerged and collapsed, and then during the Heisei recession. Neither has it been able to make concrete and effective proposals for reforming the Japanese economic system.

Indeed, it appears that actual developments have moved far beyond many of the theories which lauded Japanese management, including CIA. The current trend is to reject all aspects of Japanese management and the Japanese form of discretionary administration. With regard to management, shareholder orientation, corporate governance and global accounting standards are emphasised. With regard to monetary and financial policies, the reform of the Bank of Japan Law of April 1998 is interpreted as having realised both the independence of the Bank of Japan and the transparency of financial policies, while the power and authority the Ministry of Finance once wielded are being undermined through a series of bureaucratic reforms. These trends are echoed in the criticism of 'crony capitalism' that was made following the Asian economic crisis. It appears that market orientation and the 'rule of law' are emerging as the basic principles of the economic system on a global scale.

A theoretical weakness can be clearly seen in the CIA that welcomed the rationality of Japanese management and the efficiency of the Japanese corporate system. A lack of positive recommendations can also be clearly seen (see, for instance, Aoki et al. eds. [1999: 21–22]). CIA was a product of the 1980s, a time when Japanese management and Japanese discretionary administration became the focus of global attention. Its theoretical weaknesses were exposed during the 1990s, a period in which the failures of corporate governance of Japanese firms (and especially financial institutions) became apparent to all. The failure of the Japanese corporate system and the failure of CIA theory were thus juxtaposed in an enlightening fashion.

In this set of circumstances, why, it might be asked, is it important once again to criticise J-Firm Theory and CIA? We believe that this criticism is indeed important, because of the theoretical failings of CIA. This is because such criticism illustrates clearly a mistake often made when analysing social systems. In particular, it makes possible a detailed examination of how social theories that have no viewpoint other than rational choice and systemic efficiency jettison the experiences and understandings of people, and become blind to the dysfunctions of systems and the various problems they produce.

This chapter will examine theoretically CIA's theory of the Japanese firm. Part 2 will first cast fundamental doubts on the approach that attempts to create a bridge between observer and participant through 'objective' theory. Next, Part 3 will provide an overview of how micro-economics and game theory – which provide the basic concepts and models for CIA – treat human actions and social systems. The core components of the CIA of Japanese firms will next be reconstructed and the tacit assumptions of CIA clarified, with an emphasis on information and incentives in Part 4 and bargaining games in Part 5. Furthermore, in Part 6, the debate on institutional complementarity – a topic given much weight in recent years – will be examined. Finally, Part 7 will ask whether J-Firm Theory is 'theory for the sake of theory,' something that exists for itself. In an appendix, I will use a model to illustrate the essential characteristics of the Nash Equilibrium in a non-cooperative game.

A 'Rational' Explanation of the Japanese Firm

There are two fundamental problems with CIA. The first is the naivety about the objectification effects of theory, and the second is the difficulties inherent in micro-economic theory and game theory.

Universal and Objective Theory?

I will start with the first issue. In reply to explanations that trot out cultural traditions such as the Japanese group orientation and the vertical society, CIA claims that Japanese management is not defined by cultural uniqueness, but can be explained by a theory that can also be applied to countries other than Japan. In other words, CIA claims to analyse Japanese management and Japanese social systems with a universal logic.

The analytical tools chosen to accomplish this task are key concepts of micro-economics and game theory: information, incentives, bargaining and contract. However, the unspoken assumption of CIA is that these concepts can thoroughly explain people's consciousness, human actions and social systems, as if they were neutral concepts of the natural sciences, and moreover that they are necessary and sufficient as an explanatory principle.

However, when only a small number of concepts are used in an attempt to explain the entirety of a social phenomena such as the Japanese firm, the concepts are at times pulled to such an extreme that the original meaning almost completely disappears. For instance, information originally signified knowledge about objective reality, but when used in terms of the exchange of information, information processing, and information structure, it grows more and more distant from the original meaning (information and information processing are technical terms with distinct definitions in physics, statistics and computer science, while game theory inherited the concept of information structure from Bayesian Statistics).

The exchange of information is sometimes used in the sense of the exchange of objective knowledge, but it is also ambiguously used to include the informal communication required to maintain good relations in the workplace where, for instance, individuals teach one another their work's vital points or determine where their areas of responsibility lie.

The same can be said for information processing. For instance, in the Toyota Production Method, quality control is not viewed as a specialist area of management. Instead, the ability of each operator to 'build quality into' the product during the production process is emphasised. For quality to be 'built into' the product, the operator must have the ability to solve problems on his (or her) own initiative, based on his (or her) experience and accumulated skill. If this is called information processing, the impression is given that all the operator's actions and intentions can be neutrally and objectively defined by technical necessity.

Furthermore, the information structure in the workplace has moved far beyond what was originally meant in Bayesian Statistics,[1] and signifies the transfer of knowledge between colleagues, ways to work in cooperation, spontaneous workplace order, and even top-down relations in the management hierarchy (for this point, see Part 4 below). The same can be said for incentives and contract. These usages are not limited to CIA, but are generally seen in micro-economic theory.

CIA might at first sight seem to provide insights into Japanese management; yet this is to a large extent explained by the objectification effects of these concepts. In other words, the impression is given that CIA has made clear the true form of Japanese management – a true form that no one was previously aware of. What is entirely discarded by what is alleged to be 'objective' theory, however, is people's experiences and interpretations.

The Ideological Effects of Theory

Those involved in economics are more than well aware that 'rational and objective' explanations of social phenomena (inevitably) have ideological effects. For instance, in a classical article by Coase in firm theory (Coase [1937]), the firm organisation is defined as a resource allocation mechanism in a complementary relationship with the price mechanism, which means that the firm organisation is viewed solely in terms of rational choice and systemic efficiency. Alchian and Demsetz have published an article that is famous for reducing the superintendence, direction and orders given in the firm organisation to a 'nexus of contracts' (Alchian and Demsetz [1972]). The contract is understood to be a social relationship created voluntarily by two parties blessed with unblemished reason and firm will, and thus is a concept loaded with positive values. Although there are today few supporters of the Nexus of Contracts theory of the firm, the tendency to view all social relations through the prism of the contract has become deeply embedded in firm theory and micro-economics.

However, the price of the objectification is the separation of theory on the one hand and concrete experience on the other. The gulf between the consciousness of the parties actually involved and theory is clearly seen in relation to information and incentives, but is particularly blatant in relation to contracts and bargaining (see Part 5). What exactly is the privilege granted to theorists that justifies their employment in explaining human actions and social systems in terms of categories that the actual parties are neither conscious of nor in reality utilise?

In other words, a crucial element is missing in CIA as social analysis. Despite the necessity of explaining why the parties involved do not think along the lines suggested by, or make decisions according to, the 'objective' theory provided by CIA, no such explanation is provided. This is because any such explanation would require society to be depicted either as an enormous unconscious system or as a system of deceit and conspiracy. Here lies the pitfall of the 'objective and rational' explanation of social systems. As Bourdieu (1980) notes, we have to objectify the objectification. That is, we must focus attention to how that which purports to be objective theory jettisons the dimension of our experience and understanding.

People's experiences, interpretations, and decision-making modes are constitutive of society, and therefore social analysis cannot and must not ignore the dimension of meaning and value. Despite this, CIA views the objects of its analysis only from the viewpoint of rational choice and systemic efficiency. The dimensions of experience and understanding that cannot be covered by this approach are ignored, and therefore the structural functional imperfections and dysfunctions, together with the anti-system potential that emerges from the system itself, are also ignored.

Although the following issues, for instance, cannot be avoided in any examination of the Japanese corporate system, the CIA does in fact ignore them: the Japanese Supreme Court's case for corporate order in which the firm is permitted to encroach upon the private lives of employees; peer group pressure at the shopfloor level; the friction between spontaneity and coercion in everyday work (which results in overtime in the service industry, death from overwork, and suicide as a result of being overworked); the inherent instability in the social technology known as '*satei*' (personnel assessment) – this constitutes the pivot of the power of Personnel Divisions; the economic dependence at the bottom-end of the *keiretsu*; the gap between formal corporate rules (such as, for instance, the importance of the General Shareholders Meeting) on the one hand and the realities of the corporate governance of Japanese firms on the other; the bank management that was actively involved in the Bubble Economy; and finally the delicate combination of competition and collusion between companies in the same industries.

Furthermore, this also leads to the fundamental position of CIA, which is that of a designer looking down on the organisations and social systems. Who is this designer? CIA may provide a useful ruling principle for some bureaucrats who cannot return to the old Japanese discretionary administration, but who also cannot fully embrace a market fundamentalism that would reject the management of the state, their *raison d'etre*. However, at the same time, those for whom the system has been designed have been overlooked.

Rationality and Efficiency

The theoretical context of CIA is provided by the new micro-economics, and in particular by post-Coase theoretical work on the firm that was the subject of much research from the 1970s onwards. In order to differentiate this from General Equilibrium Theory, it will here be labelled Micro-economics Mark II. Both General Equilibrium Theory and Micro-economics Mark II are closed systems that are concerned with the two postulates of rational choice and systemic efficiency.

Micro-economics Mark II

In addition to these two fundamental postulates, General Equilibrium Theory, the basic outline of which was completed by the late 1950s, created a model of the market mechanism based on the assumption of perfect markets where markets exist for all goods and services, where perfect competition rules all markets, and where price information is instantly and freely available. However, universal markets and perfect information are of course alien to the realities of the market. Indeed, what is truly universal are the imperfections and failures of the market. The research strategy chosen by micro-economics in the face of this problem was to focus on individual cases of market transactions, leaving to one side the clarification of the adjustment mechanism across many markets, and to research the imperfect information that leads to market failure, the incentives to exploit weaknesses in economic systems, such as free-riding of public goods, transaction costs, and strategic behaviour in bargaining.

In this research, it is assumed that the rules of market transactions and economic relationships are created by those involved after fully taking into consideration asymmetric information and their strategically mutually dependent relationship. These voluntary rules are called governance structures or contracts. However, it is important to note that this concept is much broader than that of the contract as used, for instance, by legal scholars. Micro-economics includes in its understanding of a contract social relations that would not normally be viewed as a legal contract (a classical contract),[2] and raises the question of what type of contract the people involved will create.

In many cases, however, it is impossible to determine in advance what all the rights and obligations of the contracting parties will be in each and every circumstance that might occur. It is not always possible to ascertain whether the other party is in fact respecting the contract due to asymmetric information, and even when it is possible to ascertain that, the costs in terms of time and effort may be too high. Therefore, contracts tend to be incomplete. The new micro-economics tackles these issues from the standpoint of rational contracting parties who make detailed plans for future contingencies (which is sometimes called *presentiation* because such plans translate something that will happen in the future into the present).[3] In short, while General Equilibrium Theory takes as its basic assumption the example of a 'perfect market,' Micro-economics Mark II assumes an 'incomplete contract.'

The Principal and Agent Model

Within the framework of the incomplete contract, the model that is most frequently used is that of principal and agent. This model allows us to grasp the basic thrust of Micro-economics Mark II. It focuses on the problem of designing an incentive scheme for an agent in conditions where the agent's behaviour cannot be directly observed by the principal (such as when a salesperson on the road cannot be supervised by a superior). Despite the best efforts of the agent – the salesperson – the results (such as sales) of this effort are beyond his (or her) complete control. If all the risks of poor sales are imposed on the agent, he (or she) will not be willing to agree to work, but if a set amount is paid in wages without regard to results there will be no incentive to work hard. An incentive scheme that provides an optimal result for the principal is designed within the parameters of these opposites. This model has been applied to relationships such as the employment relationship, franchising, and the shareholder and manager relationship. In the CIA of the Japanese firm, the *keiretsu* relationship between parent firm and sub-contractor, or between main bank and client firm, has been viewed as a principal and agent relationship.

Note that the principal-agent model makes use of almost all major tools provided by the paradigm of the incomplete contract. The principal must take into account the response of the agent when designing an incentive scheme (i.e. strategic rationality). At the same time, it is impossible to observe directly the behaviour of the agent (i.e. asymmetric information), and there is an uncontrollable element between the agent's efforts and results (i.e. risk). Under these conditions, the principal will consider in advance all possibilities (i.e. presentiation), and create an optimal incentive scheme (i.e. mechanism design). Finally, under an optimal incentive scheme, the principal must calculate the minimum agency costs, or, in other words, calculate to what degree the principal's gains will decline at the least when compared with a situation where information is perfect (i.e. the principle of efficiency).

It is possible to counter this choice of basic concepts with an alternative set of basic concepts. For instance, instead of strategic rationality, communicative rationality (which aims for consensus and understanding) or custom; instead of the asymmetric information, the distortion of communication; instead of risk, uncertainty (where probability cannot be defined); instead of presentiation of contract, relational contract; instead of mechanism design, participation; instead of the principle of efficiency, the principles of fairness and justice. The choice of one rather than the other of these alternative concepts will have important theoretical consequences.

As a social theory, the range of Micro-economics Mark II, or the paradigm of the incomplete contract, is a question that requires a great deal of thought (for this point, see Takeda [1998]). However, CIA chooses Micro-economics Mark II as a theoretical tool of analysis in the field of Japanese corporate theory and thus tests its effective range. It is possible to ascertain the utility of the micro-economic viewpoint, which focuses only on rationality and efficiency, through an examination of CIA.

Information and Incentives

The Main Story of J-Firm Theory

The main story of the CIA of the Japanese firm can be summarised as follows. First, the high productivity of Japanese firms is a product of the problem-solving ability and incentive of the group on the shop-floor. This in turn is a product of the 'Horizontal Information Structure' and 'shared knowledge' in which productivity, quality control, and technical training work together in cooperation, and of the 'vertical incentive structure' or 'ranking hierarchy' in which employees' incentive to work is stimulated by the positive and negative sanctions (such as promotion or demotion) of the long-term personnel assessment. The 'Horizontal Information Structure' refers to, for instance, the kanban system, team production, QC (quality control) activities, and the job rotation system that promotes technical training of the Toyota Production Method, with regard to blue-collar workers, and also to the 'contextual skills' – the skill required to pay attention to human relations within the organisation and at the same time to solve problems in a flexible fashion according to circumstances – of the so-called generalist with regard to white-collar workers. 'Ranking hierarchy' refers to the status ladder within the organisation that exists independently of job-type and which one ascends as experience and skills are accumulated.

Second, with regard to the management of the firm (for instance, the decisions over investment and wages), shareholders and the employees as a group oppose one other, while managers arbitrate between them. Some interests of both opposing sides coincide, others do not. There is therefore room for bargaining, and both use agents for these negotiations. Management or the main bank acts as the agent of the shareholders, while the labour union acts on behalf of the employees. The managers thus at times negotiate with labour unions as the agent of shareholders or the main bank, and at times do not actually negotiate, instead unveiling management policies that embody a balance of the powers of bargaining of both parties or a fair arbitration. Furthermore, the main story joins with parts of the system such as the financial system, bureaucratic structure, external labour markets, so completing the CIA of the Japanese firm.

Horizontal Information Structure

Let us start with information. What exactly is meant by the 'Horizontal Information Structure' and 'shared knowledge' of the workplace as emphasised by J-Firm Theory?

Horizontal Information Structure takes as its model the main features of the Toyota Production Method: the *kanban* system, the team system, multi-skilled operators with problem-solving ability, and the QC circle. The first point to be stressed is that Horizontal Information Structure has two different meanings. The first indicates production coordination such as the *kanban* system. The second is related to communication understood in the broad sense in the production process and workplace. In both, 'horizontal' suggests the devolution of the decision-making power in the production process, but this is misleading as far as the kanban system is concerned.

For information (i.e. the *kanban*) to flow 'horizontally' between the various manufacturing processes means that production coordination between each shop is not based on directives from above but occurs as an inventory and production coordination system in the factory. That does not mean however that the decision-making of each shop is autonomous. In other words, it has nothing whatsoever to do with the devolution of power and authority in the production process.[4]

With regards to communication in the workplace, J-Firm Theory argues as follows. The team system in the Toyota Production Method is one that delegates much power to the workplace. It uses OJT (on the job training) to impart the skill (called the 'capacity to process information' or 'intellectual skills') to operators on the production line to respond in a flexible fashion to emergency situations, and to be able to use varying types of machines when and as necessary. It even encourages workers to improve their own labour processes through QC activities. Therefore, goes the argument, the power to make decisions has been delegated downwards, and in this type of workplace communication is not a top-down form of directives, but occurs in relationships between equals working in co-operation with one another. (The Toyota Production Method interacted with total quality control or TQC – TQC emerged from the American statistical quality control, or STC, in the 1960s to become a whole company management control movement – and in the 1980s rapidly spread through Japanese firms, including banks, construction companies, and firms in the service sector.)

In order to examine the pros and cons of this line of thought, let us begin with Taylorism. The essential point of Taylorism is the discovery that the most basal layer element in the managerial hierarchy is not the individual operator but the individual movements of the operator. Rather than labour being viewed as an independent action of the operator, as occurring through a natural physical rhythm and desire to work, it was instead reduced to a series of movements, and these movements were used by management after a push for standardization and greater efficiency in terms of speed and strength. Since a series of movements can be standardised, the need for control over the labour process by the operator becomes redundant, and the labour process becomes for the operator something that is felt to be external coercion.

The Toyota Production Method

The Toyota Production Method is similar to Taylorism in that it reduces autonomous labour into a series of movements (see Nomura [1993]), but differs in that the reduction of labour itself is entrusted to small groups in the workplace. These small groups are required to make continuous small reforms to the work processes and placement of machinery through QC activities while at the same time maintaining productivity levels by overcoming the various obstacles that emerge in the daily production process. For this to be made possible, a wide variety of mechanisms are mobilised, including peer group pressure, solidarity, self-sacrifice, and the desire to work and to reform. The goals of maintaining productivity levels and the push to increase efficiency are imposed from above, the team is allowed to assume joint responsibility to independently accomplish the realisation of the goals. This means that the imposition of control from above as seen in Taylorism is replaced by control from within (control from within the workplace and/or control from within each individual operator). As a result, the Toyota Production Method and TQC are implemented as a type of social movement that involves the entire company, although it is initiated by the upper levels of management (see Tokumaru [1999]).

In other words, the innovation of the Toyota Production Method can be described as the discovery of a life-world that management can use as a resource (life-world here refers to desire, dedication, solidarity, and the natural communication and authority in the small group). In the Toyota Production Method, unlike the classic model of wage labour, there is no exchange of a set number of work hours and a wage. Labourers have to offer not just labour hours, but also the resources of the life-world.

Here lies the reason the Toyota Production Method is the most important innovation in labour control technique since Taylorism. Indeed, in the 1980s many US companies studied and adopted the Toyota Production Method as 'lean production,' and it lies behind many innovations in production processes, labour processes and management techniques in US firms today, beginning with restructuring and downsizing. The ideal of the flexible firm where the aims and goals alone are imposed from above, but the methods and organisational forms needed to realise them are left blank, and the employees themselves are allowed to discover the most appropriate methods and organisation forms. From the viewpoint of the employees, this flexible firm pretends to be one where the power to make decisions is decentralised but in reality is one where a formidable micro-power is exercised. This is an amorphous form of power where 'power is concentrated without being centralised' (see Sennett [1998]).

Thus the 'Horizontal Information Structure' and 'shared knowledge' are in fact a new type of managerial control which directly intervenes into the life-world of employees, a new type of power, and from the viewpoint of employees is experienced as 'a coerced solidarity' and 'an autonomy ordered from above.' This apparent contradiction in terms is a contradiction actually experienced. As reported in many surveys, the Toyota Production Method and Lean Production are accompanied by a labour backlash, such as the internal friction between coercion and spontaneity, internal disquiet and dissent about management policy, dropping out of the labour force, sabotage, and open resistance (see Kumazawa [1997], and Graham [1994]).

Incentives

Next we will briefly mention incentives. In J-Firm Theory, the ranking hierarchy of Japanese firms is viewed as a mechanism that stimulates loyalty to the firm and the incentive to work. This mechanism is assumed to work by exposing the employees, who have been reduced to individuals, to a long-term competition for promotion. Thus the ranking hierarchy is viewed as one source of the efficiency of the Japanese firm – although this depends on one's definition of 'efficiency.' For instance, if the costs of the individual sacrifices made by employees when they are moved to another section within the same workplace or to another work place were taken into account, and a cost-benefit analysis done on Japanese labour and personnel management, it is certainly possible that the conclusion drawn would be that Japanese firms are extremely inefficient organisations.

Moreover, the ranking hierarchy has problems that cannot be reduced to the issue of costs. To operate any such hierarchy completely depends on the social technique we know as personnel assessment which, as Endō Kōshi (1999) details, has many problems. The most obvious problem is that it has become a tool used to discriminate on the basis of gender or political beliefs. Even compared to the situation in the USA, the Japanese assessment system cannot be said to be administered in a fair and objective manner.

The social technique of assessment is an area where our instinctive feelings of fairness and equality intersect with the logic of management and organisation, and thus a tension between values – a tension that cannot easily be resolved – is an intrinsic element of assessment. As the belief in meritocracy spreads, the limits of this technique will inevitably become a greater issue.

The Bargaining Game

The model that lies at the center of the CIA of Japanese firms is that of the bargaining game between shareholders and employees. It is assumed that one of the parties concerned consists of the shareholders, the main bank, and the managers, while the other consists of the individual employees and the labour union.

The Basic Structure of the Bargaining Game

1. According to CIA, the relationship between shareholders and the main bank is a principal-agent one. This, however, is a highly tenuous assumption to make. Even if the main bank does in fact monitor the management of the firm, why would it be interested in defending the interests of the shareholders of client firms? Since the bank itself is a shareholder, it is theoretically possible that as a consequence of the bank's endeavour to secure the interests of the shareholder, the interests of the powerless individual who owns shares will also

be protected. However, the main bank in reality does not deal with the firm in order to secure the interests of the shareholder.

Furthermore, according to CIA, the main bank imposes discipline on the firm's management by continuously monitoring it. When the firm gets into difficulties, the main bank dispatches top management to run the firm or hands down managerial directions, and at times even saves the firm. This notion of the main bank does not enjoy broad support, however. According to Mark Scher's (1997) survey, the aim of the bank in becoming a main bank is to secure income via transaction fees. The alleged principal-agent relationship between shareholders and the main bank should therefore be understood as a theoretical claim required for the fictitious bargaining game to run.

2. The arguments about the other party in the bargaining game, the labour union, are also tenuous. The explanation of where the basis of the power of the labour union lies appears to be confused. Although each individual employee is already caught up in the ranking hierarchy, the bargaining game opens suddenly with a discussion on individual negotiations. The basis of these individual negotiations seems to be the notion that the employment relationship is a tacit and incomplete contract: i.e. the notion that it is impossible to reach a consensus on each and every possible eventuality in the future, and therefore that a renegotiation is required each time a new problem emerges. However, in the post-Coase discourse on the theory of 'employment as an incomplete contract,' the interpretation has been that within set limits employees will obey the authority of management *because* it is impossible to reach a consensus on each and every possible eventuality. Indeed, unless the employee has a specialised skill, it is impossible for the individual to negotiate directly with the Personnel Division of a Japanese firm.

This unsubstantiated notion of individual bargaining forms the foundation of the collective bargaining of the labour union. The cross bargaining that is impossible in individual bargaining is thus entrusted to the labour union. In J-Firm Theory, therefore, employees work together 'sharing knowledge' with colleagues *on the shop floor* to solve problems, but *in their hearts* view these colleagues as competitors in the race for promotion, and *in the firm* as a whole support the labour union which protects the interests of all employees.

3. Finally, regarding the bargaining game itself, it should be noted that Aoki's writings are strangely ambiguous. It is not at all clear whether the bargaining game is a theoretical expression for an actual collective bargaining where the managers are either one of the parties or are arbitrators, or whether it is a 'hypothetical bargaining' carried out inside the minds of managers who embody fair mediation principles. There are sections of Aoki's writings that suggest that he believes that it does not matter which interpretation is chosen, or implies that he thinks that his theory will stand in either case.

The Fiction of Hypothetical Bargaining

This ambiguity is in fact indicative of a double fiction in the bargaining game of J-Firm theory. In game theory, it should be noted, the game itself is not played. That is, game theorists pose the problem of what combination of strategies are mutually consistent once the tastes (utility functions) and beliefs (subjective probability distributions over the opponent's strategies) of the players as well as the rules of the game (the information structure and payoff function of each player), are given, and focus their attention on this compatible combination, or, in other words, the equilibrium of the game. The problems of what path to follow if the game moves away from equilibrium, or what result will eventually be reached, are completely beyond the scope of current game theory (Binmore [1990], Kreps [1990]). In game theory, a leap is made from the premises of the game (the players' tastes and beliefs and the game's rules) to equilibrium. The process that leads from premise to equilibrium is not the object of theoretical discussion. A concrete analysis of the background of negotiations that actually occur, the processes, and the results, are viewed as being the focus of political, historical and sociological studies.

Furthermore, and importantly, the leap from the game's premises to equilibrium is in the cooperative game tacitly projected onto the players themselves and, in the non-cooperative game, is explicitly guaranteed through the hypothesis of 'common knowledge.' Game theory must hypothesise that the players will follow the same reasoning as the game theorist to reach the same conclusions (in comparison, the evolution game views the player's actions in terms of a model of bacteria, or an automatic machine that passively responds to circumstances). This unique epistemological structure in which the parties involved can take the viewpoint of the observer derives from a reduction of communication to information transmission, and a reduction of actions to psychological processes such as calculation and deduction. One frank game theorist admits that game theory does not deal with real bargaining, contracts and social relations, but with (the game theorist's) perceptions of these social realities (Rubinstein [1991]). This is neatly indicated by Nash's axiomatic approach to the cooperative bargaining game and Rubinstein's model of the non-cooperative bargaining game (for the latter, see the appendix to this chapter). In short, bargaining games in game theory are all hypothetical negotiations.

Institutional Indeterminacy

The fiction of bargaining in this theory is superimposed on a second fiction about the Japanese firm. This is the fiction that Japanese management stands balanced over the rival interests of the two great stakeholders, the shareholders and employees.

This second fiction is to a degree complicated. We must first pay attention to the gap between the notion of the stock company as expressed in company law and the actual relationship between shareholder and managers. Or, to be more exact, company law itself should be seen as a patchwork of a plurality of notions. Space does not permit the author to examine this issue further here (see Bratton [1989], DeMott [1988], and Frug [1984]). With regard to the stock company, since Berle and Means proclaimed the collapse of the classical concept of ownership, several explanatory theories have opposed one another about the relationship between shareholders and managers either in different academic fields, or in the same research area. It is impossible to understand the stock company with any abstract and single logic.

For instance, shareholders have not voluntarily transferred the power to run the firm to managers, nor can they reclaim the power when necessary, and therefore it is impossible to view managers as agents (in the legal sense) of shareholders. The relationship between the two is a fiduciary one, and although some see managers as trustees of shareholders, this lacks persuasion; for managers have only to obey the 'duty of due care,' and are not required always to sacrifice their own interests in order to promote those of shareholders. Managers cannot also be considered specialists in management, and shareholders cannot be viewed as their clients; managerial decisions are not a specialist ability that can be objectively defined like accounting and legal affairs, but of necessity involve an element of discretion. There is also a problem with the model of judicial review where the law intervenes in order to determine the rights and wrongs of management. This is because courts lack the ability to question the rights and wrongs of managerial decisions (the so-called 'business judgement rule'). Furthermore, in the recent 'Law and Economics' approach to company law, there is a view that argues that managerial discipline should be entrusted to market efficiency. According to this approach, the fear of takeovers will force managers to adopt a managerial policy that emphasises the shareholder. This, however, remains a mere theoretical hypothesis, and it is not clear whether or not those interested in taking over other firms will really perform this function. For instance, the 'hubris hypothesis' argues that there are no guarantees that management will always improve after a takeover. Finally, there is the theory of the stakeholder firm. According to this theory, several interested parties bargain in corporate board meetings, and therefore the results of this bargaining will be a fair balance of the various social concerns. This is, in effect, a political model of the management of the firm. The CIA of Japanese firms is an example of this position.[5]

Having reviewed the various explanatory schemata of the stock company, all of which have problems, it is difficult to choose any as the model to be adopted. Not only is this true at the theoretical level, but, even more importantly, it is also true in terms of the legal system and actual management. This means that there is great latitude in terms of which model or position the management of stock companies is based on. In this sense, there is an institutional indeterminacy in the stock company.

The Fiction of the Stockholder

In addition to this institutional indeterminacy in the general sense of term, there is also a particularity that is a product of the history of each country. In prewar Japan, traditional forms of organisation and organisational modes of thought were first adapted to the imported social system of the stock company. The style of Japanese management was formed following the rise in the postwar labour movement, and the taming of labour by management from the 1960s.

The characteristics of Japanese management emerge from the notion of multi-layered community. The community can be defined in a number of ways depending on which stakeholders are included.

For instance, moving outwards, stakeholders can include the family of the founder of the enterprise, the core group of managers, full-time tenured employees, major shareholders, the main bank, client firms that own shares in the enterprise, main customers, subcontractors and company groups lower down in the keiretsu, part-time workers and non-tenured (contract) employees. Furthermore, just as then underprivileged blue-collar workers were embraced as fully-fledged company employees in the postwar era, so the concentric circle that defines the firm community has spread outwards, or, in a reverse move, the concentric circle may retreat if – as is the case today – much of the labour force is out-sourced. Furthermore, in a crisis, there are cases where the insiders, who in fact make the decisions, are reduced to the president and four or five others in the firm (see, for instance, the process that led to the bankruptcy of Yamaichi Securities and the Long-term Credit Bank of Japan). In cases where boundaries that divided the stakeholder and the non-stakeholder can move outwards or shrink inwards according to circumstances, it becomes difficult to define clearly even the interests of stakeholders which are the premise of bargaining. For instance, are the interests of the employee, as defined separately from the interests of the firm, clearly understood by the employee himself (or herself) as being separate?

This point becomes clear when Japanese management is compared with the co-determination in large German firms. In the case of the co-determination system, the rivalry and antagonism between labour and management becomes a reality through the labour laws, the institutionalisation of labour skill, and the powerful labour union movement. In this sense, it is not meaningless to discuss bargaining at the level of an industry or firm in Germany. However, even in Germany, vagueness cannot be avoided as seen in the discussion about whether the role of the employees' representative on supervisory boards ought to adopt the viewpoint of management or take the position of the employees (Däubler [1995], Markovits [1986], Streeck [1996].)

Another characteristic of Japanese management revolves around running the system. Japanese management appears to have a paternalistic streak in that it endeavours to maintain employment. However, the small number of individuals in the firm that do not fit in and are branded as trouble makers are ruthlessly oppressed. At the same time, the 'implicit contract' that is lifetime employment (a contract that the employees alone believed to exist) has been easily cast aside with the retrenchment of middle-aged and older workers. Today, managers are promoting a management that emphasises shareholders and the price of company shares, and doing so in the name of global standards.

Thus, a Japanese firm exists within a multi-layered community, and its operating principles are spread across a spectrum that includes at one extreme symbolic rule through gift exchange and at the other a cold-hearted exercise of power.

In comparison, CIA assumes that Japanese management has an in-built mechanism to suppress rivalry between interests, and this is because decisions on managerial policy are made in the expectation of the alignment of interests. The Japanese firm is viewed as a stakeholder firm, and Japanese management is assumed to mediate the conflicting interests of stakeholders through fictitious negotiations. The blind jump which the bargaining model of the Japanese firm makes in attempting to bridge the twin indeterminacies of the stock company system and Japanese management should now be clear.

Since the bargaining game is a dual fiction (the fiction of hypothetical bargaining and the fiction of the stakeholder), it is of course impossible to provide even a single piece of evidence for the bargaining game. How, after all, are we ever to ascertain that a fair bargaining is taking place in the minds of managers?

Finally, I would like to draw attention to one aspect of the interpretation of the bargaining game. According to Aoki's interpretation, the axiomatic approach to the Nash bargaining game expresses fairness. This is an interpretation derived from the axiom of the symmetricity of the game's players. However, it hardly needs to be said that the Nash bargaining game is defined in response to a given threat-point. Therefore, there is almost no sense in the claim that the game's symmetricity guarantees fairness in cases where the position of the threat-point is, when viewed from some standards, to the great disadvantage of one of the players. For instance, let us assume that the threat-point expresses the following circumstances. The only duty imposed on management with regard to important managerial policies is the duty to inform the labour union about what has been decided, and the labour union is in fact unable to organise a strike. Even if a 'fair' bargaining game took place from this starting point, how can the totality be viewed as fair?

Institutional Complementarity[6]

Centering around the firm, CIA arrays parts of the system along one vector – the firm group (keiretsu), shareholders, the main bank, the financial system, industry bodies, bureaucratic organisations – and other parts along another vector– the labour union and internal and external labour markets. The entire system is broken into individual system parts. So long as the entirety works efficiently when constructed by joining the parts together, it will (it is claimed) form a consistent structural whole.

Why the Lack of an Analysis of Dysfunctions

However, the system's parts will not always fulfill their functions. It is possible that they may at times work in a dysfunctional way. The entire system may fall into a state of imperfect function, or even stop functioning altogether. Why does CIA completely lack the analytical tools to tackle this issue?

I believe there are two reasons for this. The first is that the micro-economics and game theory that CIA is based on cannot analyse any condition other than one in which equilibrium has already been reached where social relations are a combination of mutually optimal acts and rules. Dysfunctions and functional imperfections have already been excluded by strategic rationality and the concept of equilibrium of micro-economics and game theory (for the notion of 'inefficient equilibrium, see below).

The second is that, so long as the Japanese corporate system was as a whole 'successful,' it was assumed that each part of the system must be well-designed, and that the parts must fit together well. (However, as has been shown, each and every part of the Japanese corporate system has serious problems.) This assumption was labelled 'institutional complementarity' and was seen as an important contribution of CIA. However, the proof of this 'institutional complementarity' skates over very thin ice.

1. It is the case that without a system of qualifications along the model of Germany, each firm will have to educate and train their labourers within the firm. In this sense, the imperfection of the

external labour market is a condition for the development of an internal labour market. However, in a situation where the external labour market is functioning sufficiently, and where white- and blue-collar workers have 'portable skills' and can move freely from firm to firm, as the 'hypothesis of efficiency wages' claims, management will endeavour to secure and retain the firm's labourers. According to Cappelli (1999), US firms today face the problem of how to retain labourers and engineers who have lost their sense of loyalty to the firm as a result of never-ending waves of downsizing and restructuring. In other words, even if an external labour market is functioning, it will not necessarily obstruct the formation of an internal labour market.

2. In CIA, the Horizontal Information Structure is coupled with the ranking hierarchy, but in some US firms today the flexible organisational form is viewed as an ideal. In such an organisation, human resources are brought together from both inside and outside the firm according to necessity for each project, a team is formed, and when the project is completed then disbanded. In other words, there is no reason why a decentralised personnel management and a Horizontal Information Structure cannot coexist.

   In the Japanese management of the past, many managerial techniques in addition to the ranking hierarchy were required to maintain the Horizontal Information Structure, including, for instance, the paternalism that intervened even into private life, the team system which burdened the entire team with responsibility, QC circles and TQC movements which were intended to ascertain and strengthen the commitment of employees rather than to realise any actual progress on the shop floor. In other words, the 'coerced solidarity' which CIA calls the Horizontal Information Structure, cannot be guaranteed merely by a ranking hierarchy. If anything, the possibility that the exposure of employees to constant competition for promotion will serve as an obstacle to true solidarity at the workplace.

3. What direct relationship is there between the main bank system and the internal organisations in each firm? The main bank system today is rapidly collapsing, and large firms increasingly rely on financial markets instead of commercial banks. However, it cannot be said that this must result in large-

scale changes to the internal organisations of the firm. While it is true that the firm's internal organisations are changing, and that new systems are being rapidly introduced in corporate governance and workplace governance – splitting companies, turning companies into holding companies, outside board members, executive board systems, downsizing of mid-management positions, the utilisation of temporary workers and the flexi-time system, and so forth – this is the product of the failure of the Japanese corporate system domestically and the intensification of international competition, not of changes in the financial system.

4. In the keiretsu system, the parent company provides technical assistance and helps to develop products. In return, the sub-contractor pays heed to the parent company in regard to increasing and decreasing production. In this sense, the keiretsu is a reciprocal, mutually beneficial relationship.

It might seem that the Toyota Production Method (as exemplified by the kanban system and Just-In-Time) could be implemented only in the keiretsu relationship between the parent company and the sub-contractors, since it requires close co-operation between them. However, as suggested by Toyota's new strategy of the 'optimum global procuring' of generic parts and by the ensuing collapse of the keiretsu, the Toyota Production method is fully compatible with arms-length relationships and competition in markets. In other words, *keiretsu* and markets are to a certain extent interchangeable in the implementation of the Toyota Production Method. This implies that system parts are not necessarily complementary, and that some parts can be substituted with new parts.

Institutional Fetishism

'Institutional complementarity' has not been induced from an observation of the Japanese corporate system. Rather, it was theoretically deduced from an assumption that the system as a whole is performing a positive function (i.e. that the Japanese corporate system is 'succeeding'). In this system, the actor is not able to deviate from a given mode of actions (such as utility maximization), and individual acts do not deviate from rules determined by the system. As a result, the system's performance is that of a machine where a set output is produced by a set input, or can be described mechanically.

In this view of a system, the mechanism which governs the mode of actions cannot change, and actions are necessarily routine. However, in actual life, dysfunctions are inevitable side-effects of systems, and sometimes the entire system will change itself. How can these facts be explained?

Indeed, there has not been even a suggestion of a CIA of the rise and fall of the Bubble Economy, nor of a CIA of the regrettable realities of the corporate governance of Japanese firms (and especially financial organisations) that became so obvious in the 1990s. In a model inhabited only by rational actors, where all social relations are efficient governance structures (agreed to by rational actors), how is it possible for a Bubble Economy to rise and fall, or for corporate governance to fail? The only theoretical possibility left for the CIA to use is to view the Bubble and the failure of corporate governance as a Pareto inefficient allocation of resources, and to use the logic of the prisoner's dilemma – in the prisoner's dilemma, prisoners are separated by prison walls, information is asymmetric and commitment is impossible, as a result of which they become suspicious of one another and confess, despite knowing it is not in their interests, or in other words, individual rationality leads to inefficiency of society as a whole. However, the prisoner's dilemma actually exposes the inherent limits of game theory. When the players know what the result is going to be, why not change the game's rules and play another game in which a more efficient outcome can be obtained? Why are the game's rules given? What are the prison walls that bind prisoners? This is a problem that cannot be solved as long as the postulate of a strategically rational actor is retained (this postulate assumes a rationality where the interests of a given self is the sole standard of evaluation and in which even social relations are the objects of manipulation).

Alternatively, if the argument is that the cause of the Bubble was a large and unforeseen shock – an unexpectedly rapid globalisation of the financial system, Black Monday, political pressure from the USA, the failure of the monetary policies of the Bank of Japan, among other things, can all be given as candidates for this shock – to the Japanese corporate system, the question that must be asked is why rational actors did not immediately change the governance structure in line with the new circumstances? If the various conditions that limit rationality are so severe, what is the point of assuming rationality in the first place? By employing game theory as its theoretical foundation, CIA has also adopted the inherent limits of game theory.

CIA not only cannot produce a satisfactory explanation of the rise and fall of the Bubble Economy or the failures of the Japanese firm in the 1990s, but also derives a frightening proposal about the future Japanese economy from the notion of institutional complementarity. CIA argues roughly as follows. Since the parts of the Japanese corporate system are in a complementary relationship, it is impossible to improve each part. If a part is to be changed, everything has to be changed. If a strategically important part, such as the financial system or the labour market, is exchanged for a new part, then, following the logic of institutional complementarity, all other parts will start to change as well (see Aoki et al. eds. [1996: chapter 13]).

All this 'Successive Waves of Reform Theory' accomplishes is an after-the-fact rationalization of the Big Bang in the financial system and the marketisation of employment relationships that are currently under way. It is silent about what reforms need to be made in what order, and about what safety nets need to be set up beforehand in order to offset these reforms. This rough reform does not bother to imagine what sort of pressure will be brought to bear on those people who shoulder the weight of the system.

Theory for the Sake of Theory?

In order to examine how the CIA of the Japanese firm has been constructed, the order in which the theory and model were created will be introduced.

It is clear that it was a cooperative bargaining game of Japanese management that was first conceived (Aoki [1980]). This was followed by a widening of the scope of analysis, to information (Aoki [1986]) and incentives, shareholders and the main bank, and bureaucratic structures (Aoki [1988, 1990, 1994]). It was not a process in which small additions were made to a basic model, but one in which theoretical requirements to justify the basic model were created as models one after the other.

There are arguments, however, in the various parts of the theory that fall apart when examined closely. For instance, in order to join two contradictory theoretical requirements, the competition for promotion and the solidarity of employees in the labour union, the highly unrealistic notion of individual bargaining with a Personnel Division is advanced; or one of the parties in the negotiating game is said to be the main bank as an agent of the shareholders because the withering away of the General Shareholders Meeting has become so obvious; or in order to demonstrate the 'logical equivalence' of managers who are fair arbitrators in the bargaining game with the managers who directly represent the interests of the shareholders in bargaining, a mathematical convergence relationship is used between the axiomatic approach of the Nash bargaining game and Rubinstein's non-cooperative bargaining game. As argued here, this type of theoretical construct eventually boils down to an argument that depicts the Japanese corporate system as an enormous teleological relationship.

Our questions about the CIA of the Japanese firm are directed at the theoretical undertaking itself as a result of our examination of the theoretical contents. Is the construction of a teleological relationship reflective of the real Japanese corporate system, or of the theory of the CIA?

Appendix: The Non-cooperative Bargaining Game

How is the theory of Micro-economics Mark II constructed? In this chapter, I have focused on the model of principal and agent. Here, I will examine Rubinstein's (1982) theory of the non-cooperative bargaining game. This is first because his theory expresses in a very clear fashion the basic structure and weaknesses of the research strategy (i.e. the Nash program) of the non-cooperative game that dominates game theory today, and second because this theory is used as the mathematical foundation for Aoki's theory of the Japanese firm.

Rubinstein's Game

The problem Rubinstein attempts to solve is one which is seen as a difficult issue for economic theory – how to 'divide a pie.' This is zero sum game in which two individuals have to divide a pie sitting before them. According to circumstances, and according to the player's character and negotiating skill, all possibilities can be thought of. There is not even a guarantee that a Pareto optimal distribution will be realised. Indeed, it was for a long time viewed as common sense in economics that there was no settled solution to the problem of bilateral monopoly.

Rubinstein attempts to solve this through the established approach of the non-cooperative game, of subgame perfection. Let us assume that the two players take turns to make proposals about how to divide the pie. Player I's proposal will be that a certain percentage (a number between 0 and 1 – let us call this x) be allocated to himself, and the rest (1–x) to Player II. Player II will either accept or reject this proposal. If Player II accepts the proposal, the game will finish. If he rejects it, he will make a counter proposal (again a figure between 0 and 1 – let us call this y). Let us say that this proposal y is the percentage Player I will take. In reply, Player I will either accept or reject this proposal. Using the same procedures, a proposal and the choice to accept or reject this proposal will be called a round, and as rounds are made the game will proceed.

In order to exclude the possibility that the game will be non-ending one, both players will be given an incentive – the desire to eat the pie quickly (a time preference). For Player I, for each round, the pie will shrink by a (0<a<1). In the same fashion, Player II has a time preference rate b.

The player's moves (strategy) are the proposals made in all rounds and the response (acceptance or rejection) to the other player's proposal. The Nash Equilibrium is a combination of both moves that are best responses to one another.

Two points are immediately clear about this game. First the original game which begins in the first round (this has the potential to be an infinite game) has exactly the same structure as the subgame which begins from round three. Again, the subgame that begins from round five also has the same structure (and so on). In other words, subgames with exactly the same structure are lined up without end. Therefore, second, if in the first three rounds, Player I's proposal x is countered by Player II's counter proposal y, and if in response Player I's counter-proposal (in round-three) is x, then the combination will be:

$$x \to y \to x$$

If this is the combination, Player II will agree to x in round one due to his (or her) time preference, and since the subgame that begins in round three will have exactly the same structure and solution, the subgame will not run, and the solution of the original game will be for both most desired. Can this sort of solution be expected?

Player II's counter-proposal y has to be at least as desirable as x from his (or her) point of view, but if 1-y is strictly better than 1-x, then it will be rejected by Player I in the next round. This implies that:

$$1-x=b(1-y)$$

In the same fashion, for Player I, the counter-proposal x in round three must be at least as desirable as proposal y in round two, and so:

$$y = a\,x$$

Therefore, $x = (1-b)/(1-ab)$.

Rubinstein has shown that this solution is also an equilibrium at the strategic level.

The Epistemological Structure of the Game

For us, the epistemological structure of the game is important. Let us focus on the following three points. First, although this game is labelled a bargaining game, no actual bargaining takes place at all. Indeed, in a non-cooperative game, speech acts are excluded beforehand as a means of transmitting information or communicating one's will. In the game, information is transmitted through simple symbols or signals or the circumstances themselves. In this bargaining game, all the players actually communicate is the percentages of the pie distribution, and it is assumed that they do not make any attempt to explain why they make the proposals they do.

The attempt to solve a problem through taking turns at making proposals and counter-proposals is reminiscent of the most basic form of speech communication – 'dialogue' and 'discussion.' However, in 'dialogue' and 'discussion,' a basis for each vocalization and criticism must be provided to make it possible to examine the justification for these speech acts. In the bargaining game, all that is offered is a percentage without any articulated justification. Unlike 'dialogue' and 'discussion,' which are created through vocalization, criticism, and counter-argument and which always have the potential to develop in unforeseen directions,

Rubinstein's bargaining game borrows merely the form of the 'dialogue' or 'discussion,' but using deductions about the latter part of the game the first proposal is made. In short, the negotiating game is a 'dialogue in reverse' (Takeda [1998]).

Indeed, in this bargaining game, Player I proposes an equilibrium solution in the first round, and Player II accepts this, thus ending the game (as will be confirmed below, it is not even necessary for Player II to accept the proposal). In this sense, the bargaining game is a 'hypothetical bargaining.'

How is this possible? Here, the second point about the epistemological structure of the non-cooperative game becomes an issue. It is assumed that at the starting point of the bargaining game, once the basic game structure is unveiled, both players immediately make logical deductions with regard to the original game and all the subgames about how their strategies will impact on the other player's moves, and what counter-effect will bounce back (in other words, they calculate the Nash Equilibrium). This means that they take steps to deal with each and every possible future eventuality. Let us call this attempt to solve all possible future problems here and now 'presentiation.'

However, when, for instance, Player I considers the effect his move would have on the other player, since speech communication is not permitted, how can he deduct what Player II's response will be? Not only must Player I have prior knowledge of the form of Player II's deductions, he must also know that Player II fully understands the rules of the game, and knows that he (Player I) also understands the game's rules, and that Player II is fully cognizant of the form of his (Player I's) deductions in developing his strategy. If this is not the case, Player II will misunderstand Player I, and may even make an unexpected move. In addition, Player II must also know all these facts.

As will be readily understood, this process of mutual recognition is a process of infinite retroaction. The situation in which limitless rounds of mutual recognition have all been made is known as 'common knowledge.' The solution of the non-cooperative game (the Nash Equilibrium) requires this common knowledge. How is this sort of limitless round of mutual recognition possible without the mediation of intersubjectivity like speech communication? On the other hand, once speech communication is allowed for, the Nash Program – the research strategy that attempts to explain the realm of all cooperation by reducing it to a non-cooperative game – collapses.

(For instance, the easiest way to realise 'common knowledge' is for the players to meet, and read out the game's rules, but this pre-play communication must be unlimitedly cooperative.) The highly limiting hypothesis of common knowledge is a necessary condition for the Nash Equilibrium. Having demonstrated this point, grave doubts must therefore be raised about the significance of the Nash Program.

The epistemological structure of Rubinstein's bargaining game has been summarised into three points – hypothetical bargaining, presentation, and common knowledge. These in fact are seen in all non-cooperative games (and therefore in the solution to these games, the Nash Equilibrium).

This is true regardless of whether the model chooses as its hypothesis perfect information or imperfect information. Let us now re-examine this problem from the point of view of participant and observer.

Let us imagine an 'objective' observer exists who is looking down on a bargaining game. This observer is all knowing, and has perfect insight into the background of the bargaining, the rules of the game, and the tastes, beliefs and inner hearts of the participants (the players). Since this observer will be able to grasp instantaneously the whole picture from the players' reasoning to the bargaining process, and to the conclusion of the bargaining, the observer will be able to calculate equilibrium as soon as he sees the game. For the observer, all the players' strategies and the entire bargaining game (which is a social relationship) appear as objective 'phenomena.'

Common knowledge enables the players themselves to gaze upon the game they are involved in through the eyes of the all-knowing observer. Since the observer perceives everything, the players through the observer can not only look into and see through their own hearts, but also that of the other players. At the same time, it is possible to know the tastes, beliefs, and reasoning of self and other, and so it is possible to foresee the conclusion of the game when it starts (i.e. presentation). The actual bargaining is not able to move away even a fraction from this simulated game, and so there is no need to actually run the game (i.e. hypothetical bargaining).

Although Micro-economics Mark II began from a criticism of General Equilibrium Theory, the theoretical basis of this version of micro-economics was thought to be provided by the theory of the non-cooperative game. Since General Equilibrium Theory viewed a Walrasian price mechanism as the invisible hand of God, it is ironic that Micro-economics Mark II while criticising General Equilibrium Theory has to assume the existence of an all-knowing observer.

Finally, it is possible to draw one more lesson from Rubinstein's bargaining game. If the time preferences of Player I and Player II are the same, the solution of the game is, for Player I, $x=1/(1+a)$, and for Player II, $1-x=a/(1+a)$. Player I clearly does better. However, since Player II can also immediately calculate the equilibrium when the game starts, why should Player II play a game he knows is to his disadvantage? Why not demand change in the rules? This problem is fundamental to game theory, and emerges in all games.

Of course, it is possible to think of a meta-game which determines the rules of the game. However, it is immediately obvious that so long as strategic rationality is assumed, a higher meta-game will be required to determine the rules of the meta-game, and yet another to determine the rules of the higher meta-game, and so on *ad infinitum*. Why are the rules of the game given? Why do players obey these rules? How are the rules determined? Game theory cannot answer these most fundamental of questions.

Notes

Chapter 1

1 I had an opportunity to interview an attorney for plaintiffs in the US court where appraisal discrimination was in dispute (Rochester, NY, 9 January 2001). At the time of the interview, she handled about 100 cases of employment discrimination. In many of these, the employees claimed appraisal discrimination. There were few cases which were fought over dismissal. Most related to pay increases, promotions and demotions. The plaintiffs at the time had no discernable characteristics such as gender, race, internal hierarchy and occupation etc (although in 13 years since she opened the office there was an increase in female plaintiffs), neither did the defendant companies in terms of the type of business and scale. According to her, companies can be forced to present all personnel records of the plaintiffs including appraisal results. Companies can also be forced to present other employees' personnel records if they are necessary for comparison between the plaintiffs and the other employees. While the trial can proceed with these as evidence, it can take 12-18 months to reach a settlement after a case is presented to the court. When I explained the state of Japanese courts, she was amazed as to how to make a case without personnel records such as appraisal results even though it is not easy to prove discrimination based on these documents.

Chapter 2

1 Aoki notes that 'The term *kanban* traditionally refers to a block of wood bearing the trademark of a merchant shop, but in the present context it refers to a card placed in a vinyl envelope.' Masahiko Aoki, *Information, Incentives and Bargaining in the Japanese Economy*, Cambridge: Cambridge University Press, 1988, p. 22.

Chapter 3

1 This chapter is an updated version of an earlier article. See Osawa Mari, (2001), 'People in Irregular Modes of Employment: Are They Really Not Subject to Discrimination?' *Social Science Japan Journal*, vol. 4, no. 2, pp. 183–199.

2 The issue is bedevilled by problems of terminology, some of which will be discussed in this chapter. The broad category of 'non-full-time employees' include a host of more-or-less insecure working arrangements, including *pāto* ('part-timers'), *arubaito* ('side-jobs' – also part-timers, but generally working shorter hours than *pāto*), *haken* (workers dispatched to the workplace by *haken gyōsha* or private employment agencies) and *shokutaku* (contract workers; often a euphemism for 'full-time part-timers').

3 The Ministry of Labour was merged with the Ministry of Health and Welfare in January 2001, as part of the restructuring of the central bureaucracy. The post-merger ministry is known in English as the Ministry of Health, Labour and Welfare (MHLW).

Chapter 4

1 This is a Japanese translation of Aoki's book entitled *Information, Incentives and Bargaining in the Japanese Economy* that was published in 1988. This quote appears on page 205 of the original English version.

2 This is from page 222 of the English version.

Chapter 5

1 This appears on page 154 of the English version.

2 The comments contained in [ ] in the cited text are the author's.

Chapter 6

Note: The most important book of Koike's regarding intellectual skill is *Shigoto no Keizaigaku* (1991), which was translated into English under the title *The Economics of Work in Japan* (LTCB International Library Foundation) in 1995. However, the translation is not literal. Koike rewrote some phrases that I criticised in 1993. Therefore, in this chapter I have cited from Koike's original Japanese version.

1 This quote appears on page 63 of the English-language edition. See *The Economics of Work in Japan*, Tokyo: LCTB Library Foundation, 1995.

2 This quote appears on page 23 of the English-language edition. See *Skill Formation in Japan and Southeast Asia*, Tokyo: University of Tokyo Press, 1990.

3 This quote appears on page 86 of the English-language edition. See *The Economics of Work in Japan*.

4 This quote appears on page 70 of the English-language edition. See *The Economics of Work in Japan*.

5 This quote appears on pp. 70–71of the English-language edition. See *The Economics of Work in Japan*.

6 This quote appears on page 72 of the English-language edition. See *The Economics of Work in Japan*.

7 This quote appears on page 63 of the English-language edition. See *The Economics of Work in Japan*.

Chapter 8

1 In Savage's approach, a decision-maker's information structure is described in terms of the specific partition of the world. See L. S. Savage (1954).

2 The difference between a classical contract and a relational contract was demonstrated by Macneil's research. See, for instance, Macneil (1978).

3 Macneil views presentiation together with discreteness as a characteristic of the classical contract. For presentiation, see the appendix to this chapter.

4 I am indebted to Kamii Yoshihiko for this point.

5 This paragraph is based on Frug (1984).

6 The following section is based partly on Takeda (2000).

References

Japanese-language books in the following list were all published in Tokyo, unless specified otherwise.

Adler, Paul S., 1992, 'The "Learning Bureaucracy": New United Motor Manufacturing Inc.', *Research in Organizational Behavior*, vol. 15.

Aichi Labour Institute, 1990, *Toyota Gurūpu no Shinsenryaku: 'Kōzō Chōsei' ka no Jidōsha Sangyō* (*The New Strategy of the Toyota Group: 'Structural Adjustment' in the Japanese Automobile Industry*), Shin Nihon Shuppansha.

Aichi Prefecture, 1987, *Chiteki Jukuren no Keisei: Aichi-ken no Kigyō* (*The Formation of Intellectual Skills: Companies in Aichi Prefecture*), Aichi-ken Rōdō-bu (written by Koike, Kazuo, Muramatsu, Kuramitsu and Hisamoto, Norio).

Alchian, Armen and Demsetz, Harold, 1972, 'Production, Information Costs, and Economic Organization', *American Economic Review*, vol. 62.

Aoki, Masahiko, 1980, 'A Model of the Firm as a Stockholder-Employee Cooperative Game', *American Economic Review*, vol. 70.

.... 1986, 'Horizontal vs. Vertical Information Structure of the Firm', *American Economic Review*, vol. 76.

.... 1988, *Information, Incentives and Bargaining in the Japanese Economy*, Cambridge: Cambridge University Press.

.... 1989, *Nihon Kigyō no Soshiki to Jōhō* (*Organization and Information of Japanese Companies*), Tōyō Keizai Shinpōsha.

.... 1990, 'Towards an Economic Model of the Japanese Firm', *Journal of Economic Literature*, vol. 28.

.... 1992, *Nihon Keizai no Seido Bunseki: Jōhō, Insentibu, Kōshō Gēmu*, Chikuma Shobō (Japanese translation of Aoki 1988).

.... 1994, 'Contingent Governance of Team Production: Analysis of Institutional Complementarity', *International Economic Review*, vol. 35.

.... 1995, *Keizai Shisutemu no Shinka to Tagenka* (*The Evolution and Plurality of Economic Systems*), Tōyō Keizai Shinpōsha.

Aoki, Masahiko and Dore, Ronald (eds), 1994, *The Japanese Firm: Sources of Competitive Strength*, Oxford and New York: Oxford University Press.

Aoki, Masahiko, Kim, Hyung-ki and Okuno, Masahiro (eds), 1996. The *Role of Government in East Asian Economic Development: Comparative Institutional Analysis.* New York: Oxford University Press.

Aoki, Masahiko, Koike, Kazuo and Nakatani, Iwao, 1986, *Nihon Kigyō no Keizaigaku* (*Economics of Japanese Companies*), TBS Britanica.

Aoki, Masahiko and Okuno, Masahiro (eds), 1996, *Keizai Shisutemu no Hikaku Seido Bunseki* (*Comparative Institutional Analysis of Economic Systems*), Tokyo Daigaku Shuppankai.

Aoki, Masahiko, Okuno, Masahiro, and Okazaki Tetsuji (eds), 1999, *Shijō no Yakuwari – Kokka no Yakuwari* (*The Role of Markets, The Role of Government*), Tōyō Keizai Shinpōsha.

Asakura, Mutsuko, 2000 [1998], 'Maruko Keihōki Jiken ni kan-suru Hojū Iken-sho' (Supplementary Opinion on the Maruko Alarm Co. Incident). *Rōdō Hōritsu Junpō* 1473: 14–20. Originally presented to the Tokyo High Court, 1 October 1998.

Asakura, Mutsuko and Kon'no, Hisako, 1977, *Josei Rōdō Hanrei Gaido* (*Guidebook on Cases of Women's Labour*), Yūhikaku.

Asanuma, Banri, 1997, *Nihon no Kigyō Soshiki, Kakushinteki Tekiō no Mekanizumu, Chōki Torihiki Kankei no Kōzō to Kinō* (*Japanese Corporate Structures: The Mechanism of Innovative Adaptation and the Structure and Function of the Long Term Relationship*), Tōyō Keizai Shinpōsha.

Asao, Uichi, 1993, 'Forukusu Wāgen-sha no Seiseki Satei Kyōyaku (Labour-Management Agreement of Performance Appraisals at the Volkswagen Company),' *Tōhō Gakushi*, vol. 22.

Asao, Uichi, Saruta, Masaki, Nohara, Hikari, Fujita, Eishi and Yamashita, Motohiko, 1999, *Shakai Kankyō no Henka to Jidōsha Seisan Shisutemu: Toyota Shisutemu wa Kawattanoka* (*Social Circumstances and Automobile Production Systems: Has the Toyota System Changed?*), Hōritsu Bunkasha.

Binmore, Ken, 1990, *Essays on the Foundations of Game Theory*, Oxford: Basic Blackwell.

Bosch, Gerhard and Lehndorff, Steffan, 1995, 'Working Time and the Japanese Challenge: The Search for a European Answer,' *International Contributions to Labour Studiese*, no. 5.

Bourdieu, Pierre, 1980, *Le Sens Pratique*, Paris: Les Édition de Minuit.

Bratton, William W. Jr., 1989, 'The "Nexus of Contract" Corporation: A Critical Appraisal', *Cornell Law Review*, vol. 74.

Cappelli, Peter, 1999, *The New Deal at Work: Managing the Market-Driven Workforce*, Boston: Harvard Business School Press.

Chiba, Toshio, 1990, ''90-nen Chinage Kekka o Keizaironteki ni Sōkatsu suru (Comments on Wage Negotiations in 1990),' *Chingin Jitsumu*, no. 641.

Chūma, Hiroyuki and Nakamura, Jirō, 1990, 'Joshi Pāto Rōdō Chingin no Kettei'in-Hedonikku Apurōchi' (Factors Deciding Wages for Female Part-time Work-a Hedonic Approach). *Nihon Rōdō Kenkyū Zasshi* 369.

Coase, Ronald, 1937, 'The Nature of the Firm', *Economica N. S.*, 4.

Danjo Kyōdō Sankaku Kaigi Eikyōchōsa Senmon Chōsakai (Specialist Committee on Gender Impact Assessment and Evaluation, Council for Gender Equality) 2002, *Raifusutairu no Sentaku to Zeisei, Shakaihoshō Seido, Koyō Shisutemu ni kansuru Hōkoku* (Report on 'Lifestyle Selection and Taxation, Social Security and Employment Systems'), Danjo Kyōdō Sankaku Kaigi Eikyō Chōsa Senmon Chōsakai.

Däubler, Wolfgang, 1995, *Das Arbeitsrecht 1*, Reinbek: Rowohlt.

DeMott, Deborah, 1988, 'Beyond Metaphor: An Analysis of Fiduciary Obligation', *Duke Law Journal*.

Endō, Kōshi, 1999, *Nihon no Jinji Satei (Personnel Assessments in Japan)*, Kyoto: Minerva Shobō.

.... 2001, 'Ginō no Shogainen to Jinji Satei (Concepts of Skills and Personnel Assessments),' *(Meiji University) Keiei Ronshū*, vol. 49, nos. 1–2.

Frug, Gerald E., 1984, 'The Ideology of Bureaucracy in American Law', *Harvard Law Review*, vol. 97.

Fujimoto, Takahiro, 1997, *Seisan Shisutemu no Shinkaron (Evolution of Production Systems)*, Yūhikaku.

.... 1999, *Evolution of Manufacturing Systems at Toyota*, New York, Oxford University Press.

Fujimoto, Takahiro and Clark, Kim B., 1991, *Product Development Performance: Strategy, Organization and Management in the World Auto Industry*, Boston, Harvard Business School Press.

.... 1993, *Seihin Kaihatsuryoku* (Japanese translation of Fujimoto and Clark 1991), Daiyamondosha

Fujimura, Hiroyuki, 1989, 'Seiseki Satei no Kokusai Hikaku (An International Comparison of Performance Appraisals),' *Nihon Rōdō Kyōkai Zasshi*, no. 362.

Furugōri, Tomoko, 1997, *Hiseiki Rōdō no Keizai Bunseki (Economic Analysis of Irregular Labour)*, Tōyō Keizai Shinpōsha.

Graham, Laurie, 1994, *On the Line at Subaru-Isuzu: The Japanese Model and American Workers*, Ithaca: ILR Press.

Hyōdō, Tsutomu, 1971, *Nihon ni okeru Rōshi Kankei no Tenkai (The Development of Industrial Relations in Japan)*, Tokyo Daigaku Shuppankai.

Imai, Ken'ichi and Komiya, Ryūtarō (eds), 1989, *Nihon no Kigyō (Japanese Companies)*, Tokyo Daigaku Shuppankai.

.... 1994, *Business Enterprise in Japan: Views of Leading Japanese Economists*; translation edited and introduced by Ronald Dore and Hugh Whittaker, Cambridge, Mass. : MIT Press.

Inoue, Masao, 1992, 'Shohyō: Koike Kazuo, 'Shigoto no Keizaigaku (Book review: Koike Kazuo, 'The Economics of Work in Japan')',' *Ōhara Shakai Mondai Kenkyūjo Zasshi*, nos. 400/401, March.

.... 1997, *Shakai Henyō to Rōdō: 'Rengō' no Seiritsu to Taishū Shakai no Seijuku (Social Transformation and Labour. The Formation of 'Rengō' and Maturity of a Mass Society)*, Bokutakusha.

.... 2000, 'Rōdō Kumiai (Labour Unions),' *Ōhara Shakai Mondai Kenkyūjo Zasshi*, no. 50.

Ishida, Mitsuo, Fujimura, Hiroyuki, Hisamoto, Norio and Matsumura, Fumito, 1997, *Nihon no Rīn Seisan Hōshiki: Jidōsha Kigyō no Jirei (Lean Production Systems in Japan: A Case Study of Automobile Companies)*, Chūō Keizaisha.

Itami, Hiroyuki and Kagono, Tadao, 1989, *Zemināru Keieigaku Nyūmon (Seminar: Introductory Business Administration)*, Nihon Keizai Shimbunsha.

.... 1993, *Zemināru Keieigaku Nyūmon (Seminar: Introductory Business Administration), 2nd edition*, Nihon Keizai Shimbunsha.

Iwashita, Tomokazu, Konno, Hisako, Takizawa, Shūichi and Matsumura, Fumio, 2000, 'Maruko Keihōki: Rinji Shain Chingin Sabetsu Soshō de

Wakai Seiritsu-Kono Soshō to Undō ga Hasshin suru Messēji' (Maruko Alarm: The Temporary Workers Wage Discrimination Suit Reaches Out-of-Court Settlement-The Message Sent Out by this Suit and the Associated Movement). *Rōdō Hōritsu Junpō* 1473.

Jinno, Naohiko and Kaneko, Masaru (eds), 1999, *'Fukushi' Seifu e no Teigen* (*A New Agenda for the 'Welfare Government'*), Iwanami Shoten.

Kamii, Yoshihiko, 1993, 'Minkan Daikigyō no Rōdō Mondai: "Nihonteki Keiei" ka no Rōdō Mondai (Labour Problems in Large Private Companies: Labour under Japanese Management),' in Totsuka, Hideo, and Tokunaga, Shigeyoshi (eds), *Gendai Nihon no Rōdō Mondai: Atarashii Paradaimu o Motomete* (*Labour Problems in Contemporary Japan: In Search of a New Paradigm*), Kyoto: Minerva Shobō.

.... 1994, *Rōdōkumiai no Shokuba Kisei: Nihon Jidōsha Sangyō no Jirei Kenkyū* (*Labour Unions' Work Regulations: A Case Study of the Japanese Automobile Industry*), Tokyo Daigaku Shuppankai.

Kaneda Hideharu, 1991, *Posuto Toyota Hōshiki* (*The Post-Toyota System*), Paru Shuppan.

Kaneko, Masaru, 1991, 'Kigyō Shakai no Keisei to Nihon Shakai: "Shisan Shoyū Minshushugi" no Kiketsu (The Formation of Company Life and the Characteristics of Japanese Society: The Result of Property Owning Democracy after the Second World War),' in Tokyo Daigaku Shakai Kagaku Kenkyūjo (ed.), *Gendai NihonShakai* (*Contemporary Japanese Society*), vol. 5, Tokyo Daigaku Shuppankai.

.... (ed.), 1996, *Gendai Shihonshugi to Sēfutī-netto* (*Contemporary Capitalism and Safetynets*), Hosei Daigaku Shuppankyoku.

.... 1997, *Shijō to Seido no Seiji Keizaigaku* (*The Political Economy of Markets and Institutions*), Tokyo Daigaku Shuppankai.

.... 1999a, *Sēfutīnetto no Seijikeizaigaku* (*Political Economy of the Safetynet*), Chikuma Shobō.

.... 1999b, *Shijō* (*The Market*), Iwanami Shoten.

.... 1999c, *Han-gurōbarizumu: Shijō Kaikaku no Senryakuteki Shikō* (*Anti-globalism: A Strategy for Market Reform*), Iwanami Shoten.

.... *Nihon Saiseiron*, (*The Arguments for Economic Revival in Japan*), NHK Bukkusu.

Kaneko, Masaru and Mori, Kiyoshi, 1993, 'Nihon Keizai no Sābisuka Sofutoka to Kigyō Kazei: Sābisuka Sofutoka to Bunshaka no Kurosuwādo (The Growth of Service Industries and the Structure of Japanese Enterprises),' *Keizai Shirin*, vol. 61, no. 1.

Kawanishi, Hirosuke, 1981, *Kigyōbetsu Kumiai no Jittai* (*The Realities of Enterprise Unions*), Nihon Hyōronsha.

Koike, Kazuo, 1977a, *Shokuba no Rōdō Kumiai to Sanka: Rōshi Kankei no Nichi-Bei Hikaku* (*Participation of Labour Unions in Management at the Workplace: A Comparison of Industrial Relations in Japan and the U.S.*), Tōyō Keizai Shinpōsha.

.... 1977b, 'Kigyōbetsu Kumiai no Hatsugenryoku: Kumazawa Makoto-shi no Hihan ni Kotaete (Influences of Enterprise Labour Unions: A reply to Kumazawa Makoto's Criticism),' *Nihon Rōdō Kyōkai Zasshi*, April.

.... 1981, *Nihon no Jukuren* (*Skills in Japan*), Yūhikaku.

.... 1983, 'Josetsu: Howaitokarāka Kumiai Moderu (A Hypothesis of the

White-collarization of Blue-collar Workers),' *80-nendai no Rōshi Kankei*, edited by Nihon Rōdō Kyōkai, Nihon Rōdō Kyōkai.

.... 1986, 'Naibu Shōshinsei no Nichi-Bei Hikaku (US-Japan Comparison of Internal Promotion System),' in Aoki, Masahiko, Koike, Kazuo, and Nakatani, Iwao, *Nihon Kigyō no Keizaigaku (The Economics of the Japanese Companies)*, TBS Britanica, 1986.

.... 1989, 'Chiteki Jukuren to Chōki no Kyōsō (Intellectual Skills and Long-Term Competition),' in Imai, Ken'ichi and Komiya, Ryūtarō (eds), *Nihon no Kigyō (Japanese Companies)*,Tokyo Daigaku Shuppankai.

.... 1991, *Shigoto no Keizaigaku (The Economics of Work in Japan)*,Tōyō Keizai Shinpōsha.

.... 1993, 'Chiteki Jukuren Sairon: Nomura Masami-shi no Hihan ni Taishite (Restatement on the Theory of Intellectual Skills: A Reply to Nomura Masami's Criticism),' *Nihon Rōdō Kenkyū Zasshi*, July.

.... 1994, 'Intellectual Skills and Long-Term Competition,' in Imai, Ken'ichi and Komiya, Ryūtarō (eds), *Business Enterprise in Japan*, Cambridge, Mass. : MIT Press 1994.

.... 1996, *The Economics of Work in Japan*, LTCB International Library Foundation.

.... 1997, *Nihon Kigyō no Jinzai Keisei: Fukakujitsusei ni Taisho suru tameno Nōhau (Skill Formation in Japanese Companies: Know-how in an Uncertain Society)*, Chūkō Shinsho.

.... 1999, *Shigoto no Keizaigaku (The Economics of Work in Japan)*, 2nd edition, Tōyō Keizai Shinpōsha.

Koike, Kazuo, Chūma, Hiroyuki and Ōta, Sōichi , 2001, *Monozukuri no Ginō: Jidōsha Sangyō no Genba de (Manufacturing Skills: From Workplaces in the Automobile Industry)*, Tōyō Keizai Shinpōsha.

Koike, Kazuo and Inoki, Takenori (eds), 1987, *Jinzai Keisei no Kokusai Hikaku (An International Comparison of Human Resource Developments: Southeast Asian Countries and Japan)*, Tōyō Keizai Shinpōsha.

Kōsei-Rōdōshō (Ministry of Health, Labour and Welfare), 2002, *Heisei 13-nen Pāto-taimu Rōdōsha Sōgō Jittai Chōsa Hōkoku (Report on the General Survey of the Conditions of Part-time Workers in 2001)*, Ministry of Finance Printing Bureau.

Kōsei-Rōdōshō (Ministry of Health, Labour and Welfare), 2003, *Heisei 14-nen-ban Josei Rōdō Hakusho (White Paper on Working Women, 2002)*, 21-seiki Shokugyō Zaidan.

Kōshiro, Kazuyoshi and Rengō Sōgō Seikatsu Kaihatsu Kenkyūjo, 1995, *Sengo 50-nen: Sangyō, Koyō, Rōdōshi (50 Years After the War: The History of Industries, Employment and Labour)*, Nihon Rōdō Kenkyū Kikō.

Kreps, David M., 1990, *Game Theory and Economic Modelling*, Oxford: Clarendon Press.

Kumazawa Makoto, 1997, *Nōryokushugi to Kigyō Shakai (Meritocracy and the Corporate System)*, Iwanami Shinsho.

Macneil, Ian, 1978, 'Contracts: Adjustment of Long-term Economic Relations Under Classical, Neoclassical, and Relational Contract Law', *Northwestern University Law Review*, vol. 72.

Markovits, Andrei, 1986, *The Politics of the West German Trade Unions*, Cambridge: Cambridge University Press.

Mizumachi, Yūichirō, 1997, *Pāto-taimu Rōdō no Hōritsu Seisaku* (*Legal Policy on Part-time Workers*). Yūhikaku.

Nagase, Nobuko, 1994, 'Kikon Joshi no Koyō Shūgyō Keitai no Sentaku ni kan-suru Jisshō Bunseki: Pāto to Seishain (Empirical Analysis of Married Women's Choices of Mode of Employment: Part-timers and Regular Employees),' *Nihon Rōdō Kenkyū Zasshi*, no. 418.

.... 1995a, 'Joshi no Shūgyō Sentaku ni tsuite' (On Women's Employment Choices). Doctoral dissertation, University of Tokyo.

.... 1995b, '"Pāto Sentaku" no Jihatsusei to Chingin Kansū (The Voluntariness of the 'Choice to Work Part-time' and the Wage Function),' *Nihon Keizai Kenkyū*, vol. 28.

Nagayoshi, Hiromi, 2000–01, 'Jinji Kōka ni taisuru Hōteki Kisei no Nichi-Bei Hikaku (US-Japan Comparison of Legal Regulations against Performance Appraisals) (1) (2),'(*Chūō University*) *Hōgaku Shinpō*, vol. 107, nos. 7–8, 9–10.

Nakamura, Jirō and Chūma, Hiroyuki, 1994, 'Hedonikku Chingin Apurōchi ni yoru Joshi Pāto-taimu Rōdōsha no Chingin Kettei' (Determining Wages for Female Part-time Workers Using the Hedonic Wage Approach). *Nihon Rōdō Kenkyū Zasshi*, no. 415.

Nakamura, Keisuke, Satō, Hiroki and Kamiya, Takuhei, 1988, *Rōdō Kumiai wa Hontō ni Yakudatte irunoka* (*Are Labour Unions Really Useful for Employees and Society?*), Sōgō Rōdō Kenkyūjo.

Nakanishi, Yō, 1982, *Zōho – Nihon ni okeru 'Shakai Seisaku, Rōdō Mondai Kenkyū: Shihonshugi Kokka to Rōshi Kankei* (*The Research History of Social Policy and Labour Problems: The Capitalist State and Industrial Relations*), Tokyo Daigaku Shuppankai.

Nakata, Yoshifumi, 1997a, 'Nihon ni okeru Kigyōkan Chingin Kakusa no Genjō: Jidōsha Sangyō ni Miru Teishōkomi Chin'ageritsu Kōshō to Kigyō Keiretsugata Rōshi Kankei no Motsu Chingin Kakusa Koteika Kōka (The Realities of Wage Disparities by Company-size: Bargaining Over Wage Increases and the Effect of Fixed Wage Disparities in Labour-management Relations in Keiretsu Firms in the Case of the Automobile Industry),' *Nihon Rōdō Kenkyū Zasshi*, no. 449.

Nakata, Yoshifumi, 1997b, 'Nihon ni okeru Danjo Chingin Kakusa no Yō'in Bunseki: Dō'itsu Shokushu ni Tsuku Danjo Rōdōsha-kan ni Chingin Kakusa wa Sonzai Suru no ka?' (Analysis of Factors in Gendered Wage Differentials in Japan: Does a Wage Differential Exist between Male and Female Workers Employed in the Same Occupational Category?), in Chūma, Hiroyuki and Suruga, Terukazu (eds), *Koyō Kankō no Henka to Josei Rōdō* (*Changing Employment Practices and Female Labour*), Tokyo Daigaku Shuppankai: 173–205.

Nihon Rōdō Kenkyū Kikō, 1994, *Chōsa Kenkyū Hōkokusho, no. 60, Neo-Kōporatizumu no Kokusai Hikaku: Atarashii Seiji Keizai Moderu no Tansaku* (*Research Report no. 60: International Comparison of Neo-corporatism*), Nihon Rōdō Kenkyū Kikō.

.... 1998, 'Kanri Shokusō no Koyō Kanri Shisutemu ni kansuru Sōgōteki Kenkyū (Comprehensive Study of Personnel Management System for Managers) (final),' *Chōsa Kenkyū Hōkokusho*, no. 107.

Nikkeiren (Nihon Keieisha Dantai Renmei) Kōhōbu (Japan Federation of

Employers' Association, Public Relations Division) (ed.), 1996, *Jinji Kōka Fōmattoshū* (*A Collection of Personnel Assessment Formats*), Nikkeiren.

Nimura, Kazuo, 1984, 'Kigyōbetsu Kumiai no Rekishiteki Haikei (The Historical Background of Enterprise Unions),' *Shiryōshitsuhō*, Hōsei Daigaku Ōhara Shakai Mondai Kenkyūjo, no. 305.

Nishiguchi, Toshihiro and Beaudet, Alexandre, 2000, 'Ba to Jiko Soshikika: Aishin Seiki Kasai to Toyota Gurūpu no Taiō (Ba and Self-Organisation: the Fire at Aisin and the Toyota Group),' in Itami, Hiroyuki et al. (eds), *Ba no Dainamizumu to Kigyō* (*Ba Dynamism and Companies*), Tōyō Keizai Shinpōsha.

Nitta, Michio, 1988, *Nihon no Rōdōsha Sanka* (*Workers' Participation in Management Decisions*), Tokyo Daigaku Shuppankai.

.... 1993, '"Pāto-taimu Rōdō" no Jittai' (Conditions of "Part-time Work"). *Jurist* 1021: 33–38.

Nohara, Hikari and Fujita, Eishi (eds), 1988, *Jidōsha Sangyō to Rōdōsha: Rōdōsha Kanri no Kōzō to Rōdōshazō* (*The Automobile Industry and its Workers: Labour and Personnel Management and the Characteristics of Workers*), Hōritsu Bunkasha.

Nomura, Masami, 1993a, *Jukuren to Bungyō: Nihon Kigyō to Teirāshugi* (*Skills and Division of Labour: Taylorism in Japanese Companies*), Ochanomizu Shobō.

.... 1993b, *Toyotizumu: Nihongata Seisan Shisutemu no Seijuku to Henyō* (*Toyotism: The Maturity and Transformation of a Japanese Production System*), Kyoto: Minerva Shobō.

.... 1994, *Shūshin Koyō* (*Life-time Employment*), Iwanami Shoten.

.... 2000, 'Chiteki Jukuren no Jisshōteki Konkyo: Koike Kazuo ni okeru Riron to Jisshō (Empirical Evidence of the Theory of Intellectual Skills: Theory and Empirical Evidence in the Case of Koike Kazuo),' *Ōhara Shakai Mondai Kenkyūjo Zasshi*, October.

.... 2001, *Chiteki Jukuren-ron Hihan: Koike Kazuo ni okeru Riron to Jisshō* (*Criticism on the Theory of Intellectual Skill – Theory and Empirical Evidence of Koike Kazuo*), Kyoto: Minerva Shobō.

.... 2003, *Nihon no Rōdō Kenkyū: Sono Fu no Isan* (*Labour Studies in Japan: Their Negative Legacies*), Kyoto: Minerva Shobō

Ogata, Keiko, 1999, 'Doitsu ni okeru Seiseki Kakyū Seido to Hōtekikisei no Kōzō (Performance-related Pay and Legal Framework of its Regulations in Germany),' *Kikan Rōdō-hō*, nos. 190–191.

Onnatachi no Ōshū Chōsadan (Women's Survey Party to Europe), 2000, *Nakusō: Pāto, Keiyaku Rōdō, Haken Sabetsu-Kintō Taigū wa Sekai no Jōshiki* (*Wipe Out Discrimination against Part-timers, Contract Workers and Agency Workers-Parity of Treatment is Global Common Sense*), Onnatachi no Ōshū Chōsadan.

Ono, Akira, 1989, *Nihonteki Koyō Kankō to Rōdō Shijō* (*Japanese-style Employment Practices and Labour Markets*), Tōyō Keizai Shinpōsha.

Ōno, Taiichi, 1978, *Toyota Seisan Hōshiki: Datsukibo no Keiei o Mezashite* (The Toyota Production System: Free from Economies-of-Scale Management), Daiyamondosha.

Ōsawa, Machiko, 1993, *Keizai Henka to Joshi Rōdō – Nichibei no Hikaku Kenkyū* (Economic Change and Women's Work-Comparative Research on Japan and America), Nihon Keizai Hyōronsha.

Ōsawa, Mari, 1994, 'Nihon no "Pāto-taimu Rōdō" towa Nanika' (What is 'Part-time Labour' in Japan?), *Kikan Rōdōhō*, 170.

Ōsawa, Mari, 1997, '"Pāto-taimu" Rōdō to Kintō Shogū Gensoku-Keizaigakuteki Apurōchi ('Part-time' Labour and the Principle of Parity of Treatment – an Economic Approach). *Nihon Rōdō-hō Gakkai-shi* 90: 95–110.

.... 2000, 'Government Approaches to Gender Equality in the mid-1990s.' *Social Science Japan Journal*, 3(1): 3–19.

Oyama Yōichi (ed.), 1985, *Kyodai Kigyō Taisei to Rōdōsha: Toyota no Jirei (Workers in Big Business: The Case of Toyota)*, Ochanomizu Shobō.

Parker, Mike and Slaughter, Jane, 1988, *Choosing Sides: Unions and the Team Concept*, A Labor Notes Book.

Rōdōshō (Ministry of Labour), 1992, *Heisei 2-nen Pāto-taimu no Jittai: Pāto-taimu Rōdōsha Sōgō Jittai Chōsa Hōkoku (Conditions of Part-timers in 1990: Report on the General Survey of the Conditions of Part-time Workers)*, Ministry of Finance Printing Bureau.

.... 1997a, *Pāto-taimu Rōdōsha Sōgō Jittai Chōsa Hōkoku Heisei 7-nen (Report on the General Survey of the Conditions of Part-time Workers 1995)*, Ministry of Finance Printing Bureau.

.... 1997b, *Pāto-taimu Rōdō ni Kakaru Chōsa Kenkyūkai Hōkoku (Report from the Survey Research Group on Part-time Labour)*, Ministry of Labour.

.... 2000a, *Pāto-taimu Rōdō ni Kakaru Koyō Kanri Kenkyūkai Hōkoku (Report from the Research Group on Employment and Management of Part-time Labour*; known as 'the Monosashi Report'), Ministry of Labour.

.... 2000b, *Heisei 12-nen-ban Rōdō Hakusho (White Paper on Labour, 2000)*, Nihon Rōdō Kenkyū Kikō.

.... 2000c, *Danjo Koyō Kikai Kintō Taisaku Kihon Hōshin (Basic Policy on Measures for Gender Equality in Employment Opportunities)*, Ministry of Labour.

Rubinstein, Ariel, 1982, 'A Perfect Equilibrium in a Bargaining Model', *Econometrica*, vol. 50.

Rubinstein, Ariel, 1991 'Comments on the Interpretation of Game Theory', *Econometrica*, vol. 59.

Saruta, Masaki, 1995, *Toyota Shisutemu to Rōmu Kanri (Labour and Personnel Management in Toyota)*, Zeimu Keiri Kyōkai.

Savage, Leonard J., 1954, *The Foundations of Statistics*, New York: John Wiley and Sons.

Scher, Mark J., 1997, *Japanese Interfirm Networks and Their Main Banks*, New York: Palgrave.

Seiyama, Kazuo, 2000, 'Jendā to Kaisō no Rekishi to Riron (Histories and Theories of Gender and Class)' in Seiyama, Kazuo (ed.), *Nihon no Kaisō Shisutemu 4 Jendā, Shijō, Kazoku (Class System in Japan Vol. 4: Gender, Market and Family)*, Tokyo Daigaku Shuppankai.

Sennett, Richard, 1998, *The Corrosion of Character*, New York: W. W. Norton & Company.

Streeck, Wofgang, 1996, 'Lean Production in the German Automobile Industry: A Test Case for Convergence Theory', in S. Berger and R. Dore (eds), *National Diversity and Global Capitalism*, Ithaca: Cornell University Press.

Sugeno, Kazuo and Suwa, Yasuo, 1998, 'Pāto-taimu Rōdō to Kintō Taigū

Gensoku-Sono Hikakuhō-teki Nōto' (Part-time Labour and the Principle of Parity of Treatment-Notes from Comparative Legal Studies), in Kitamura, Ichirō (ed.), *Gendai Yōroppa-hō no Tenbō* (*Prospects for Contemporary European Law*), Tokyo Daigaku Shuppankai: 113–134.

Tachibanaki, Toshiaki and Rengō Sōgō Seikatsu Kaihatsu Kenkyūjo (eds), 1993, *Rōdō Kumiai no Keizaigaku: Kitai to Genjitsu* (*The Economics of Labour Unions: Expectations and Realities*), Tōyō Keizai Shinpōsha.

Takahashi, Yūkichi, 1998, 'Nihonteki Keiei no Henbō to Rōdō Kumiai no Yukue (Changing Japanese-style Management and the Future of Labour Unions),' *Nihon Rōdō Shakaigakkai Nenpō, no. 9, Rōdō Kumiai ni Mirai wa aruka*, Nihon Rōdō Shakaigakkai.

Takeda, Shigeo, 1998 'Strategy and Community: Critical Notes on the Post-Walrasian Microeconomics', Working Paper No. 67, Institute of Comparative Economic Studies, Hōsei University.

.... 2000, 'Shijō o Rikai suru tame ni – Kōi, Mekanizumu, Seido no Shiten kara' (Understanding markets: From the viewpoint of actions, mechanisms, and institutions), in Yoshinori Shiozawa ed., *Hōhō to shite no Shinka* (*Evolution as Methodology*), Springer Verlag Tokyo.

Tanaka, Hirohide, 1982, 'Rensai Intabyū: Nihonteki Koyō Kankō o Kizuita Hitotachi = Sono 2, Yamamoto Keimei shi ni Kiku (3) (Interview Series: The People who Established Japanese Employment Practices, No.2, Interviewee – Yamamoto Keimei),' *Nihon Rōdō Kyōkai Zasshi*, September.

Tokumaru, Sōya, 1999, *Nihon teki Keiei no Kōbō – TQC wa Wareware ni nani o Motarashita no ka* (*The Rise and Fall of Japanese Management: What Has TQC Done to Us?*), Daiyamondosha.

Tōnai, Kazuhiro, 1995, 'Doitsu ni okeru Jinji Kōka Seido no Unyō Jittai (The Realities of the Operating Performance Appraisal System in Germany),' *Nihon Rōmu Gakkai Nenpō*, no. 24.

Uchiyama, Mitsuo, 1954, *Kanbu Tōsō kara Taishū Tōsō e* (*From a Leaders' Struggle to a Mass Struggle*), Rōdō Junpōsha.

Ueda, Hirofumi, 1989, 'Jidōsha Sangyō no Kigyō Kaisō Kōzō: Jidōsha Mēkā to Ichiji Buhin Mēkā no Ketsugō Kankei (1) (The Hierarchical Supplier System in the Japanese Automobile Industry (1)),' (Osaka City University) *Kikan Keizai Kenkyū*, vol. 12, no. 3.

.... 1992, 'Jidōsha Buhin Mēkā ni okeru Furekishibiritī no Keisei to Rōshi Kankei (1) (Flexibility of Parts Suppliers and their Industrial Relations),' (Osaka City University), *Kikan Keizai Kenkyū*, vol. 15, no. 3.

.... 1995, 'Jidōsha Buhin Mēkā to Kaihatsu Shisutemu (Product Development in Automobile Parts Manufacturers),' in Akashi, Yoshihiko and Ueda, Hirofumi (eds), *Nihon Kigyō no Kenkyū Kaihatsu Shisutemu* (*Research and Product Development System in Japanese Manufacturing Companies*), Tokyo Daigaku Shuppankai.

.... 1998, 'The Subcontracting System during the Japanese Wartime Economy', *Japanese Yearbook on Business History*, vol.13.

.... 2000a, 'Genchi Seisan, Kaihatsu to Sapuraiya Shisutemu: Eikoku Nikkei Jidōsha Kigyō no Jirei (The Supplier System in Japanese Automotive Transplants in the UK),' in Morisawa, Keiko and Ueda, Hirofumi (eds), *Gurōbaru Kyōsō to Rōkaraizēshon* (*Global Competition and Localisation*), Tokyo Daigaku Shuppankai.

.... 2000b, 'Sapuraiya-ron ni Kansuru Ichikōsatsu (A Study of the Supplier System),' (Osaka City University) *Kikan Keizai Kenkyū*, vol. 23, no. 2.

.... 2001, 'Jidōsha Seisan no Mojūruka to Sapuraiya (Modularization and Suppliers in the Automotive Industry),' (Chūō University) *Keizaigaku Ronsan*, vol. 41, no. 5.

Ujihara, Shōjirō, 1953, 'Waga Kuni ni okeru Daikōjō Rōdōsha no Seikaku (Social Characters of Factory Workers in Large Companies in Japan),' Nihon Jinbun Kagakkai, *Shakaiteki Kinchō no Kenkyū (Social Tensions)*, Yūhikaku.

Wada, Hajime, 2000, 'Pāto-Taimu Rōdōsha no "Kintō Taigū – Pāto-Taimu Rōdōhō Shian ni tsuite ('Equal Treatment' of Part-timers. On a Private Draft of Part-time Labour Law), *Rōdō Hōritsu Junpō*, 148.

Watanabe, Yukio, 1997, *Nihon Kikai Kōgyō no Shakaiteki Bungyō Kōzō (Social Division of Labour in the Japanese Machinery Industry)*, Yūhikaku.

Yoshikawa, Hiroshi, 1994, 'Rōdō Bunpairitsu to Nihon Keizai no Seichō, Junkan (Labour's Share and Economic Development of the Japanese Economy),' in Ishikawa, Tsuneo (ed.), *Nihon no Shotoku to Tomi no Bunpai (Wages and the Distribution of Wealth in Japan)*, Tokyo Daigaku Shuppankai.

Subject Index

absenteeism 20–29, 110, 124, 127
allowance time 34, 36, 37
asymmetric information 148, 149
autonomy 86, 88, 89, 99, 123, 124, 126, 130, 131, 137, 153
autonomy ordered from above 153

bargaining power 82–101, 125, 131, 132, 139
bubble economy 36, 82, 90, 121, 122, 132, 135, 136, 138, 140, 142, 147, 164, 165
Bayesian statistics 144, 145

career 7, 86, 102, 103, 105
casualisation of employment 39
collective bargaining 83, 84, 93, 155, 156
common knowledge 113, 156, 169, 170
communicative rationality 149
comparative institutional analysis 11, 58, 142–166
contract
  classical contract 148
  implicit contract 129, 131, 160
  incomplete contract 148, 149, 155
  relational contract 149

corporate governance 121, 142, 143, 147, 163, 164
corporate tax 136
cross-shareholding 124, 133, 136, 137
cycle time 25, 37

decentralization 20–27, 31, 38, 86, 124, 153, 162
design
  design approved 71–78, 134
  design supplied 71–78
development costs 74, 79, 134
discrimination 1–19, 39, 40, 49, 50, 61, 95, 96, 101, 128, 132, 154
dispatched worker (*haken*) 41
duality principle 123, 127, 132, 140

egalitarianism 87, 88
employment
  irregular modes of employment 39–42, 47, 51, 53, 54, 57, 60, 63, 100, 101, 132
  lifetime employment 106, 160
  long-term employment 57, 106, 114, 115, 129, 131, 132
enterprise union 82–101, 106, 107, 115, 116, 129, 138–140
equal treatment 49, 50, 54, 55, 57, 60–63

fallacy of composition 139
fictitious negotiations 160
foreman 21, 24, 25, 28, 29,
    32, 87, 88, 117, 127,
    130

game
  bargaining game 82–85,
    90, 91, 100, 129, 134,
    143, 154–157, 160, 161,
    165, 166, 168–171
  cooperative game 125, 130,
    133 156
  non-cooperative game 143,
    156, 166–170
  epistemological structure
    of the game 168–171
guild 116

hierarchical incentive 123,
    125, 127, 130
hierarchical information 124
human capital hypothesis 51,
    90, 114
hypothetical bargaining 84,
    100, 156, 160, 169, 170

implicit commitment 83, 129
incentive 52, 69, 73, 78–80,
    84, 85, 96, 105, 123–
    125, 127–130, 142–150,
    153, 165, 167
individual bargaining 84,
    155, 166
industrial democracy 52, 53,
    58, 87, 131, 132, 134
information
  information sharing 22, 23,
    31, 86, 124
  horizontal information
    structure 20–38, 86,

123–127, 130, 133, 134,
    150, 151, 153, 162
  vertical information
    structure 21, 86
institutional
  complementarity 135,
    143, 161, 163, 165
institutional fetishism 163

job analysis 14
job matrix chart 3, 6, 7, 11,
    103–105, 116–120
job posting 8

kaizen 28, 32–33, 48, 78, 127
kaizen team 28, 36, 127
kanban 22, 26, 27, 30, 71,
    123, 127, 133, 150, 151,
    163
keiretsu 68, 76, 123–125,
    132–134, 136–138, 146,
    149, 159, 161, 163

labour-management
  consultation 96–99
labour market 51, 52, 53,
    54, 57, 58, 59, 61, 82,
    113–115, 132, 150, 161,
    162, 165
  dual labour market 51, 65
  internal labour market 54,
    57, 58, 82, 113–115,
    162
  segmented labour market
    51, 58, 59, 61
labour productivity 51, 92,
    131, 139, 140
labour share 92, 93
long-term business relations
    26, 66, 69, 75, 79, 81,
    134, 137

main bank 132–138, 149, 150, 154, 155, 159, 161, 162, 165, 166
management by stress 33
Maruko Alarm case 50, 54–59, 62
microeconomics 69, 142, 147, 148, 161
mutual trust 98
myth surrounding land 137

neo-classical school 53, 121, 122, 124, 125

Off-JT 111, 112, 126
oil shock 93, 97, 116, 131, 133, 137, 138, 139, 140
OJT 1, 3, 111, 112, 123, 126, 151
overtime 34–36, 41, 56, 57, 63, 87, 88, 90, 146

part-timer 39–63, 100, 132
performance appraisal 1, 2, 4, 9, 12, 15, 18, 19
personnel assessment 1–19, 85, 95, 96, 113, 117, 119, 128, 130, 132, 138, 146, 150, 154
personnel division 7, 8, 10, 11, 15, 16, 32, 88, 146, 155, 166
presentiation 148, 149, 169, 170
principal-agent model 136, 148–150, 154, 155, 157, 166
prisoner's dilemma 164
productivity standards principle 92, 131, 139, 140

quasi-rent 79, 80, 81, 125, 129, 130, 134, 135
QC activities 150–152, 162

rank hierarchy 21, 84, 85, 86, 123, 125, 127, 130, 134, 150, 153, 154, 155, 162
reliefman 20, 21, 24, 29, 85, 127
rent 123, 125, 126, 130, 133
risk-sharing 64–81, 89, 90, 134

semi-autonomous work collective 87, 88
seniority 116, 131, 132
shareholder 121, 125, 133, 135, 136, 142, 147, 149, 150, 154, 155, 157–161, 165, 166
shuntō 91–95
skill
  contextual skill 83, 85, 86, 89, 91, 123, 126, 128, 129, 135, 150
  firm-specific skill 62, 89, 90, 106
  intellectual skill 2, 7, 28, 85, 89–91, 102–120, 126, 128, 129, 151
  relational skill 72, 73
specialist 20, 21, 23, 29–31, 44, 85, 104, 109–114, 126, 127, 128, 145, 158
stakeholder 157–160
standard time 36, 37, 109
strategic management decision 84, 90, 96, 98, 100
strategic rationality 149, 161, 171

subcontracting 64–81, 132,
    134
supervisor 32–34, 38, 85, 88,
    127

Taylorism 111, 152, 153
transfer of worker (*haichi
    tenkan*) 3, 34, 36, 56, 87,
    88, 102
transaction costs 123, 148

union regulation 86, 89
union shop agreement 101
unit price 70, 71, 74, 75, 78,
    79

wage
  compensation wage
      hypothesis 51, 54, 56, 59,
      63
  efficiency wage hypothesis
      52, 59, 162
  hedonic wage hypothesis 51,
      56
  seniority-based wage (*nenkō
      wage*) 8, 54, 61, 106,
      107, 113, 114, 128
  economy-compatible wage
      policy 93, 139

Author Index

Adler, Paul S. 37
Alchian, Armen 145
Aoki, Masahiko 4, 7, 8, 9,
    11, 12, 15, 18, 19, 20–38,
    52–54, 58, 59, 65, 67,
    79–86, 89–91, 95, 96,
    100, 102, 105, 110, 111,
    121–166
Asakura, Mutsuko 58, 63
Asanuma, Banri 64–81, 134
Asao, Uichi 4, 20, 28, 37, 86,
    126, 127

Beaudet, Alexandre 75
Binmore, Ken 156
Bosch, Gerhard 35
Bourdieu, Pierre 146
Bratton, William W. Jr. 157

Cappelli, Peter 162
Chiba, Toshio 93
Chūma, Hiroyuki 51, 56, 105
Clark, Kim B. 67
Coase, Ronald 145, 147, 155

Däubler, Wolfgang 159
DeMott, Deborah 157
Demsetz, Harold 145

Endō, Kōshi, 2, 4, 7, 12, 14,
    95, 104, 117, 128, 154

Frug, Gerald E. 157
Fujimura, Hiroyuki 9, 10, 15

Fujimoto, Takahiro 67, 74,
    75, 78
Fujita, Eishi 34
Furugōri, Tomoko 51, 59, 62

Graham, Laurie 153

Hyōdō, Tsutomu 115

Inoki, Takenori 89, 103, 112
Inoue, Masao 96, 100, 114
Ishida, Mitsuo 33
Itami, Hiroyuki 10, 15, 16,
    125

Kagono, Tadao 10, 15, 16
Kamii, Yoshihiko 88, 95, 98,
    129, 131
Kamiya, Takuhei 91
Kaneda, Hideharu 33
Kaneko, Masaru 30, 122, 128,
    133, 134, 141
Kawanishi, Hirosuke 82
Kikutani Tatsuya 69, 70
Koike, Kazuo 1–11, 12, 18,
    19, 28, 29, 34, 82, 85,
    86–91, 94, 96, 100, 102–
    120, 121, 122, 123, 126,
    127, 128
Komiya, Ryūtarō 6, 125
Kōshiro, Kazuyoshi 92
Kreps, David M. 156
Kumagai, Hisao 92
Kumazawa, Makoto 153

Lehndorff, Steffan 35

Markovits, Andrei 159
Mizumachi, Yūichirō 56, 57, 59, 63

Nagase, Nobuko 41, 42, 55, 56, 59, 62, 63
Nagayoshi, Hiromi 4
Nakamura, Jirō 51, 56
Nakamura, Keisuke 91
Nakanishi, Yō 115
Nakata, Yoshifumi 61, 62, 94
Nakatani, Iwao 4, 8
Nimura, Kazuo 115, 116
Nishiguchi, Toshihiro 75
Nitta, Michio 50, 55, 97
Nohara, Hikari 34
Nomura, Masami 7, 28, 34, 36, 37, 87, 102, 103, 108, 113, 115, 117, 119, 122, 126, 128, 152

Ogata, Keiko 4
Okuno, Masahiro 11, 105
Ono, Akira 114
Ōno, Taiichi 32
Ōsawa, Machiko 52, 55
Ōsawa, Mari 44, 55, 132
Ōta, Sōichi 105
Ōwaki, Masako 50
Oyama Yōichi 34

Parker, Mike 33

Rubinstein, Ariel 157, 166–171

Saruta, Masaki 34, 38
Satō, Hiroki 59, 91
Scher, Mark J. 155

Seike, Atsushi 50, 51, 62
Seiyama, Kazuo 62
Sennett, Richard 153
Slaughter, Jane 33
Streeck, Wofgang 159
Sugeno, Kazuo 57, 58, 61, 63
Sumiya, Mikio 92
Suwa, Yasuo 57, 58, 61, 63

Tachibanaki, Toshiaki 91
Takahashi, Yūkichi 101
Takase, Saburō 12
Takeda, Shigeo 84, 122, 149, 169
Tokumaru, Sōya 152
Tōnai, Kazuhiro 4

Uchiyama, Mitsuo 89
Ueda, Hirofumi 65, 69, 74, 76, 78, 81, 94, 134
Ujihara, Shōjirō 88

Wada, Hajime 63
Watanabe, Yukio 64, 66

Yoshikawa, Hiroshi 92